#518071
LF
D1320172
3 2 157 7237
The University of Memphis
University Libraries
Special
Wynn
ND
467
.F55
copy 2
Lorraine Hogan
April, 1970

Rossetti and the Pre-Raphaelite Brotherhood

BY THE SAME AUTHOR

George Alfred Lawrence
and the Victorian Sensation Novel

G. H. FLEMING

Rossetti and the Pre-Raphaelite Brotherhood

RUPERT HART-DAVIS

© G. H. Fleming 1967
First published 1967
Rupert Hart-Davis Ltd
1–3 *Upper James Street, London W*1

Printed in Great Britain by
Western Printing Services Ltd, Bristol

For Mey

CONTENTS

	Preface	xi
1	Young Rossetti	1
2	Poet or Painter?	17
3	Madox Brown and Holman Hunt	33
4	Millais, the Reluctant Brother	52
5	The Formation of the Brotherhood	63
6	The Fruits of a Year	83
7	*The Germ* and the Launching of a Poet	108
8	The Battle of 1850	128
9	Ruskin Intervenes	144
10	The Turn of the Tide	165
11	The End of the Brotherhood	191
12	Postscript	213
	Select Bibliography	221
	Index	225

PLATES

(*between pages 64–65*)

The Eve of St Agnes
The Departure of Hagar
The Sacrifice of Isaac
Ford Madox Brown
John Everett Millais
Dante Gabriel Rossetti
Holman Hunt
Cordelia Watching at the Bedside of Lear
The Girlhood of Mary Virgin
Lorenzo and Isabella
Ecce Ancilla Domini

(*between pages 128–129*)

A Converted British Family
The Carpenter Shop
Mariana
The Woodman's Daughter
Valentine Rescuing Sylvia from Proteus
Convent Thoughts
Wickliffe Reading his Translation of the Bible
The Death of Ophelia

(*between pages 192–193*)

The Hireling Shepherd
The Huguenot
Christ Washing Peter's Feet
Beatrice at a Marriage Feast
Dante Drawing an Angel
Claudio and Isabella
The Strayed Sheep
The Order of Release

PREFACE

In the April 1959 issue of *Connoisseur* there is a single paragraph headed 'Return of the Pre-Raphaelites?' which begins thus: 'A brief generation ago, Dante Gabriel Rossetti and the Pre-Raphaelites were considered as sentimentalists and dismissed as misguided dreamers. Today they may be returning to fashion.'

Although their 'return' might be challenged by some knowledgeable persons, such as Leslie Parris, Assistant Keeper of the Tate Gallery, who on 8 November 1965 wrote that 'interest in [the Pre-Raphaelites] seems to have been fairly constant,' surely no one would now deny that Rossetti and his friends are in fashion. And most of Mr Parris' peers would, I think, agree that recent Pre-Raphaelite sales, exhibitions, and publications do signify a revival of interest which stands out even within the general artistic renascence of which it is a part. This renewed interest, moreover, seems not to be merely another passing fancy, but probably reflects, in the words of one scholar of the period, Morse Peckham, 'a growing recognition of the importance of what [Pre-Raphaelitism] did at the time and its subsequent effect on English art', and a realization that 'they did, for all their faults, paint a number of paintings which we can now recognize as strikingly beautiful and profoundly original'. Some authorities indeed feel that we have not yet seen the peak of Pre-Raphaelite popularity. Peter Cannon Brookes, for example, Keeper of the Department of Art at the Birmingham City Art Gallery, on 5 November 1965, stated, 'I believe that the next few years will show such a fast re-evaluation of the Pre-Raphaelites that the works they produced during their earliest years of association will be revealed as a central and highly important facet of European painting of the nineteenth century and possibly as far reaching in their effects as the more highly lauded movements in French art in the last quarter of the century'.

This is not the appropriate place to assert why Rossetti and his associates are receiving, and deserve to receive, recognition; at this point I shall merely observe that the current interest in them establishes a basis for re-examining their lives and works. Another, and more compelling, reason for re-assessing the Pre-Raphaelites is that far from being dealt with definitively, they have not yet been subjected to a satisfactory scrutiny. There is of course no shortage of written material on the Pre-Raphaelite movement and its principal personages. As far back as 1947, Terence Robsjohn-Gibbings complained in *Mona Lisa's Moustache* that 'there have been more than enough books on the subject'. Truly said, but with one exception none of these volumes even approach a deterring standard of excellence. The best of them, such as A. C. Benson's *Rossetti* and Henry C. Marillier's splendidly illustrated study of Rossetti are inadequate and outdated. The others are either excessively adulatory, such as the biographies of Rossetti written by his friend William Sharp and by his niece Helen Angeli; or inexcusably inaccurate, such as Esther Wood's biography of Rossetti and Evelyn Waugh's books on Rossetti and the Pre-Raphaelite Brotherhood; or shallow and superficial, such as Lucien Pissarro's study of Rossetti and most of the biographies of Millais and Hunt; or semi-fictional, such as Frances Winwar's *Poor Splendid Wings* and William Gaunt's *Pre-Raphaelite Tragedy*; or sensationally fictitious, such as David Larg's *Trial by Virgins*, and, perhaps the worst book ever written on any aspect of the Pre-Raphaelite movement, Violet Hunt's *Wife of Rossetti*.

The exceptional book alluded to above is Oswald Doughty's biography of Rossetti, *A Victorian Romantic*, which for sixteen years has stood as a ponderable barrier on the path of potential biographers of the most famous Pre-Raphaelite. In his 'Author's Note', however, Mr Doughty explicitly states that he has not written '1. A History of Preraphaelitism or of the Preraphaelites. 2. A critical study of the Preraphaelites' (or of Rossetti's) painting and poetry.' What Mr Doughty said his book *is not*, I hope that my two volumes *will be*. (Volume II will begin immediately upon the conclusion of the present volume, in the spring of 1854.) My concern, as the title implies, is predominantly with Rossetti, not only because he was clearly the most personally fascinating Pre-Raphaelite, but also because without Rossetti there would have been no Pre-Raphaelite movement. (It also is probable that without the Pre-Raphaelites there would have been few if any Rossettian achievements worth writing about.)

I have mentioned broadly the pertinent literature available when I began the present study, and now I should like to refer more particularly to three works which have appeared since the completion of my manuscript: the first two volumes of the *Letters of Dante Gabriel Rossetti,* edited by Oswald Doughty and John Robert Wahl; *Pre-Raphaelitism: A Bibliocritical Study,* by William E. Fredeman; and *Portrait of Rossetti,* by Rosalie Grylls. (Gale Pedrick's *Life with Rossetti,* published in 1965, deals with a period later than 1854 and does not fall within our immediate purview.)

The two volumes of Rossetti letters are well edited, and they conveniently include more than one thousand entries which had been scattered throughout dozens of published and unpublished sources. It should be noted, however, that for various reasons Rossetti's letters provide only a small indication of the character and personality of the man who wrote them.

Although Mr Fredeman's *Pre-Raphaelitism* is marked by some surprising inclusions and even more surprising omissions, although it contains at least one significant factual error, although it is not free from affectations, such as its repeated references to 'Signora' Angeli who in fact is a native-born English daughter of a native-born Englishman, and although some of its 'bibliocritical' comments are questionable, the book is a unique bibliography of the Pre-Raphaelite movement and certainly will be an indispensable reference tool for all of Mr Fredeman's fellow specialists. Its value to the layman, however, is at best doubtful.

Unlike Mr Fredeman's exhaustive and exhausting study, *Portrait of Rossetti* is directed to the general reader. Only twenty-eight of its pages are allotted to the years with which we will be concerned in the present volume—according to Miss Grylls the Pre-Raphaelite movement was no more than 'a hilarious lark'—but we cannot disregard this book, for its well-known author is regarded by some people, including William E. Fredeman, as the high priestess of Rossettiana. Miss Gryll's 'portrait' is egregiously eulogistic. Her position is clearly established in her preface: 'In several instances . . . I have taken the unusual step of explicitly disagreeing with conclusions reached by Professor Doughty in his biography of Rossetti. He often proffers hostile interpretations of Rossetti's motives which can be disproved by facts. It seems to me extraordinary for a biographer not to give his "hero" the benefit of the doubt.' My own reading of *Portrait of Rossetti* has not uncovered any of Mr Doughty's conclusions that have been disproved by 'facts'. I have, however, been startled by some of Miss Gryll's factual inaccuracies. It seems to me, moreover, extraordinary to expect a biographer to resolve all, or any, doubts in favour of his subject, who, properly speaking, is a 'hero' only in the sense of being the principal personage of his study. The biographer's only obligation, I submit, is to present a fair, accurate picture of his subject, and only when to do otherwise would violate this obligation, should he resolve a 'doubt' in favour of his 'hero'. As Lytton Strachey said in his justly celebrated preface to *Eminent Victorians*, 'It is not [the biographer's] business to be complimentary; it is his business to lay bare the facts of the case, as he understands them.'

The books by Mr Fredeman and Miss Grylls and the volumes edited by Messrs Doughty and Wahl appeared too late to affect my text, but I have been influenced by other individuals, living and dead, and to them I should like to express my thanks and appreciation.

I am indebted, first of all, to several of the Pre-Raphaelites themselves, their friends, and their immediate descendants, whose notebooks, diaries, journals, letters, and biographical studies are invaluable source material for students of Pre-Raphaelitism. I should like particularly to mention William Holman Hunt, Frederic George Stephens, Ford Madox Brown, William Bell Scott, John G. Millais, William Sharp, Joseph Knight, and, above all, William Michael Rossetti. As for the living, I thank the Research Council of Louisiana State University for two grants-in-aid; the library staffs of the British Museum, the Bodleian Library, the Guildhall, the Royal Academy, Louisiana State University in Baton Rouge, and Louisiana State University in New Orleans, for much assistance; Michael Rinehart, Witt Librarian at the Courtauld Institute of Art, Alister Grieve, a Courtauld student, and Sidney C. Hutchison, librarian at the Royal Academy, for information; Mary Bennett, Peter Cannon Brookes, Hans Fletcher, Richard Ormond, Leslie Parris, Donald Piper, Mr and Mrs Harold F. Rossetti, and Mrs Virginia Surtees for answers to inquiries; John Paul Smith, a colleague of mine at Louisiana State University in New Orleans, for suggestions and patient answers to questions; Morse Peckham, of the University of Pennsylvania, for a most helpful critical reading of the manuscript; Cecil Y. Lang, of the University of Chicago, for advice and encouragement after his careful reading of the manuscript; John M. Guideau, head librarian of Louisiana State University in New Orleans, for assistance and co-operation beyond the call of duty; and my wife, for her constant encouragement during the preparation and writing of this book.

G.H.F.

1

Young Rossetti

Without Dante Gabriel Rossetti there would have been no Pre-Raphaelite Brotherhood. Thus to tell properly the story of the Brotherhood, we must begin at the beginning, with the story of Rossetti—or perhaps, for perspective's sake, a generation earlier.

Rossetti's father, Gabriele—whose own parents were a village blacksmith and the illiterate daughter of a shoemaker—was born in 1783 in the Adriatic town of Vasto. At twenty-one he went to Naples, through the patronage of the Marquis of Vasto, who had admired the young man's poems enough to employ him as a private secretary and to send him to the University of Naples.

In that city young Gabriele devoted himself to poetry, publishing a volume that brought him some acclaim, and to a job as librettist with the San Carlo opera company. When Napoleon entered Italy, causing the flight of King Ferdinand and his court, including the Marquis, Gabriele continued as before. He was rapidly consolidating his Neapolitan reputation (some laudatory verses addressed to the French may have helped), and was making valuable contacts through a new job as sub-curator in the Bourbonic Museum, taken on when the tempestuous opera world became too much for him. At the museum he met and befriended several politically or artistically eminent people who were to prove helpful to him later—including Lady Dora Moore, wife of Admiral Sir Graham Moore, commander-in-chief of the British Mediterranean Fleet.

After Waterloo, when Ferdinand returned to Italy and his throne, Gabriele became involved in politics (about which, he admitted, he knew and cared little): he adopted the principles of the *Risorgimento*, the Italian independence movement, and composed passionate poems in defence of liberty and against tyranny. As a leading bard of the *Risorgimento*, he became famous throughout Italy when the uprising of 1820 forced the king to sign a moderate constitution; but, also as a bard of independence, he had to flee the country when the king crushed the movement in 1821.

He fled to Malta—assisted in his escape by Lady Dora Moore. After a stay of three years on the island—where he used to the full his talent for attracting the attention and friendship of the wealthy and influential, such as Malta's governor John Hookham Frere—he followed many of his fellow Italian exiles to England. The English had been shocked by the occurrences in Italy into providing material benefits for the political refugees who sought asylum in Britain. Gabriele took none of the charity, but took advantage of the pro-refugee atmosphere, the general friendliness that was being shown to Italians. Letters of introduction—from the Admiral and Lady Dora, from Frere and others—opened many useful doors, including those of Holland House, the London home of Lord Holland, whose dinner table was always graced by the distinguished and influential. There Gabriele met Samuel Taylor Coleridge, the almost equally famous poet Thomas Campbell, the banker-poet Samuel Rogers, and the leading translator of Dante, Rev. Francis Cary.

At this time Gabriele was living in a cheap rooming house in Soho and earning a meagre living teaching Italian to young men and women of well-to-do families—for whom a smattering of Italian, along with French, was a necessary part of their cultural equipment. Among the exiles, competition was fierce; there were barely enough students to go round all the Italian teachers, and here again Gabriele's influential acquaintances came to his aid. These contacts soon furnished him with enough students to give him a comfortable living.

But while Gabriele lived off Englishmen, he lived with Italians. One of the most prominent of his Italian friends in London was Gaetano Polidori, a language teacher, poet, author, and translator (he had rendered all of Milton into Italian). Polidori had settled in Britain some years before, had married an English wife, and had fathered eight children. Gabriele paid frequent visits to his home—and paid much attention to one of the daughters, Frances. She was twenty-five, quiet, unassuming and placid, not unattractive but no beauty. She was also an avid reader who was deeply concerned with intellectual matters; as she said, years later, 'My wish was that my husband should be distinguished for intellect.' She got her wish: she and Gabriele Rossetti were married in 1826. (And, later still, she commented: 'I now wish there was a little less intellect in the family, so as to allow for a little more common sense.')

So the lonely exile's life of Gabriele ended. By the time Frances was pregnant, the couple had found a house in Charlotte Street,[1] an area then in slow decline, mingling the respectable and the shabby genteel with the outright disorderly. (The building that stands today on the site of their first house bears a plaque announcing that this was the birthplace of Dante Gabriel Rossetti—and annoying some literary pilgrims by making no mention of his sister Christina.) Gabriele continued to teach Italian, and in a few years managed to enhance his status by becoming Professor of Italian at the newly-created King's College in the Strand. Frances, in those years, bore children: Maria in 1827; Gabriel Charles Dante (who later dropped the Charles and reversed the two other names) in 1828; William in 1829; Christina in 1830.

The children's early upbringing was almost entirely Frances's responsibility, for the luxuries of nursemaid or governess were beyond the Rossetti means. She gave the boys their pre-school education, and gave the girls their *entire* education;[2] she ensured that their religious and moral training followed the precepts of the Church of England. Though Gabriele was devoted to his children, Frances was by far the strongest influence on their early lives.

Gabriele's life was occupied in other ways. His teaching filled his days; arguing politics and poetry with Italian friends who dropped in took almost every evening; and his *magnum opus* claimed the rest of his waking hours. This was a vast commentary on *The Divine Comedy*—a commentary that sought to prove that the entire poem was in fact political, and that Dante's strictures against tyranny, against the papacy, and on behalf of freedom showed him to have been a fourteenth-century Freemason. Indeed, Gabriele was convinced that not only Dante but Petrarch, Boccaccio and others had been members of a far-ranging secret society devoted to ideals of independence and freedom. Naturally, these ideas would be buried deep in their writings

[1] The street on which the Rossettis lived should not be confused with the identically named street six blocks to the east, which still exists as Charlotte Street. The Rossettis lived at what is now 110 Hallam Street.

[2] Since Mrs Rossetti always spoke English, the children were raised in a truly bilingual home: they spoke Italian to their father and English to their mother.

—for any unambiguous expression of them would have meant banishment or death. So Gabriele tortuously dug into the 'symbolism' of almost every line of Dante to uncover its 'real' intent.

Thanks to the enthusiasm of Charles Lyell, father of the geologist, who was Gabriele's principal financial benefactor, the money was raised—six hundred pounds were needed—to pay for the publication of Gabriele's *Comento Analitico* on the Inferno. (The Purgatorio commentary was later written but never published; the Paradiso commentary was never written.) This published work, along with other shorter volumes by Gabriele on Dante, was either ignored or ridiculed: no one, not even Lyell, could accept the 'conspiracy' theory—but disagreement and indifference merely strengthened Gabriele's defiant conviction that his ideas were right.

In spite of all these preoccupations, Gabriele still managed to remain a warmly affectionate family man. He always spent some time each day playing with his children, and the children always ate their evening meal with their parents (which was a breach of the nineteenth-century English custom). Also, the Rossettis lacked not only a nursemaid but a nursery: so when the meal was over, whether guests had arrived or whether Gabriele was buried in scholarly labours, the children were not hurried off out of the adults' sight but joined their parents in the parlour. The Rossetti home was, in short, a closely knit family circle; and, naturally, since cultural and intellectual concerns predominated in that circle, the children were infected early by their exposure to art and literature.

Maria, the eldest, was reading easily when she was five, and read (like her mother) voraciously all her life. William, the second son, shared the family's general enthusiasm for books. But neither of these children showed much creative ability; it was clear that the artists in the family were Christina and young Gabriel Dante. They too were avid readers; but Christina was also writing quite passable verse when very young, and Gabriel was precociously devoted to drawing. (There is a frequently told story of a milkman who one day saw the five-year-old Gabriel sitting sketching a chair, and said to the servant in amazement: 'I saw a baby making a picture!') Not that Gabriel was a child prodigy. His early drawings, including his imaginative work (such as his conceptions of Shakespearean characters) as well as his representational, showed that he had talent worth developing, but were not extraordinary in themselves. He was no John Everett

Millais, who as a child drew and painted pictures with some intrinsic merit. For that matter, he was no Christina either: where her first poems had considerable inherent value, as verse, his writings were those of a gifted child but little more.

The child Gabriel Dante was as individualistic and independent as was the man Dante Gabriel. He was uninhibited and outspoken, and usually had things his own way: not unnaturally, for in that art-oriented family he was of course the favourite, being the artistic boy; thus perhaps less restraint and discipline came his way than was imposed on the more quiet, obedient William. A reaction against his environment produced in Gabriel a permanent disinterest in politics, and at least a temporary dislike of Old Masters[1] and of Dante. Also, he cared little for such boyish occupations as athletics, handicrafts and so on—though he enjoyed playing simple games with his brother and sisters, and had a mischievous sense of humour (the other side of the coin from his moodiness, wilfulness, and quick temper).[2]

Gabriel had little contact with children outside his own family until he was eight, in 1836, when he began school—first attending a local school, afterwards transferring to King's College School. His father was still the Professor of Italian at the College, which position gave his elder son free tuition and his second, William, reduced fees. King's College School, a public school with an enrolment of about 400, was a strange and largely unpleasant new world for young Gabriel. To the other boys he was a foreigner,[3] and a poorly dressed one at that; and

[1] William related that when Gabriel was a child, 'some one gave him a book of rather large outline engravings from Scripture, after the Old Masters—emptyish-looking things which he frequently inspected, with little real sympathy. I have always thought that his indifference to the respectable conventions of Old-Masterhood, leading to the Pre-raphaelite movement, had something to do with this book.' *Dante Gabriel Rossetti, His Family Letters*, vol. I, pp. 61–62.

[2] 'He [Gabriel] had a theory, which I have heard him express at various periods of life, that men who have an originating gift—or, in a broad sense, what we call men of genius—are all selfish in that same mood of being self-centred. He would say it of such poets as Dante, Milton, Goethe, Wordsworth, Shelley, or of Shakespeare if the facts of his life were adequately known—of such painters and sculptors as Titian, Cellini, Rembrandt, Blake and Turner.' Ibid., p. 75.

[3] Few refugees could afford the cost of a public school education (even the great Mazzini for a while was compelled to earn a living by selling sausages), and so foreign pupils in good English schools were rarities. The plight of most Italian boys in London is suggested by a brief item, under the heading 'Cruelty to Italian Boys', in the 23 December 1843, issue of *The Illustrated London News*, which told of how 'Italian and English gentlemen of influence' had gathered 'in furtherance of a plan for establishing an institution for the care and protection of destitute Italian boys', and of how they had heard 'several affecting statements . . . detailing various acts of gross cruelty, alleged to have been committed upon these boys by their "masters".'

he was set even further apart from them by his lack of interest in organized games and sports, and his dislike of the usual playground scuffling and fighting. Also, he detested his schoolmates' tendency towards deceitfulness and smutty conversation—though he never took a stand against it. Indeed, as William wrote later, 'we deteriorated and were conscious of deteriorating'.

Still, he did not remain entirely aloof from the other boys—nor did they entirely dislike him. His personal charm, always as abundant as his father's, made him some friends; and his skilful little sketches of people and incidents at school drew some admirers. So he was not made wholly unhappy at King's College. For him, the worst thing about school was the boredom. He enjoyed the drawing classes and the language classes (they studied Greek, Latin, French and German as well as English), but loathed the rest—especially the mathematical and scientific sides of the curriculum. He also detested the discipline, though it was considerably less rigorous than at more famous public schools, and the school routine—which by comparison with the lively and unconventional life of the Rossetti home must indeed have seemed monotonous. In fact, Gabriel's main pleasure during his school days was the two-mile walk through the crowded, exciting streets of London between Charlotte Street and King's College, in the Strand.

After five years of attendance at King's College, Gabriel, then thirteen, decided he had had enough of conventional education and announced his decision to attend an art school. His family, as usual, gave him his own way: they had always expected him to be an artist, and thirteen was not then thought too young for one to become an art student. So Gabriel enrolled at a local academy, properly called The School of Art but usually known as 'Sass's Academy'. It had been founded by the portrait painter Henry Sass, and after his death was run by a minor artist named F. S. Cary. Sass's held some prominence as a leading 'preparatory' school for the Royal Academy Schools of Art—which were the objective of all young art students. As such, Sass's concerned itself less with stimulating and training creativity than with providing instruction in the conventional, accepted methods and techniques of art—i.e., simply training its students to pass the R.A. qualifying examination.

The Royal Academy at this time was the ultimate authority and fountainhead of British art, and had been virtually since its establishment in 1768. Its membership consisted of forty Royal Academicians (R.A.'s), who were presumably the nation's most eminent painters, sculptors, architects, and, eventually, engravers, and twenty Associates (A.R.A.'s), from whom vacancies in the ranks of the R.A.'s were filled. As an institution the Academy was as rigid and conservative as it was prestigious. It owed its existence and its strength to Sir Joshua Reynolds, the celebrated English eighteenth-century artist, whose personal prestige had enabled him to weld the individual members of the Academy into a functioning unit, and to establish the nature of the instruction in the Academy's schools. He achieved the latter by means of his famous *Discourses*—fifteen addresses delivered between 1769 and 1792 to fellow Academicians and students. The Discourses contained the pattern for what Reynolds considered to be the proper approach to the teaching of art. But unfortunately the pattern petrified: it was still dominating the Academy's thinking generations later when Rossetti entered it as a student. It is worth while looking briefly at Reynolds's statements, in order to glimpse through them the artistic climate of nineteenth-century England.

Reynolds's advice to the student of art was contained in three basic precepts: (1) study the works of your predecessors; (2) observe the generally accepted rules of art; (3) follow your own judgment when working. Unfortunately, the R.A.'s rather lost sight of (3), but were perhaps even more devoted than Reynolds to (1) and (2).

The principal advantage of an Academy [Reynolds wrote] is, that besides furnishing able men to direct the Student, it will be a repository for the great examples of the Art. . . . By studying these authentic models, that idea of excellence which is the result of the accumulated experience of past ages, may be at once acquired. . . . Those models, which have passed through the approbation of ages, should be considered by [art students] as perfect and infallible guides; as subjects for their imitation, not their criticism.

(Discourse I)

As for the 'generally accepted rules', Reynolds said:

I would chiefly recommend, that an implicit obedience to the *Rules* of Art, as established by the practice of the great MASTERS, should be exacted from the *young* Students. . . . Every opportunity should be taken to discountenance that false and vulgar opinion that rules are the fetters of genius. They are fetters only to men of no genius: as that armour, which upon the strong is an ornament and a defence, upon the weak and mis-shapen becomes a load, and cripples the body which it was made to protect. (I)

Clearly the third dictum, concerning the artist's individual judgment, was not to be taken as an invitation to individualistic extremes:

> There is one precept . . . in which I shall only be opposed by the vain, the ignorant, and the idle. I am not afraid that I shall repeat it too often. You must have no dependence on your own genius. If you have great talents, industry will improve them; if you have but moderate abilities, industry will supply their deficiency. Nothing is denied to well directed labour; nothing is to be obtained without it. (II)

> The purport of this discourse, and, indeed, of most of my other discourses, is, to caution you against that false opinion, but too prevalent among artists, of the imaginary power of native genius, and its sufficiency in great works. This opinion . . . almost always produces, either a vain confidence or a sluggish despair, both equally fatal to all proficiency. (VI)

These statements were, of course, good typical eighteenth-century thinking, with which no one in the Enlightenment would have disagreed. Certainly not Pope:

> You then whose judgment the right course would steer
> Know well each ancient's proper character,
> His fable, subject, scope in every page. . .
>
> Learn hence for ancient rules a just esteem;
> To copy Nature is to copy them.
>
> (*Essay on Criticism*)

Reynolds's undoubtedly good influence in the eighteenth century had become largely pernicious by the mid-nineteenth—the more so because his words, like all useful generalities, were consistently misread, misunderstood, and misapplied. Few people remembered that Reynolds was talking for and about students, not mature artists. More important, even fewer understood that Reynolds was not *unqualifiedly* recommending rigorous, submissive copying of great works of art as the best training (although the quotations thus far given might make it seem so). He insisted on an understanding of the principles and conceptions underlying these masterpieces, but he did not expect students to imitate the individual mannerisms of other artists. He believed that 'Invention is one of the great marks of genius'; and though he added, 'if we consult experience, we shall find, that it is by being conversant with the inventions of others that we learn to invent' (VI) he qualified this with a warning to 'guard against an implicit submission to the authority of any one master however excellent' (III). Nor did he advocate 'an entire dependence upon former masters', for, he said, 'I do not desire that you should get others to do your business, or think for you' (XII). His insistence on rules, too, was directed at students, and at younger ones especially.

Reynolds, then, did not prescribe an inflexible code of laws; it was the influential R.A.'s in the first half of the nineteenth century who imposed inflexibility. They lost sight of Reynolds's distinction between studying basic principles of antique works and an out-and-out copying of the works; they came to see the copying as not a means but an end. Nature, to Reynolds 'the fountain . . . from which all excellencies originally flow' (VI), received only lip service from the Academicians —most of whose own training had come from studying pictures and sculpture. Holman Hunt, when in his seventies and reminiscing about his early days as a painter, remarked that at the time 'All adduced Phidias and Raphael as prophets to sanctify their course, and all revolted at any suggestion that the solid ground beneath their feet was the foundation on which sincere workers must stand.'

The course, sanctified by Phidias and Raphael, was also clearly marked out by a host of rules of technique. These specified, for instance, that every picture must have firm, solid outlines; that its composition must take the form of either an 'S' or a triangle; that its human figures must be represented freed from all deformities; that the most appropriate colours are low and subdued, and for landscapes, the prescribed colour is brown;[1] that light and shadow must show a ratio of one to three or one to four. Rules circumscribed even the technique of applying oils to canvas: the artist was required first to paint the tone values, then the half lights, and finally the deep shadows and high lights.

So it is easy to imagine what happened when a painter allowed his originality to exceed these bounds. As an anonymous pamphleteer (who may have suffered for such a reason) wrote of the molders of art opinion: '*Their* only standards are old pictures; hence if the new production fails to remind them of somewhat they have seen before, it is instantly condemned. . . . Men will stoop to condemn his talents with virulence which ought to be reserved for criminal actions.' Before 1850 the most serious condemnation of this kind was directed at J. M. W. Turner. So long as he was considered a traditional painter,

[1] The reason for this rule was that landscapes in old Italian pictures were usually brown. It seems not to have occurred to the legislators of art that the colour of these canvases might have been due to age, not the original pigment.

Turner was acclaimed by influential writers. But when he began to show himself as a nonconformist—in his colour combinations, his proportions of light and shade, his figure drawing, and his foregrounds and backgrounds—the commendations were quickly replaced by denunciations. Various art critics said that his colours were inharmonious, unrestrained, and lurid; his designs delicate, vague, and hazy; and they described his work as a 'confused dream', 'frantic puzzle', and 'gorgeous monstrosities'.

The Academy, as the Establishment of art, was also an important bulwark of the broader Establishment that dominated English society generally. There was no doubt of the extraordinary social as well as artistic importance of the annual R.A. exhibition of contemporary art. At the dinner held before the opening, the guests might include royalty (often the Prince of Wales), high nobility, Cabinet ministers and M.P.s, foreign ambassadors and other equally distinguished men. As for the opening itself, few other occasions were of greater consequence to polite society.

The exhibition, however, also sparked off much of the adverse criticism levelled at the Academy in the nineteenth century. From 1837 until 1869, when it moved into its present home in Burlington House, the R.A. had to share a building with the National Gallery in Trafalgar Square, and because of a shortage of space artists complained that not all the acceptable pictures could be hung, and not all of those hung could be placed in desirable positions.[1] Accusations of capricious, dictatorial methods flew at the R.A. More generally, it was accused of being provincial and intolerant; of pandering to the aristocracy; of ignoring creative accomplishments that were unconnected with wealth or power; of driving artists to insanity and suicide.

Some of these attacks undoubtedly came from unsuccessful artists seeking a scapegoat—but not all. Consider the favouritism that occurred on the pre-exhibition 'varnishing days'. Academicians and Associates were permitted three full days for cleaning, finishing, and re-touching their pictures to bring them into harmony with the light and their hanging positions. Other exhibitors were allotted only half

[1] The noted nineteenth-century painter W. P. Frith, in his book of recollections *A Victorian Canvas*, commented on the chore given to those who were charged with hanging pictures in an Academy Exhibition: 'In the days of which I am writing the Hanging Committee was composed of three men, whose duties consisted in cramming into small rooms in Trafalgar Square as many pictures as they would hold, totally, indeed necessarily, regardless whether any could be seen without telescopes or not.'

a day. (This special R.A. privilege was, incidentally, abolished in 1852 —the year after the death of Turner, who had been its most outspoken defender.)[1] Furthermore, R.A.s had the absolute right to have eight pictures hung without first being judged by the Royal Academy Council.[2]

But the Academy's influence on English art was the target for far more serious complaints than those relating to varnishing days or selection committees. In 1821 John Constable had declared, 'In thirty years English art will have ceased to exist.' By the 1840's his prophecy looked as if it were coming true. As William Rossetti wrote, concerning conditions in 1848, 'The British school of painting . . . had sunk far below what it had been in the days of Hogarth, Reynolds, Gainsborough, and Blake, and its ordinary average had come to be something for which commonplace is a laudatory term, and imbecility a not excessive one.' It seems more than coincidence that English painting declined as the R.A. and the attitudes it inspired gained power and prestige.

Most leading painters in the 1840's were technicians who had more or less mastered the mechanics of their art, but at the expense of freshness or imagination. Holman Hunt comments, in his observations on the Exhibition of 1848:

. . . there was such a lack of courage and individualism in the painting of these things, and so slavish an adherence to one technical formula, that it would not have been difficult to believe that half the pictures were the work of a single competent and laborious hand.

And again:

The fault we found in this younger school was that every scene was planned as for the stage with second-rate actors to play the parts, striving to look

[1] A few years later the Academy inaugurated its practice of giving separate varnishing days to members and non-members.

[2] Frith reported the following revealing incident: 'When Constable was a member of the selecting Council, a small landscape was brought to judgment; it was not received with favour. The first judge said: "That's a poor thing"; the next muttering: "It's very green"; in short, the picture had to stand the fire of animadversion from everybody but Constable, the last remark being: "It's devilish bad—cross it." Constable rose, took a couple of steps in front, turned round, and faced the Council.

' "That picture," said he, "was painted by me. I had a notion that some of you didn't like my work, and this is a pretty convincing proof. I am very much obliged to you," making a low bow.

' "Dear, dear!' said the President to the head-carpenter, "how came that picture amongst the outsiders? Bring it back: it must be admitted, of course."

' "No! it must not!" said Constable; "out it goes!" and in spite of apology and entreaty, out it went. This story was told me by Cooper, who witnessed the scene.' *A Victorian Canvas*, pp. 83–84.

not like sober live men, but like pageant statues of waxwork. Knights were frowning and staring as none but hired supernumeraries could stare; the pious had vitreous tears on their reverential cheeks; innkeepers were ever round and red-faced; peasants had complexions of dainty pink; shepherdesses were facsimiled from Dresden-china toys; homely couples were ever reading the Family Bible to a circle of most exemplary children; all alike from king to plebeian were arrayed in clothes fresh from a bandbox. With this artificiality, the drawing was often of a pattern that left anatomy and the science of perspective but poorly demonstrated.

And John Ruskin supplied a contemptuous note:

Behold the 'cattle-pieces', and 'sea-pieces', and 'family-pieces', the eternal brown cows in ditches, and white sails in squalls, and sliced lemons in saucers, and foolish faces in simpers, and try to feel what we are, and what we might have been.

Yet the R.A. exhibitions contained the best there was in British art at the time. Other institutions and exhibiting bodies (of which there were many) followed the R.A.'s lead in terms of standards, directed their students to learn the rules and copy old masters, and hung pictures which had been declined by the Academy. Second in importance to the R.A. was the British Institution, and of its 1847 exhibition the *Athenaeum*'s reviewer wrote:

The British Institution has become the emporium for the perpetuation of platitudes and versions of the most accidental human forms, ordinary landscapes, costume pictures, and uninteresting still life. . . . No exercise of the imagination—no high employment of the faculties of the human mind—is called into action by the execution of such works.[1]

Another prominent exhibition was offered annually by the Society of British Artists, which had been formed in 1823 by a group of painters (including the celebrated historical painter Haydon) who had quarrelled with the Royal Academy—not because they disagreed with its principles but because they thought it had treated them badly. Rebels without a real cause, their exhibitions exceeded in mediocrity even those of the British Institution.

One other exhibition deserves mention because of its role in Rossetti's early professional life: the Association to Promote the Free Exhibition of Modern Art—popularly called the Free Exhibition—

[1] R.A.s even had some control over selecting and hanging pictures in the British Institution Exhibitions since the President of the Academy was an ex officio member of the Institution, whose by-laws provided that all entries received from Academicians would be accepted without preliminary examination.

which was first held in 1847 in Piccadilly, and in 1848 moved to the Chinese Gallery in Hyde Park Corner. The exhibition was free neither to visitors, who paid a shilling for admission. nor to artists, who were charged for each foot of wall space they used. It was 'free' only in that anyone who paid the fee could exhibit his pictures.

So the picture of English art in the first half of the nineteenth century was one of conventionality, mediocrity and decline—justifying Constable's gloomy prophecy. Yet the gloom was broken by occasional bright patches, such as the growth of provincial art societies in Liverpool, Birmingham and Manchester, which showed (perhaps because they were far enough away from the Royal Academy) rather more tolerance for artistic non-conformity than London. Also, though the quality of English painting had declined, there is no doubt that the quantity had increased—i.e., that interest in and desire for art was growing. Artists may have lived precariously around the turn of the century, but by the 1840's established artists could make handsome livings.[1] The *nouveaux riches* of the Industrial Revolution were building grand houses and buying contemporary paintings for the walls; the government was setting up competitions of cartoon drawings suitable for decorating the new Parliament building, and offering worthwhile prizes to the winners. And in these, held in Westminster Hall between 1843 and 1845, the Establishment suffered a mild setback: because entries were submitted anonymously, few were received from R.A.s and A.R.A.s, not one of whom won a prize.

Perhaps this was a straw in the wind; or perhaps it merely seems so in the artificial focus of hindsight, by which we know that the times were overripe for change. In poetry the battle against the rules had been fought and won a generation or two earlier. The arts were beginning to be democratized, as a new class of wealthy patrons arose who did not belong to polite society; discontent of all kinds, not only artistic, was spreading through Europe on the threshold of the revolutionary year of 1848. Change was in the air—and, whether or not the Royal Academy knew it, the question was no longer *if* their power would be challenged, but when, and by whom.

. . .

[1] George D. Leslie, for example, said that his father, Charles Robert Leslie, who died in 1859, 'made more by his paintings during the last twelve years of his life than he had earned throughout almost the whole of the rest of his career; it was the only period of his life in which he was enabled to put by money at all'. *The Inner Life of the Royal Academy*, p. 273.

But that question was certainly undreamed of in the halls of Sass's Academy, where young Rossetti was suffering with the conventionalized, uninspired teaching. Holman Hunt, who refused to attend Sass's, gives an indication of the quality of its training:

> Many students who worked there shaded their drawings with the most regular cross hatching, putting a dot in every empty space; thus the figure was blocked out into flat, angular surfaces, which ultimately blended by half-tints, produced the required modelling; for all such systems I had neither time nor inclination.

Nor had Gabriel Rossetti. He chafed at the tedious copying of bones and casts, and the rigid rules that governed the copying. He grew rebellious, drawing caricatures of the ancient figures that served as models, and, though his teacher explicitly forbade the practice, repeatedly drew thick, solid outlines in charcoal, instead of the required Italian chalk. He grew insolent, talking and singing in class, refusing to work when at the school and often simply staying away for days.

But it was art school that bored him, not art. Away from Sass's and the inhibiting supervision of his teachers, he drew incessantly, even joining a student sketching club in 1843, from which he 'derived great improvement'; and he drew what he wanted to draw—most often images inspired by his reading, from Scott, Shakespeare, Goldsmith and other writers. He also regularly attended art shows, such as the first Westminster Hall Exhibition of cartoons for decorating the new Houses of Parliament, which opened in July 1843. His parents were then in Paris hoping to find temporary relief for Mr Rossetti's ill health, and in a letter to his mother Gabriel wrote, 'It is indeed a splendid sight; by far the most interesting exhibition in fact at which I have ever been, more so even than the Royal Academy.' The subject matter alone of the cartoons would have been enough to please Gabriel: one-third of the works were inspired by Milton, and many others depicted scenes from Shakespeare and Spenser. But it was the exhibiting artists themselves that most forcibly impressed him. The exhibition was competitive, with a number of prizes awarded by the government, and most of the prize winners were comparatively young painters whose work exhilarated the youthful Rossetti: 'Taken on the whole, this exhibition may be considered as a proof that High Art and high talent are not confined to the Continent. . . . Almost all the successful competitors are young men who now appear for the first time before the public, thus directly giving the lie to the vile snarling assertion that British Art is slowly but surely falling, never more to rise.' The exhibitor who most pleased Gabriel was the highly rebellious George Frederick Watts, who now for the first time achieved recognition by winning one of the top prizes (three hundred pounds) with his *Caractacus led captive through the Streets of Rome.* If this letter reveals Gabriel's attraction to nonconformists, it also indicates that he had not yet become an insurgent, for by saying he had enjoyed this exhibition 'more so even than the Royal Academy', he implied that he also had received more than a little pleasure from the conservative shows in Trafalgar Square.

Unfortunately, but unavoidably, in his rejection of the methods of Sass's he also rejected, or simply failed to learn, some of the necessary and fundamental principles of drawing. He was aware of his technical inability, complaining in a letter of 1843 of his 'knowledge of anatomy, in spite of my efforts at improvement, being at present less than imperfect'. But the efforts were themselves less than strenuous; so, during the four years at Sass's, Rossetti added only a rudimentary technical proficiency to his natural talent.

There was no prescribed period of matriculation for a Sassite; students stayed at the school until they either felt ready to take the R.A. entrance examination, or gave up the study of art. John Millais was at Sass's for only sixteen months—but then Millais was an extraordinary prodigy.[1] Talented but less precocious artists such as W. P. Frith and John Calcott Horsley studied at Sass's for two years, a more usual length of time for a pre-R.A. preparation. Rossetti, however, in spite of his gifts and his ambitions, lingered on for four years. The reason is clear: he held back from the R.A. examination because of a fear of failure. In August 1843, after more than two years at Sass's, he wrote to his mother that he might take the next semi-annual examination, in December—'though certainly not unless I feel sure of success, for a rejection is a thing I should by no means relish.' And, after commenting on the formidable nature of the examination, he repeated: 'I shall certainly decline making the attempt at Christmas unless by that time I shall be fully competent to the ordeal.'

His anxiety was by no means groundless. Examinees, in the Antique School of the Academy, were required to produce three

[1] John Everett Millais was a student in the Antique School of the Royal Academy at the age of eleven.

drawings in chalk—an antique figure, an anatomical figure, and a skeleton. Then their work was evaluated in the prevailing spirit of the mid-century R.A., as Harry Quilter described it, writing in 1892:

. . . the result is judged not by the manner in which the drawing had caught the spirit of the original, but by the smoothness of the shading, the 'polish', so to speak, with which the light and shade are rendered. No more stupid and absolutely futile method of selecting a student could be conceived; no more certain manner of preventing an artist in after life understanding and enjoying the beauty of antique art could be adopted than this making him labour for weeks, without help or explanation, to reproduce the delicacies of light and shade, and the details of modelling which he has neither learnt to see, enjoy or understand.[1]

If the drawings received the judges' approval, the students would be accepted as probationary students in the Academy. After about three to five months they would undergo a second examination; those that passed this second test would become full-fledged students in the Antique School. This was the first stage of training: one progressed from copying statuary and casts in the Antique School to drawing from living models in the Life School to, finally, the Painting School where, incidentally, until 1853 no living model was permitted to enter.

It was not until June 1845 that Gabriel Rossetti summoned up the courage to submit his three drawings to the Academy's board of examiners. His work was viewed with favour—and in July he became a probationary student at the R.A.

[1] *Preferences in Art, Life and Literature*, p. 28.

2

Poet or Painter?

A well-known story describes how the young Rossetti attracted attention on his very first day as a student at the Academy. The Keeper of the Antique School, George Jones R.A., assembled the new students and asked each to introduce himself. Rossetti, in his turn, announced himself sonorously as 'Gabriel—Charles—Dante—Rossetti!' Jones, taken by surprise, replied, 'Dear me, sir, you have a fine name!'

The seventeen-year-old Rossetti's personality was as flamboyant and attention-getting as his name. Because some Sassites who had preceded him to Trafalgar Square had spoken of the eccentricities of their former school-mate, he was perhaps the Academy's best known probationer. From the moment of his arrival he was an object of curiosity. His striking features and bearing were described later by a man who in 1845 had been an Academy student:

I saw Rossetti . . . enter the school with a knot of Probationers, who, as if to keep each other in countenance, herded together. All their forerunners turned . . . to the door of the room, and noticed among the freshmen the saturnine, thin, and . . . not well-developed tyro other 'Caryites' had talked of as a poet . . . and whom they described as a clever sketcher of chivalric and satiric subjects, who, in addition, did all sorts of things in all sorts of unconventional ways. Thick, beautiful, and closely curled masses of rich brown, much neglected hair fell about an ample brow, and almost to the wearer's shoulders; strong eyebrows marked their dark shadows a pair of rather sunken eyes, in which a sort of fire, instinct of what may be called proud cynicism, burned with a furtive kind of energy, and was distinctly, if somewhat luridly glowing. His rather high cheek-bones were the more observable because his cheeks were roseless and hollow enough to indicate the waste of life and midnight oil to which the youth was addicted; close shaving left bare his very full, not to say sensuous lips and square-cut masculine chin. Rather below the middle height, and with a slightly rolling gait, Rossetti came forward among his fellows with a jerky step, tossed the falling hair back from his face, and, having both hands in his pockets, faced the student world with an insouciant air which savoured of defiance, mental pride and thorough self-reliance. A bare throat, a falling, ill-kept collar, boots not over familiar with brushes, black and well-worn habiliments, including, not the ordinary frock or jacket 'of the period', but a very loose dresscoat which had once been new—these were the outward and visible signs of a mood which cared even less for appearance than the art-student of those days was accustomed to care, which undoubtedly was little enough.[1]

Holman Hunt, writing two and a half years later, makes it clear that outward rebelliousness was not all there was to young Rossetti:

. . . with his pushing stride and careless exclamations, a special scrutiny would have been needed to discern the refinement and tenderness that dwelt in the breast of the defiant youth; but anyone who approached and addressed him was struck with surprise to find all critical impressions dissipated in a moment, for the language of the painter was wealthy and polished, and he proved to be courteous, gentle, and winsome, generous in compliment, rich in interest in the pursuits of others, while he talked much about his own, and in every respect, as far as could be shown by the outward manner, a cultured gentleman.[2]

The Antique School held its classes in the rear of the building in the large Sculpture Room, which was inadequate for the exhibition of sculpture but made a satisfactory classroom. Two rows of seats were arranged in a semicircle, in the centre of which stood specimens from the Academy's collection of casts of nearly all extant masterpieces of antiquity. The students sat with pencils and crayons and white paper from ten until dusk, hour after hour, day after day, laboriously and scrupulously copying statues while faithfully observing the 'rules of art'. The teaching in the Antique School was highly perfunctory. Those enrolled in the two higher schools (Life and Painting) were taught primarily by Visitors, prominent R.A.s each of whom served for a term of one month. Their presence provided students with certain benefits: the advantages of being directed by established painters, and the greater likelihood of some neophytes' receiving understanding and encouragement when their work was examined by numerous and diverse teachers rather than one. In the Antique School, however, all of the instruction was performed by one person, the Keeper. Rossetti's Keeper, George Jones, was popular with and

[1] Quoted in F. G. Stephens, *Dante Gabriel Rossetti*, pp. 26–28.
[2] *Pre-Raphaelites and the Pre-Raphaelite Brotherhood*, vol. I, pp. 144–5.

fond of his students, but because of his duties he could give little attention to individuals. In essence his teaching was confined to sententious words of advice and a few corrective suggestions made during his daily half-hour rounds of the classroom.

Rossetti, for all his surface eccentricities, seems to have been on his best behaviour during his probationary period; and after passing the second examination, he was admitted on 19 December as a student in good standing entitled to pursue a complete course of free instruction in the schools of the Royal Academy. For a brief period he applied himself eagerly to work; but soon the routine, as wearisome as that of Sass's, began to have its effect—the more so because of his great expectations upon entering the Antique School. After what must have seemed like a lifetime of studying the rudiments of drawing, Gabriel was impatient to start expressing in art some of the many ideas seething within him. He had not balked at going over familiar ground while he was a probationer, for he thought he was merely preparing for the second and final entrance examination; when this hurdle had been cleared he expected to be able freely to indulge his talents. He was appalled to realize that he would have to spend about two or three more years copying ancient statues.

An R.A. student was given ten years in which to complete his studies, but otherwise the Academy, like Sass's, prescribed no fixed term of instruction. A pupil in the Antique School, according to the earliest 'Laws and Regulations for Students', was obliged to 'continue to draw after the plaister-casts, till the Keeper and Visitor judge him qualified to draw after the living models'. When Rossetti reached the Academy, the requirements for admission to the second school were more explicitly laid down in the 'Laws and Regulations':

> When any Student . . . in the Antique School shall desire to be admitted to draw from the Nude Living Model . . . he shall deliver to the Keeper a finished Drawing of a Statue or Group, accompanied by a finished Drawing as large as nature of a Hand and Foot. He shall also be required by the Keeper to make a Drawing in twelve consecutive sittings of two hours each from a Statue especially placed for that purpose, which if approved by the Keeper, shall be submitted to the Council; and if the Student shall be thought qualified, he shall be admitted to draw from the Living Model accordingly. . . .
>
> The length of the Course will depend entirely on the aptitude shown by the Student.

Gabriel's conduct as an Academic student was predictable—even by himself. Nearly ten years after he had left the Academy, he told his brother, 'As soon as a thing is imposed on me as an obligation, my aptitude for doing it is gone; what I *ought* to do is what I can't do!' In the Antique School there were many things that he ought to have done. He responded by complaining of the 'lifeless conventionality of the schools'; by staying away from classes; by taking little notice of advice from Jones or his fellow students, especially when it embodied adverse criticism of what lay on his drawing board (criticism which was often justified, for, as he himself well knew, he was still technically deficient in drawing). Unlike most of his contemporaries, Gabriel showed no reverence for the Royal Academy; he had simply hoped that in Trafalgar Square he would find a direct and speedy means to an end. But he quickly concluded that the Academy schools offered only 'a toil rigidly exact and dealing with trifles'.

Nor was he alone in his opinion, or his rebellious behaviour. Contemporary reports describe the R.A. students in the 1840's as unruly, mischievous and often insubordinate. Their obstreperousness finally, in 1851, brought about the appointment of a curator to help the Keeper maintain discipline. More important, the Academy's teaching methods were then receiving considerable censure from established artists, even from R.A.s. The talented George Frederic Watts, for example, who was enrolled in the Antique School for a while in the 1830's, said, 'Finding there was no teaching, I very soon ceased to attend.' When the future Royal Academician George Dunlop Leslie entered the Antique School, he found that the instruction, 'though probably beneficial to the well-coached dullards, was looked upon as so much wasted time by the more highly gifted'. Leslie asserted that 'stricter and more efficient tests ought to have been made for the admission of probationers, tests which would have served to weed out those who were merely painstaking incompetents or "well-coached" incompetents'.[1]

Perhaps the most telling criticism of the R.A. Schools came from George Leslie's father, Charles Robert Leslie, one of the most celebrated British painters of the century, Professor of Painting in the Academy, and author of the widely read and influential *Handbook for Young Painters*. In this book, which was based on a series of lectures delivered in 1848, Leslie wrote:

From the time of Raphael to our own, it is indisputable that those painters who have devoted the most time to the study of the Antique have always

[1] George Dunlop Leslie, *The Inner Life of the Royal Academy*, pp. 64–65, 68.

been the least excellent in colour; while the greatest colourists of all schools have rarely had any acquaintance with ancient sculpture; in our own school, for example, neither Hogarth, Reynolds, nor Gainsborough ever drew or painted except from nature. . . .

Life is much too short for the mode of study now practised by many young painters. I mean devoting two or three years to drawing from the Antique, and as many to the Life, before they begin to paint. Students may often be seen in the Academy and other schools twenty years of age and more, who have scarcely had a palette in their hands. . . . It is true that our Academy requires a certain proficiency in the power of drawing from the Antique before it admits the student to the study of the living model. But this proficiency, I am convinced, might be much sooner acquired than it usually is were the students to set themselves seriously to work. I mean were they to set their *minds* to work as well as their eyes and their fingers. . . .

No one could have agreed more than Rossetti that 'life is much too short for the mode of study now practised by many young painters'; but so long as he could see no other way to become a famous painter, he remained a student in good standing. While he was enrolled in the Antique School, he made some artistic progress—but less from obligatory drawing exercises than from his own personally directed and eclectic practice. Of his Academic days, he once said, 'I cared even too little for what could be taught me by others; and my original designs greatly outnumbered my school drawings.' These 'original designs', done mostly in 1847, comprised a number of pencil-drawings, several water-colours, and his first attempt at an oil-painting. Again, as at Sass's, his reading supplied the subjects for most of his sketches, especially heroic and chivalric scenes; but he also drew portraits of Christina, William, and Aunt Charlotte Polidori, and a fine self-portrait, which now hangs in the National Portrait Gallery. Christina's portrait served as frontispiece to a small, privately-printed volume *Verses by Christina G. Rossetti*, for which Gabriel also supplied illus-rations for four of his sister's poems. One of William's observations on these drawings is interesting:

A noteworthy point about the designs is the total absence of any feeling for costume. There are clothes, but of that nondescript kind which, in the male figures, is evidenced by little more than a slight line at the throat, and two others at the wrists. Tasso and Leonora might be anybody or nobody.[1]

The unfinished oil was a fairly large picture whose title later was borne by one of *The House of Life* sonnets, '*Retro me Sathana*' (Get

[1] *Dante Gabriel Rossetti, His Family Letters*, vol. I, p. 99.

thee behind me, Satan). After he had worked on it for three or four months, without practice or instruction in the use of pigments, he showed it to the distinguished Keeper of the National Gallery and future President of the Royal Academy, Charles Eastlake—whose response could not have been encouraging, for Gabriel immediately abandoned and destroyed the picture. According to William, the painting 'formed a group of three mediaeval-costumed figures—an aged churchman and a youthful lady, and the devil slinking behind them baffled. He was a human being with a tail.'

It was typical of Gabriel to undertake an oil-painting when he knew almost nothing about the techniques of working in oils, and still had much to learn about drawing. This cavalier attitude towards the necessary fundamentals of drawing and painting was mostly due to his temperament, but it may also have arisen partly from the fact that, during nearly all of his Academic career, Gabriel was unsure whether he was primarily a painter or a poet. He continued to devote much of his time to literature, both reading and writing. As a reader he ignored subjects in which he felt no interest, such as politics, philosophy, history, and science, but within the boundaries of literature he travelled widely and deeply, poring over plays, novels, and poems in several languages written by every conceivable type of author. Among non-English writers, his favourite, whom he rediscovered when he was sixteen, was the focus of his father's monomania, Dante Alighieri, who provided young Rossetti with nothing but pleasure and, as the years passed, an immense influence upon his creative work, pictorial and literary. But his most extensive reading was done in English poetry. He was familiar with the works of the standard poets, but was especially excited by almost anything that was fanciful, individualistic, or unconventional, such as old romances and early ballads. Among the more recent poets he was especially enthralled by four who were then not widely appreciated: Blake, Shelley, Keats, and Browning.

Blake and Browning were probably the most potent early artistic and literary influences upon Rossetti. Early in 1847, in the manuscript room of the British Museum, he came across the virtually unknown poet-artist William Blake, whose verse, audaciously unconventional, and prose, teeming with fresh, original ideas on art, he found enchanting. In April 1847, an attendant at the Museum showed him a large manuscript book replete with Blake's verse, prose, and designs, which he had procured in a second-hand bookstore and offered to sell for ten shillings. Gabriel borrowed the money from dependable William and bought the book, which became one of his most cherished possessions. He was excited by Blake's poetry and also, as William disclosed, by his art criticism:

His ownership of this truly precious volume certainly stimulated in some degree his disregard or scorn of some aspects of art held in reverence by *dilettanti* and routine-students, and thus conduced to the Pre-Raphaelite movement; for he found here the most outspoken (and no doubt, in a sense, most irrational) epigrams and jeers against such painters as Correggio, Titian, Rubens, Rembrandt, Reynolds, and Gainsborough—any men whom Blake regarded as fulsomely florid, or lax, or swamping ideas in mere manipulation. These were balsam to Rossetti's soul, and grist to his mill.

Because of the lasting influence of this volume on Rossetti, we should glance briefly at the particular selection that probably most strongly moved him, the refreshingly irreverent 'Annotations to Sir Joshua Reynolds's Discourses.' Blake made clear his attitude toward this almost sacred work by calling it 'the Simulations of the Hypocrite who smiles particularly where he means to betray' and by saying that he 'always considered True Art & True Artists to be particularly Insulted & Degraded by the Reputation of these Discourses'. Repeatedly Reynolds's maxims are followed by such succinct comments as 'What Nonsense!' 'How Ignorant!' 'A Lie!' 'Villainy!' 'What Folly!' 'Infernal Falsehood!' and 'Damned Fool!' As for individual Discourses, the Third, according to Blake 'is particularly Interesting to Block heads, as it endeavours to prove that . . . any Man of a plain Understanding may by Thieving from Others become a Mich. Angelo', while the Fourth and Fifth 'are Particularly Calculated for the Setting Ignorant & Vulgar Artists as Models of Execution in Art'. Blake then defiantly declared, 'Let him who will, follow such advice. I will not.'

Instead of Reynolds, whom or what, then, would Blake follow? The following assertions, typical of many such statements scattered throughout the 'Annotations', point to the road on which Blake was determined to travel:

'The Man who on Examining his own Mind finds nothing of Inspiration ought not to dare to be an Artist.'

'Reynolds thinks that Man Learns all that he knows. I say on the Contrary that Man Brings All that he has or can have Into the World with him. Man is Born Like a Garden ready Planted & Sown.'

'The Man who never in his Mind and Thoughts Travel'd to Heaven Is No Artist.'

'What has Reasoning to do with the Art of Painting?'

'Knowledge of Ideal Beauty is not to be Aquired. It is Born with us.'

Blake did not always disagree with the author of the Discourses. Thus when Reynolds said, 'I would particularly recommend that after your return from the Academy . . . you would endeavour to draw the figure by memory,' Blake commented, 'Good advice!' And an emphatic 'True!' followed the declaration that 'Few have been taught to any purpose who have not been their own teacher.'

Blake did not, then, as certain other dissidents would do, replace Reynolds with nature. He turned inward, to himself. For him the inspiration and source of all good art was the uniquely subjective creative imagination of the artist. We should not lose sight of this doctrine as we follow the artistic development of one of William Blake's most avid devotees.

Later in 1847, Gabriel exhilaratingly discovered another poet whose works as yet lay shrouded in obscurity, Robert Browning. Of Browning's effect on his brother, William wrote:

> At last everything took a secondary place in comparison with Robert Browning. . . . Here were passion, observation, aspiration, mediaevalism, the dramatic perception of character, act, and incident. In short, if at this date Rossetti had been accomplished in the art of painting, he would have carried out in that art very much the same range of subject and treatment which he found in Browning's poetry; and it speaks something for his originality and self-respecting independence that, when it came to verse-writing, he never based himself upon Browning to any appreciable extent, and for the most part pursued a wholly diverse path.[1]

Writing as well as reading diverted Gabriel from the R.A. classroom and ancient statuary. While at Sass's, Gabriel had produced two prose tales (including a *Faust*-like novel called *Sorrentino*, with the devil as protagonist, which was abandoned and destroyed after four or five chapters), a ballad, and a verse translation of Gottfried Burger's *Leonora*. Now, at the Academy, he wrote two of his most famous poems, 'The Blessed Damozel' and 'My Sister's Sleep'; five other important pieces, 'The Portrait' and four *House of Life* sonnets ('Retro Me, Sathana!' and the three sonnets collectively titled 'The Choice'); and two or three minor works, including the only poem

[1] *Dante Gabriel Rossetti, His Family Letters*, vol. I, pp. 101–2.

Rossetti ever wrote 'to order', commemorative verses entitled 'Sacred to the Memory of Algernon R. G. Stanhope, Natus est 1838, obit. 1847', composed at the request of a friend of the Stanhope family. He also composed portions of several highly praised poems—'Jenny', 'Dante at Verona', 'A Last Confession', and 'The Bride's Prelude'; and he translated into English verse a generous amount of Italian poetry, including a substantial part of Dante's *Vita Nuova*.

Among his early poems, Gabriel's own favourite was 'My Sister's Sleep'. He sent a copy of it to his Aunt Charlotte in June 1848, and in an accompanying note he wrote, 'It is one of my precious performances which is, I think, the most likely to please you as to style and subject. Indeed I think myself it is perhaps my best thing as yet, being more simple and like nature.'

Although none of these works was published at this time, and all were revised at least once before publication, most of them were basically products of 1847. Rossetti was justifiably proud of 'My Sister's Sleep' and 'The Blessed Damozel',[1] which show his remarkable imaginative powers, and also underline the contrast between his poetic and his artistic development. He was creating finished, high-quality products in poetry, while at the same time struggling to become proficient in basic fundamentals in another art whose technique was immeasurably more complex and exacting than that of writing verse. He had acquired poetic dexterity effortlessly, without a long drawn-out monotonous period of preparation. And of course speedy maturation of this talent aggravated the frustration he felt in the Academy. As a poet he was self-directed, unchecked by rules or supervision or restraint on his creativity and inventiveness. As a visual artist he sat copying casts without, as yet, even approaching dexterity. No wonder he was a discouraged and disgruntled art student.

Just as Rossetti the young artist led a divided life, so was Rossetti the young man a contradictory personality. He could be pleasant and

[1] The only extant source for the first version of 'The Blessed Damozel' is a manuscript in the Pierpont Morgan Library signed 'D.G.R., 1847'. Even though the manuscript is dated later than 1847, its genuineness was established by Paull E. Baum in his definitive edition of the poem. It is worth comparing the 1847 text of this poem and the version usually anthologized, that of 1870. Not one of the twenty stanzas in the earlier version (entitled 'The Blessed Damsel') was deleted; and only four were added. Further, only one change was made in the stanzaic order of the 1847 text. Of the 120 lines of the poem, ninety remain unaltered, eleven contain a minor change of one word, and nearly half of the remaining lines show relatively minor modification. Thus we can say that 'The Blessed Damozel' as we know it was written when Rossetti was nineteen. Of the other completed poems mentioned, only 'The Portrait' was substantially altered for publication.

gregarious, or irritable and reclusive. Despite his frequent disagreeableness, his personal magnetism remained strong, and without consciously trying to do so, he easily attracted people willing to overlook his faults. The minor poet William Bell Scott, who was to become acquainted with him early in 1848, related that the 'fascination of the personality of D.G.R. . . . makes one accept certain peculiarities in him', which 'all his intimate associates did . . . placing him in a position different from themselves.' At the Academy he was the leader of a small but clamorous group of admiring students, whose association with him was founded on his uncontested leadership and their unquestioning compliance. Rossetti's instinctive and perpetual dominance over others, which A. C. Benson called 'a natural kingliness', was something that had to be accepted by his friends. 'On that footing', William Rossetti said, 'he was easy and agreeable; any other footing would have been troublesome to himself, and not long to be pursued by others.'

Gabriel's leading passion at this time, after art and literature, was the theatre. In the late 40's, he spent much of his own time and his brother's cash in one or another of London's twenty theatrical houses, where he escaped from the tediousness of the Antique School. Catholic by taste, he enjoyed anything that was entertaining—melodramas in the Queen's Theatre, farces in the Lyceum, serious contemporary plays in the Theatre Royal, and Shakespearean productions in the celebrated Drury Lane Theatre. Among the performers he was captivated above all by the popular, talented, and versatile Miss Woolgar, who sang and danced and acted in burlesques, farces and comedies at the Adelphi Theatre, in the Strand.[1] When he attended the theatre with one or more friends, the evening's entertainment seldom ended with the final curtain. Before going home, they usually visited a supper room, or a coffee house, or an oyster shop in Leicester Square or Piccadilly, in the Strand or Fleet Street. When eventually Gabriel arrived back at his home he might sit up reading or sketching

[1] Although he was held spellbound by Miss Woolgar, and although he liked some simple tunes and popular songs, Gabriel did not care for serious music. In August, 1847, he was given two highly coveted tickets to a recital by the world's most famous singer, Jenny Lind, but, he wrote in a letter, 'As I abhor concerts, I gave them to the Heimanns.' After attending a performance of the opera *Lucrezia*, in 1848, he commented that 'Grisi screamed continuously for about two minutes.' In describing a production of *The Messiah*, he said it seemed as if 'everybody got up and shouted as loudly as possible'. As Holman Hunt declared, 'Music Rossetti regarded as positively offensive; for him it was nothing but a noisy nuisance.'

until after three o'clock. His sleeping habits affected both his school attendance and his physical appearance.

During this period Gabriel had cause, too, to worry about the state of his family. Rossetti senior, declining in health, had had to give up teaching, and the family was hard pressed financially. Mrs Rossetti tutored young ladies in French and Italian, Maria worked as a governess, and the frail Christina did much of the housework. Young William, who had shown some brilliance at school and had thought of studying medicine, ended his studies and took a job in the Internal Revenue Office. In comparison with his unselfish brother Gabriel seemed almost callously indifferent to the plight of his family. When he learned that William was about to give up his ambition to become a doctor, Gabriel began a letter to him by saying, 'I was rejoiced to hear of the prospect of employment which has opened for you. Let us hope that it will be permanent.' Gabriel himself contemplated no such drastic or unselfish move. He only felt more dissatisfied with the Academy—because there was now a further reason, aside from his own ambitions, for him to seek the quick road to success and wealth. He saw little likelihood of the R.A. opening that road. Perhaps, then, his poetry would. But, even if in fact he were highly talented, he might be foolish to think he could support himself with his pen. What he needed was professional advice and criticism: and so with characteristic impulsiveness he wrote letters to two established poets.

The first letter, dated 25 November 1847, went to a thirty-six-year-old Scotsman named William Bell Scott, who after eight years of trying to earn a living from poetry and painting in London had moved in 1844 to Newcastle to become a teacher in a Government art school. Gabriel's letter was an encomium in honour of Scott's verse. A few years earlier, he related, he had encountered two of Scott's poems, which were 'so beautiful, so original', he 'could think of little else for several days'. He had looked for other poems by Scott, but had searched unsuccessfully until this year, when he came upon the recently published *The Year of the World*, which he 'fell upon like a vulture'. He then described his response to the book:

You may be pretty certain that you had in me one of those readers who read the volume at a single sitting. A finer, more dignitous, a more deeply thoughtful production, a work that is more truly a *work*—has seldom, indeed, shed its light upon me. To me I can truly say that it revealed 'some depth unknown, some inner life unlived'.

Rossetti concluded by saying that because his efforts to obtain additional works of this fine poet had caused him to neglect his studies and his other daily affairs, he was asking Scott to send information about his other compositions and 'to excuse this, but for my profound admiration, unwarrantable intrusion'.

This letter was wholly devoted to the poetry of Scott; nothing was said about the poetry of Rossetti. Although he had an ulterior motive for writing, and although his praise was extravagant, it would be unjust to charge Gabriel with insincerity. He had been genuinely delighted by the poetry of this unknown Scotsman, just as he had been genuinely delighted by the poetry of Robert Browning, who was not much better known—and to whom Gabriel had also written a letter of admiration.

Happily surprised that a stranger in London should even have heard of him, Scott replied cordially, and Rossetti immediately dispatched to Newcastle a bundle of manuscripts of his own poems. Scott's reply did not survive, but from his reflections on the episode in his autobiography, one can conjecture as to its contents. 'It may easily be allowed', he declared, 'that I must have written with extraordinary delight. The mastery in rhythm and the invention in these poems were both equally astonishing to me, especially in a youth of manifest immaturity, as apparent in certain peculiarities evidently cherished as his favourite characteristics. . . . I looked forward with anxiety to meeting . . . this wonderfully gifted boy.'[1]

Scott's earliest opportunity to meet Rossetti came on a visit to London in the following spring, when he and Gabriel began an enduring friendship. But before the two men became personally acquainted with each other, Rossetti had written to a second poet. He had been jubilant over the letter from Newcastle, but although he liked Scott's poetry, he knew nothing of his critical faculties. Furthermore, Scott had said nothing about the practical aspects of a literary career. Now that he had received the highly favourable response of a published poet, he felt no timidity about asking advice from an acclaimed man of letters. And so without hesitation he wrote to Leigh Hunt.

Hunt was then widely renowned (or, depending upon one's point of view, notorious) as a poet, essayist, editor, and critic—a discerning, liberal-minded critic who had encouraged a number of unknown or critically assaulted but talented young poets, including Byron,

[1] William Bell Scott, *Autobiographical Notes*, vol. I, pp. 289–90.

Shelley, Keats, and Tennyson. In 1847 Hunt was living in Kensington, on a pension, as an elder statesman of literature. Rossetti's letter to Hunt began, characteristically, with lavish praise of the addressee:

> It was four years ago, at the age of fifteen, that I became acquainted for the first time with some of your writings. Since then I have read more and more of them; and having read once, I have read again. I possess all the old editions of your poems and both the more modern ones, together with several of your prose works. You have delighted me—strengthened me—instructed me: you do so still. How then could I consider you otherwise than as a personal friend, or address you otherwise?

Gabriel then told his 'personal friend' that although he had been studying painting, he was also attracted to poetry as a possible career, and could not decide on which of the two arts to concentrate his efforts. He therefore had enclosed some of his original poems and translations and asked if he would be well-advised to choose as his profession poetry rather than painting. Hunt was tardy in replying, but when his letter finally was delivered, on 1 April, it proved to be worth waiting for:

> My Dear Sir,
>
> I have at length had the pleasure of reading your manuscripts, but am still forced to be very brief. I hope the agreeableness of my remarks will make amends for their shortness, since you have been good enough to constitute me a judge of powers of which you ought to have no doubt. I felt perplexed, it is true, at first, by the translations, which, though containing evidences of a strong feeling of the truth and simplicity of the originals, appeared to me harsh, and want correctness in the versification. I guess indeed that you are altogether not so musical as pictorial. But, when I came to the originals of your own, I recognized an unquestionable poet, thoughtful, imaginative, and with rare powers of expression. I hailed you as such at once, without any misgiving; and, besides your Dantesque heavens (without any hell to spoil them), admired the complete and genial round of your sympathies with humanity. I know not what sort of painter you are. If you paint as well as you write, you may be a rich man; or at all events, if you do not care to be rich, may get leisure enough to cultivate your writing. But I hardly need tell you that poetry, even the very best—naturally, the best, in this respect, is apt to be the worst—is not a thing for a man to live upon while he is in the flesh, however immortal it may render him in spirit. When I have succeeded in finding another house, I hope you will give me the pleasure of your acquaintance: and meantime I am, Dear Sir, with hearty zeal in the welfare of your genius,
>
> Your obliged and faithful Servant,
>
> Leigh Hunt.

It is not difficult to imagine young Rossetti's reaction to these words from the man who had been the first important person to recognize the genius of Keats. On 12 April he wrote to Aunt Charlotte that he had been 'for some days in a state of considerable exhilaration' because of Hunt's letter, which, he said, was 'so flattering that I cannot quote any part of it, lest it should seem like conceit'.

Hunt's letter strengthened Rossetti's confidence in himself as a poet; it also dismissed whatever doubt he may have felt concerning one of his recent decisions. He did not need to be reminded by Hunt of the perils of poetry. Hunt himself was an object lesson for would-be poets: after a lifetime of hardship he was only now, in his sixty-fourth year, free of money problems. Rossetti had mainly wanted from Hunt a critical evaluation of his verse from a man whose judgment he respected. For already, before hearing from Hunt, he had committed himself to a career in painting. But this did not mean that he was obediently copying statuary: by the time Hunt's letter reached 50 Charlotte Street Rossetti had permanently severed his ties with the Royal Academy.

He was sick of the Academic routine. If he continued as a student, he would probably spend another year in the Antique School, followed by two or three years in the Life School; and only then, perhaps four years later, would he be permitted to hold a brush and mix and use colours.[1] He had already put in six and a half years as a drawing student, and now he wanted to be a productive artist, to express himself with a brush as well as a pen. Even if he subdued his impatience and did as he was told, might he not stifle his inventiveness? Then there was his family, whose very presence was a daily admonition that he was a non-productive student. The question was settled; he would quit the Academy.

Gabriel knew that he could not become a painter until he had taken care of his technical deficiencies. But would he have to learn his craft in an organized classroom? Why not, like many of his predecessors, serve his apprenticeship under an established artist? After a few months of instruction in the essentials of painting, surely he would be able to embody his thoughts on paper or canvas. But first he had to

[1] Rossetti's complaint about having to spend four or five years as an Academic student before being allowed to paint was not unreasonable. Visitors in the Painting School frequently grumbled about their students' ability to use a palette and brush, and shortly after moving into Burlington House, in 1869, the Academy created a Lower School of Painting for graduates of the Antique School.

persuade an artist to accept him, and he needed the means to pay for his instruction. His immediate family obviously could give him no financial help; and so he turned to the person who would often be his benefactress, his generous Aunt Charlotte Polidori. As a comparatively well paid governess to the Marchioness of Bath, she was Gabriel's only relative with money to spare, and in February 1848, he wrote to her, requesting the help she had once said she would gladly provide:

The motive which has induced me to lay myself under so great an obligation to you is the knowledge that, unless I obtain by some means the advantage which you have offered me, my artistic career will be incalculably retarded, if not altogether frustrated. Every time I attempt to express my ideas in colour I find myself baffled, not by want of ability—I feel this, and why should I not say it?—but by ignorance of certain apparently insignificant technicalities which, with the guidance of an experienced artist, might soon be acquired. Such an artist is not very easy to find, out of the ranks of those whose fame either makes them careless of obtaining pupils, or renders their charges for instruction exorbitant. I have got however two men in my eye who, possessing abilities equal to the most celebrated, have by some unaccountable accident not obtained, except among their brother artists, that renown which they merited. These therefore would, I should think, be the persons to apply to . . .

Aunt Charlotte promptly promised to furnish whatever her nephew would need to become an artist. He now could communicate with one of the 'two men' he had in mind.

The man to whom he did *not* write has never positively been identified,[1] but probably he was Gabriel's second choice—for in March he sent the following letter to Ford Madox Brown:

Sir,

I am a student in the Antique School of the Royal Academy. Since the first time I ever went to an exhibition (which was several years ago, and when I saw a picture of yours from Byron's 'Giaour') I have always listened with avidity if your name happened to be mentioned, and rushed first of all to your number in the Catalogues. The *Parisina*, the study in the manner of the early master, *Our Lady of Saturday Night*, and the other glorious works you have exhibited, have successively raised my admiration, and kept me standing on the same spot for fabulous lengths of time. The outline from your *Abstract of Representation of Justice* which appeared in one of the illustrated papers, constitutes, together with an engraving after that great painter Von Holst, the sole pictorial adornment of my room. And as for the *Mary Queen*

[1] William conjectured that the man might have been C. H. Lear or W. D. Kennedy.

of Scots, if ever I do anything in the art it will certainly be attributable in a great degree to the constant study of that work.

It is not therefore to be wondered at if, wishing to obtain some knowledge of colour (which I have as yet scarcely attempted), the hope suggests itself that you *may* possibly admit pupils to profit by your invaluable assistance. If such being the case, you would do me the honour to inform me what your terms would be for six months' instruction, I feel convinced that I should then have some chance in the art.

I remain, Sir

Very truly yours,

Gabriel C. Rossetti

3

Madox Brown and Holman Hunt

Ford Madox Brown, who was later to become something of a godfather to the P.R.B., was born in Calais in 1821, the son of a retired British naval officer. Having shown artistic abilities, he was sent in the 1830's to Belgium, where he studied under such well-known instructors of painting as Professor Gregorius in Bruges, Professor Van Hanselaer in Ghent, and, his most influential teacher, the celebrated fresco painter Baron Wappers, director of the Academy in Antwerp where Brown was a student from the end of 1837 until the end of 1839. The technical facility he acquired then distinguished him, as *The Athenaeum* said in its obituary notice on 14 October 1893,

> . . . from the majority of the contemporaries of his youth in England. . . . It made him a master of all the processes of the art, from etching and lithography to painting in pastels, fresco encaustic, oils, and water-colours. He was enabled to distinguish himself in all these directions because he thoroughly understood the techniques of each method.

Brown's parents both died in 1839, leaving him an income barely sufficient to support himself and his wife, whom he married in 1840. Brown spent the early 40's in Paris where, because he could not find a congenial teacher, he studied and copied paintings by Rembrandt and the Spanish Masters in the Louvre.[1] It was during these years in Paris that he discovered and developed his predilection for realism in painting. The health of his wife was never good, and when it worsened in 1845, the couple travelled to Rome, stopping briefly in Basle, Switzerland, where Brown became acquainted with the work

[1] When his 1842 painting *Parisina's Sleep* was exhibited in 1865, Brown wrote for the catalogue, 'The style has its origin in the Spanish pictures and in Rembrandt.'

of the sixteenth-century German painter Hans Holbein the younger. Holbein was not then a highly esteemed artist, but his realism, his independence and originality, and his rich colours excited Brown, whose first painting upon returning to England was subtitled 'A Holbein of the Nineteenth Century'. The Browns remained for nine months in Italy, where he was deeply moved by the determination, earnestness, and sincerity he saw in the works of early Renaissance masters whose very names were scarcely known in England—such men as Giotto, Masaccio, Fra Angelico, Uccello, and Pollaiuolo. On 3 January 1865, Brown would refer to the early influences on his art in a letter to a Pre-Raphaelite patron, George Rae, who was about to depart for the Continent and had asked for advice on the paintings he should see:

> . . . what remains strongest printed in my mind are the wall-paintings of Giotto, . . . the frescoes of Masaccio in the Brancacci Chapel at Florence; the Museum at Bâle, in Switzerland, where some of the very finest of Holbein's paintings are to be seen; the *Last Supper* and the other works of Leonardo, at Milan, and also some wonderful *heads* by his pupil Luini. . . .
>
> The paintings of Fra Angelico, executed on the walls of his convent in Florence . . . and of course the great works of Rafäel and Michael Angelo in Rome, and lastly, but not least, all the pictures by Titian that can be seen everywhere.

Because of Mrs Brown's declining health, they departed for England presumably so she could spend her last days in her native land; but she died before they reached home, and he returned with the body and settled in England.

When Brown arrived in London, he was already an artistic revolutionary. Since none of his schooling or training had taken place in England, he had been little influenced by British artists, and owed no allegiance to Academic traditions—in fact believing that servile adherence to them was largely responsible for the mediocrity of most contemporary British painting. The salvation of British art, in Brown's view, lay in the direction of realism. He admired nothing in a work of art more than sincerity; and sincerity in a painting, he concluded, necessarily meant the faithful representation of life as it appears to the eyes of its creator. An artist painting an incident from life should think not of how the scene must be portrayed according to Academic rules, but of how in actuality the occurrence probably would have taken place. He should endeavour to depict genuine, realistic drama within a setting of absolute verisimilitude. Twelve years after Brown had returned to England, a writer in *Fraser's Magazine* declared that he 'really did initiate modern art', for he 'seems to have been the first man in modern days to see or to put in practice the theory that aesthetic salvation was to be found, not in changing his method of looking at and rendering the visible world. He began trying to paint what he saw.' Illustrative of his attempt to 'paint what he saw' was his attitude toward lighting in pictures. When he was only twenty, in Paris, he formulated the idea of lighting pictures realistically rather than conventionally, and of his 1840 painting of *Manfred on the Jungfrau* when it was exhibited in the 1865 Piccadilly Exhibition, a reviewer said, 'Such as it was, it was a first, though not very recognizable, attempt at outdoor effect of light.' He thus rebelled against the practice of using asphaltum, which inevitably darkened paintings, and he resisted such dicta as that which insisted a picture must contain twice as much shadow as light. His early concern for realistic lighting is often revealed in his diary, as, for example, in his entry for 12 October 1847: '. . . went and bought stuff for a blind, to have two lights if necessary, to give the appearance, to those figures which are not in the sunlight, of being in the open air.' Brown would have to wait several years, however, before he could fully put into practice his ideas of realistic lighting.

Before moving to England, Brown had completed more than thirty pictures, mostly oils, of which seven had been exhibited in London. Rossetti had seen each of the seven, beginning with *The Death-Bed of the Giaour*, based on Byron's 'The Giaour', which was Brown's only painting thus far accepted by the Academy, where it had hung in 1841. Rossetti approached Brown's subsequent works with absorption and enthusiasm: he saw in them an artist possessing independence, originality, and a powerful intellect, whose works were notable for composition and colours, for pathos and drama, for fidelity to nature and disregard of conventions. Rossetti's judgment of Brown was honest, but even more eccentric and more highly subjective than his opinion of the poetry of William Bell Scott. These pictures, to be sure, are well drawn, dramatic, and realistic, but their virtues are offset by glaring defects, such as exaggerated, overemphasized gestures and actions to which young Rossetti was blind. Brown had not yet begun his truly fine paintings, such as *Christ Washing Peter's Feet*, *The Last of England*, and *Work*.

In 1848 Rossetti may have been Brown's only devotee: the older man, poor and struggling, had received almost no recognition from the general public, the reviewers, or the exhibitors. He had competed twice, without winning an award, in the Westminster competitions; every picture he had submitted to the Academy except *The Death-Bed of the Giaour* had been rejected; his contributions to other exhibitions sometimes had been declined and sometimes had been hung in a bad light near the ceiling or the floor. Reviewers took no note of his paintings or at best dealt with them cursorily. One of his best notices was a single sentence in an *Illustrated London News* account of the 1845 Westminster competition: 'Mr Ford Brown has a Cartoon of "Justice", which though grotesque and deficient in simplicity, shows that the artist professes vigour of conception and hand.'[1] Brown's frame of mind in March 1848 led him to prepare a picture for the Free Exhibitition, which, as we have noted, was open to anyone willing to pay for his wall space.

Although he could be cheerful and occasionally even jovial, Brown was by nature a solitary, introverted man. Four of his earliest works were based on poems of Byron:[2] *The Death-Bed of Giaour*; a portrayal of The Prisoner of Chillon; and two representations of the most typically Byronic of all Byronic heroes, Manfred. Somewhat of a Byronic hero himself, Brown refused to truckle to anyone or do anything that might call attention to himself or his painting. By 1848, because of the continued neglect of his pictures and because of the death of his wife, Brown had become as morose and misanthropic as Manfred. He sent much of his small inherited income to Gravesend, where relatives cared for his young daughter, and he lived and worked alone on slumlike Clipstone Street in dingy, cramped, insanitary quarters that once had served as a carpenter's shop, angry with himself and society. In this state of mind, early in March, he received the letter from Rossetti.

His subsequent reaction suggests that he became, in rapid succession, astonished, incensed, and curious. A person whose work had

[1] At least one artist privately took note of Brown's cartoon—Benjamin Robert Haydon, who on 3 July 1845, wrote this in his diary: 'Passed the morning in Westminster Hall. The only bit of fresco fit to look at is by Ford Brown. It is a figure of Justice, and is exquisite, as far as the figure goes.'

[2] His grandson, Ford Madox Ford, wrote that 'the one modern English poet with whose works Madox Brown would either boast of or wish for acquaintance was Lord Byron' *Ford Madox Brown: A Record of His Life and Work*, pp. 30–31.

rarely received even moderate praise could only have been dumbfounded by Rossetti's panegyric: the embittered, irascible Brown probably thought it was an impudent joke by some derisive R.A. students or fellow artists seeking amusement at his expense. And being bracketed with von Holst must have seemed insulting, for who could seriously refer to Theodore von Holst as 'that great painter'? Who could this person be who inexplicably knew of every work he had exhibited in London, and who bore the improbable name of Gabriel C. Rossetti? Were the name and address themselves part of a hoax? This question, at least, could easly be answered. Brown's studio at 20½ Clipstone Street lay only three short blocks to the south-east of 50 Charlotte Street, and so early in the evening of the day on which he received the letter he reached for his coat and walking stick and set out for the Rossetti home. There he rapped on the door with his stick and told the servant who greeted him that he wished to see Mr Gabriel C. Rossetti, but he would not give his own name or go into the parlour; he stood waiting in the entrance-way just inside the front door.

When Rossetti came to the door he confronted a largish, forceful-looking man with a handsome but also stern and forbidding face, which at this moment exhibited its almost habitual scowl. This stranger wasted no time on formalities. Thrusting out the letter, he asked, 'Is your name Rossetti, and is this your writing?' Rossetti acquiesced. Brown asked, 'What do you mean by it?' Rossetti said that he meant just what he had written.

Throughout the scene Rossetti seemed composed and self-possessed; but when he first saw Brown, as he told William Bell Scott later, 'I began to shake in my shoes.' He also informed Scott that Brown had held his walking stick 'menacingly'—and from this some commentators have imagined that he shook in his shoes for fear of being beaten. Out of this idea has come the imaginative conclusion that Brown had in fact set out with his stick to thrash the prankster who had perpetrated this hoax. That Brown actually planned to attack Rossetti in his own home is almost inconceivable; the more likely, though prosaic, reason for his carrying a walking stick was that for which the article had been created.

Gabriel's nervousness upon suddenly coming face to face with one of his heroes, with or without a walking stick, is easy to understand, but it was only momentary. Rossetti's personal charm, coupled with his beautiful voice (both inherited from his father), had their effect on

Brown. After he had listened for a few minutes to this young man, and had observed his courteousness, unaffectedness, and sincerity, 'the fact dawned on Brown', Rossetti told Scott, 'that the letter wasn't a hoax, but an honest compliment; he suddenly changed from a deadly antagonist to the sweetest of friends'. Shortly the ungregarious Ford Madox Brown, who had never given instruction to anyone, found himself agreeing to tutor Rossetti in his own studio, for which, moreover, he would accept no payment.

On the following day, Rossetti walked over to Clipstone Street, which was even more dilapidated than Charlotte Street, and visited Brown in what the latter called his 'rascally barn of a studio'. Its roof contained a large skylight, and its front was made largely of glass; with hangings and blinds Brown let in or kept out light. Scattered about the untidy studio were pieces of tattered household furniture and the paraphernalia of painting. Rossetti was unconcerned about the state of his teacher's house; he was simply exhilarated that now at last he was really beginning his professional career as an artist. He expected that Brown would quickly remedy his technical shortcomings and instruct him in the fundamentals of painting so that within months he could be doing what would have taken years at the Academy.

After looking over samples of Rossetti's work, Brown advised him to enrol in a drawing academy on Maddox Street, just below Hanover Square, where on four nights a week a class met with a living model. Gabriel readily agreed; his Aunt Charlotte just as readily agreed to pay the monthly tuition of half a guinea; and (delayed by an attack of boils and possibly by a disinclination to return to a classroom) on 11 April he attended his first session on Maddox Street.

For Rossetti's initial assignment, Brown gathered up several red and green bottles, a palette and brushes, and two cylindrical objects, and told him to do a still-life oil-painting. This exercise hardly sent Rossetti into a transport of delight, for his artistic hopes had not included prosaic sketches of miscellaneous articles; but he resigned himself to the task. And, considering that it was probably his first completed oil-painting, the picture, notable for its vivid colours, is commendable.[1] Later, Holman Hunt contended that the discipline of painting bottles

[1] The framed picture of an eye-filling, sleeping young lady with well-formed bare arms, which stands in the background behind the bottles and other objects, according to Holman Hunt, was 'sketched years afterwards'.

Rossetti had found so abhorrent that it had tormented his soul beyond power of endurance. Thus disheartened, he had given up painting for the time and had turned for counsel to Leigh Hunt, asking him to read his small collection of poems . . .[1]

But one must consider that this passage was written more than fifty years afterwards by a man who was never especially friendly towards Brown. The letter to Leigh Hunt, as we have noted, was posted before Rossetti met Brown, and Rossetti's correspondence hardly suggests that his soul had been tormented. Several letters from his 'Brown period' have survived, and none of them contains a hint of dejection. As late as June, he wrote to Aunt Charlotte:

I continue going to the Life-school in Maddox Street, where I enjoy my studies much. During the day I paint at Mr Brown's, who is an invaluable acquisition to me as regards the art, and moreover a most delightful friend. We are already quite confidential. His kindness, and the trouble he takes about me, are really astonishing; I cannot imagine what I have done to deserve them.

These two temperamental opposites very quickly became boon companions, and for the rest of his life Gabriel's first tutor was his most devoted friend. And Brown soon found his long dormant affability regenerated by his relations with the exuberant Rossetti, who spent more time in the studio talking than painting. They chatted on any subject that interested Gabriel, and, besides art, their main topic of discourse was literature. A well-read man, especially in poetry, Brown also had written verse, and the two men happily read and commented on each other's poems. Brown's interest in English poetry showed itself in one of his two major unfinished paintings, a large work which he had begun in Rome in 1845, and continued in London in 1846, but which he would not complete until 1851: *Chaucer at the Court of Edward III.* Some of the soon-to-be-formulated principles of Pre-Raphaelitism are foreshadowed in Brown's following remark concerning *Chaucer*:

This picture is the first in which I endeavoured to carry out the notion, long before conceived, of treating the light and shade absolutely as it exists at any one moment instead of approximately or in generalized style. Sunlight, not too bright, such as is pleasant to sit in out-of-doors, is here depicted.

Brown surely must often have expressed to his pupil views such a these on realism in painting, but there is nothing to indicate that the made much of an impression on Rossetti.

[1] *Pre-Raphaelitism and the Pre-Raphaelite Brotherhood*, vol. I, p. 108.

Brown's other uncompleted painting, which would hang in the coming Free Exhibition, was *Wickliffe Reading His Translation of the New Testament to John of Gaunt.*[1] This picture, which he designed in 1845, in Rome, and after meticulously working out all of its details began painting in November 1847, was another harbinger of the Pre-Raphaelite movement. The scene is presented as Brown imagined it might actually have occurred, and especially noteworthy are the carefully arranged composition; the mediaeval costumes, which the painter had studied closely; the vivid, realistic heads; and the many carefully delineated details, extending to subordinate figures and minute and seemingly insignificant objects.[2] We do not know precisely what Gabriel Rossetti thought of this painting but William called it a

> highly interesting and important painting . . . which, in its bright but rather pale colouring, lightness of surface, and general feeling of quietism had beyond doubt served in some respects to mould the ideas and beacon the practice of the Pre-Raphaelites.

F. G. Stephens also considered the picture a precursor of things to come:

> A happy combination of Italian taste and technique of the Low Countries of the pre-Rubensian epoch, the gravity, energy, high finish and pure and brilliant colouration of this noble piece had profound effects on the painters of the Pre-Raphaelite Brotherhood.

[1] In his biography of Rossetti, first published in 1894, F. G. Stephens said that Rossetti, had written to Brown after seeing *Wickliffe* in the Free Exhibition. Several subsequent writers, including Brown's grandson, the novelist Ford Madox Ford, and more recently Rosalie Grylls in *Portrait of Rossetti* have repeated this statement, apparently without thinking it strange that in his letter Rossetti did not mention the painting. In 1848 the Free Exhibition opened on 24 April, at least twenty-four days after Rossetti had written his letter.

[2] Illustrative of Brown's working methods are the April 1848, entries in his diary:

14th(April). Painted the head of Wicklif till half past ten from old Coulton . . . began painting the female ln the spandril at nine: worked till half past twelve (eleven hours' work).

16th. My birthday; twenty-seven today, alas!

19th.—Got up at six; set off with my picture to the gallery, Hyde Park Corner. Got there by nine. Ten o'clock before framed, and that did not fit. Tonight I had all day to work, but found we were all to decamp at ten. Got leave to wait till the sweeping was done, and set to work again at twelve to six. Improved the general appearance much by glazing etc. Slept next door at a tavern, to be able to be at work next morning at six, to finish it before the private view.

20th. Up at quarter to six; to work by half past. Painted at the house of John of Gaunt, and put in some trees—too green.

21st. Went to the gallery at about eleven: repainted the trees till two.

As a painter Brown's working methods contrasted strikingly with Rossetti's. Since his early student days, Brown had been a methodical, indefatigable worker, thinking nothing of putting in ten or twelve uninterrupted hours a day for a stretch of several weeks. A sign of his orderliness is the red-covered notebook in which, throughout his life, he kept a running account of the particulars of each of his works as he executed them. Rossetti's work habits, on the other hand, were still what they had been at Sass's and at the Academy. Sometimes he would begin a dozen pictures at once, would paint furiously and haphazardly for hours—and then, faced with what he considered an insurmountable difficulty, he might collapse and sit or lie on the floor groaning. Then for hours or days he might just talk and watch Brown. The following typical occurrence from this period in Rossetti's life was related by Brown:

> Rossetti had a most beastly bit of alpaca for the drapery of his lay figure, which would not make folds nor sit properly. He would work at this for a whole week, and it seemed that he would go mad. I told him to leave it alone, that that piece of alpaca would never make proper folds. He exlaimed, 'God Almighty, what am I to do? it's the colour, it must do; I can't get anything else.' It finished in this way—he got a little china palette and stuck this on his easel, and then sat on the ground with his drawing-board, leaning against the easel, when down came the whole lot, and the china palette breaking, cut his hands. 'This has ended it all,' he cried out; 'I shall have lockjaw, and a very good thing too. I have had quite enough of this work.' I said, 'Nonsense, Gabriel, people don't have lock-jaw simply because they cut their thumbs.' 'If people cut their thumbs,' he said, 'they always have lock-jaw: well, I'm glad, I shall never touch this picture again,' and he never did.

It would have been out of character for Rossetti to be a conscientious student—as it would have been for Brown to condone his indolence and erratic ways. Brown's methods of instruction were only what might have been expected of someone whose own art education had been typified by his career at the Antwerp Academy, where for two years he toiled unrelentingly from dawn till dusk. He knew of no easy road to proficiency; with him, Rossetti could look forward only to unremitting work on art fundamentals and a series of unexciting studies like his already completed still-life. Holman Hunt said that Brown's instruction was 'in accord with all sound precedent', but this may have been a left-handed-compliment—since Hunt recognized that Rossetti was unlikely ever to profit from anything that was in accord with sound precedent. Now that he had learned something of mixing colours and putting them to proper use, and had completed an oil-painting, he was more intolerant than ever of discipline or restraint, and unwilling to apply himself to tasks he considered dull and unimaginative. He never completed a second painting under Brown's direction; and when his initial excitement had run its course, he ceased going to the studio with any degree of regularity.

Although he was still far from being a technically facile painter there is no question that Rossetti benefited from his days on Clipstone Street. In a letter to Brown nearly twenty years later, he alluded to 'the great obligations under which you have laid me in early life, and which were real ones'. Some of these obligations were immediately practical. When Rossetti approached Brown, he knew almost nothing about the technique of painting; in a short time he had completed a still-life and had begun an oil-portrait of his father which he finished soon after leaving Brown's studio. Rossetti profited from his teacher's advice on composition, and he even improved his drawing.

Somewhat less direct and tangible were Rossetti's greatest obligations to Brown. It was of inestimable value to be able to fraternize with a truly independent artist, though this relationship encouraged Rossetti to continue to be self-reliant and self-directing, even to the point of disregarding Brown's own instructions. It was also extremely helpful to know a sympathetic, understanding person who was always ready and willing to discuss any problem, artistic or non-artistic. Nor was the value of the relationship all one way: Brown drew pleasure and encouragement from hearing, perhaps for the first time since his wife's death, someone enthusiastically praise his work. The end of their formal teacher-student relationship in no way affected their friendship, to which Rossetti paid tribute in a letter of 1866, saluting Brown as 'you, whom I regard as so much the most intimate and dearest of my friends, that I might call you by comparison the only one I have'.

When Rossetti decided against following the training programme prescribed by Brown, he gained permission from an Academy sculpturing student, John Hancock, to work in his studio. There, with Hancock at school, he necessarily worked alone—and accomplished very little, for he was neither temperamentally nor artistically qualified to be a solitary painter. And so, in May, barely two months after he had written to Brown, Rossetti was again looking for a studio furnished with an instructor.

Meanwhile, the eightieth exhibition of the Royal Academy had opened. Rossetti attended The Exhibition, but did not find it stimulating or inspiring, nor was he particularly impressed by any of the numerous creations of R.A.s or A.R.A.s. Among the 1,474 works contributed by 840 artists, the one that most forcibly arrested his attention was Number 804, a medium-sized painting hanging rather high, but in a good light, in the Architectural Room. It depicted the final incident in Keats's 'The Eve of St Agnes', the escape from the castle by Madeleine and Porphyro:

> They glide, like phantoms, into the wide hall;
> Like phantoms, to the iron porch, they glide;
> Where lay the Porter, in uneasy sprawl,
> With a huge empty flagon by his side:
> The wakeful bloodhound rose, and shook his hide,
> But his sagacious eye an inmate owns:
> By one, and one, the bolts full easy slide:—
> The chains lie silent on the footworn stone;—
> The key turns, and the door upon its hinges groan.

After gazing appreciatively for a few moments at the painting, Rossetti noticed its creator, a young man who had become an Academic student a year before him and now was enrolled in the School for the Living Model, William Holman Hunt. Although he was only thirteen months older than Rossetti, Hunt was almost a seasoned exhibitor, being at that time represented on the walls of the Royal Academy for the third successive year. (Additionally, in 1847 he had exhibited at the British Institution.) Rossetti approached his former schoolmate, commended him for selecting a subject from Keats, and loudly and emphatically proclaimed his picture to be easily the best in the exhibition. Hunt, a shy person, was embarrassed by these extravagant praises, and by the gesticulations of the speaker and the stares of other spectators. When Rossetti asked if he might visit Hunt's home to see more of his work, Hunt quickly assented and with relief watched his noisy acquaintance depart.

In his typically hyperbolic but sincere outburst, Rossetti clearly magnified the merits of *The Eve of St Agnes* when he called it the finest picture in the exhibition; but from his viewpoint, the subject matter alone would have been almost enough to justify his excitement. To confront suddenly a scene from a poem of one of his idols, a poet who was almost universally neglected, must have been gratifying. Still, the picture itself had, besides its literary origin, much to commend it. It was skilfully imagined and composed and the scene as a whole is a vivid, dramatic realization of Keats's lines. Hunt himself reported that on the morning of the opening the picture drew several accolades from fellow exhibitors.

Rossetti must have been pleased not only to see Hunt's painting but to see the painter himself. He had been working aimlessly and spasmodically: a day with Brown, a session in Hancock's studio, then perhaps a day or two of idleness. He was disenchanted with Brown's instruction; but still aware of his continuing need for guidance with technique. Making contact with Hunt indicated a solution to his problems.

Although Hunt and Rossetti had spent many months together in the same classroom, they were only casual acquaintances. For a short time, while they had been students together, both belonged to a sketching club called the Cyclographic Society, whose members passed around their drawings to each other for written criticism. Despite its high-sounding name, it was a highly informal organization which seldom held meetings and carried on no activities. But naturally they had talked together informally, and in his reminiscences Hunt recalled one brief conversation of theirs which was prophetic of things to come. Rossetti had been sitting alone copying a cast of one of Lorenzo Ghiberti's celebrated Biblical bas-reliefs, which adorn the bronze doors of the Baptistery in Florence, completed more than thirty years before the birth of Raphael. Ghiberti then was by no means well known, and so Hunt had been surprised to see what Rossetti was doing—for he too, perhaps alone among Gabriel's schoolmates, had drawn from these doors. For a few minutes the two students had conversed on this shared interest. But this talk had not led to a friendship. Neither had ever visited the other's home, nor had they ever taken part together in any social event. The reserved, sober-minded, earnest Hunt avoided Rossetti and his noisy followers, who, he thought, were not sufficiently serious about art. As for Rossetti, a man like Hunt would have seemed too solemn for his kind of companionship.

The son of a poorly-paid City warehouse manager, Hunt had grown up in the drab north-eastern suburb of Haggerston, a crowded place of factories, almshouses, gas works, and the modest homes of artisans.

Like Rossetti, from early childhood he was fascinated by artistic matters: he enjoyed colouring theatrical prints and sketching for hours without cessation, and he used what little spending money he had to pay for drawing lessons. So long as this interest in art seemed only to be a pastime, Hunt's father encouraged him and paid for his supplies. At the end of 1839, however, when the boy was twelve and a half years old, the father suddenly realized that his son was obviously thinking of art as a profession; and because of the stories he had heard about starving artists, he decided to remove his son from school and place him in a warehouse (not his own), where the hours of employment, from nine till eight, would leave him little time for playing with his drawing equipment.

But Hunt was a step ahead of his father: hearing of an opening for a clerk in the office of an estate agent who was also an amateur painter, he applied for the position, was accepted, and got Mr Hunt's grudging consent to his proposal. This post, which he held until his employer retired from business a little over a year later, enabled Hunt to combine business and pleasure: his employer discussed art with him, gave him painting lessons, encouraged him to attend an evening drawing class, and occasionally permitted him to draw and paint during working hours.

After the office had closed permanently, Hunt's father again threatened to place him in a warehouse, but the boy came up with another counter proposal. Mr Hunt again agreed, and Holman went to work in the London office of a Manchester calico concern, where he could spend an occasional leisure hour drawing or painting, and where sometimes he was asked to create ornamental designs for cloth patterns. During his commercial career Hunt never lost his desire to become a professional artist, and he was permitted to spend a portion of his meagre earnings on weekly painting lessons from a minor portraitist who had unquestioned faith in the Academic rules and conventions. Hunt learned much from him that was technically valuable, but, as he later confessed, he also acquired 'certain habits and practices which afterwards cost me pain to eradicate'. On favourable Sundays he painted landscapes—one of which, when shown to his teacher, produced a prophetic conflict:

'Oh, dear,' he exclaimed. 'You haven't any idea of the key in which nature has to be treated; you must not paint foliage green like a cabbage; that'll never do. You say that the ivy on the tower, and still more the grass below, was very bright green, but no one with a true eye for colour sees them so. Constable, who is just lately dead, tried to paint landscape green, but he only proved his wrong-headedness; in fact he had no eye for colour. I'll show you a small picture I did when last in the country; there now, you see all the trees and grass, which an ignorant person would paint with greens, I've mellowed into soft yellows and rich browns.' It was so, and it looked most masterly and exemplary. I could not say that nature ever put on that aspect towards me, but he said encouragingly that if I worked in the right way, an eye for nature might come at last.[1]

In January 1841, not long after he had begun his painting lessons, the thirteen-year-old Hunt paid his first visit to the National Gallery, where he eagerly looked forward to

see with my actual eyes the great masters of whose glory I had read with longing fancy. When the mere description of their beauties had given such delight, how wonderful, I thought, would be the perfection of the works themselves when I stood before what every panegyrist declared to be beyond the power of words to express!

After he had passed through all of the rooms, he ingenuously asked an official, 'I am wanting to find the really grand paintings of the great masters; will you direct me?' To his disappointment, he was told that he had just been looking at 'the really grand paintings'. The attendant pointed to Titian's famous *Bacchus and Ariadne* and asked, 'Can't you see its beauty, sir?' Hunt replied, 'Not much, I must confess. It is as brown as my grandmother's painted tea-tray.' He was similarly unimpressed by such other highly esteemed paintings as Sebastian del Piombo's *Raising of Lazarus* and Guido Reni's *The Toilet of Venus*, which 'offended' him by 'its empty pretension'. He also was left cold by the works of celebrated artists like Parmigiano, Rubens, and Van Dyck, some of whose pictures he regarded as 'vapid canvases'. In fact, Holman thought that some of his teacher's portraits were on a par with most of the best pictures in the building.

He was not, however, indifferent or antipathetic to everything in the National Gallery. He enjoyed one portrait, by Gevartius, and Francia's *Dead Christ*, he said, 'kept me before it a long time'. He was also pleased with Hogath's *Marriage à la Mode* series, whose 'every touch seemed everlasting and clear as if done in enamel'. On later visits to the Gallery, he related, 'the unaffected work which I saw in Francia, Ludovico Mazzolini, and their schools, also the newly acquired Van Eyck [*Jan Arnolfini and His Wife*] became dear to me,

[1] *Pre-Raphaelitism and the Pre-Raphaelite Brotherhood*, vol. I, pp. 25–26.

as examples of painting most profitable for youthful emulation'. He even found something to admire in Titian's *Bacchus and Ariadne*: 'the flowers—notably the purple flags—were edifying examples of the spirit [of humility and self-restraint] in the great masters, wilfully overlooked by modern students.' London's second most important collection of paintings was housed across the river in the Dulwich Gallery. There Hunt observed that an early portrait of his mother by Rubens 'had surprisingly the characteristics of care and humility', and where, he said, 'a portrait of a man with a stubbly white beard by Holbein fascinated me with its delicate painting.'

One morning when Holman's employer was out of town, a middle-aged woman orange-vendor appeared, and Hunt, who could not afford to buy an orange, offered instead to paint her portrait. A few days later, his employer returned and saw the still incomplete water-colour picture of the pedlar with a basket resting on her head and two oranges held in one hand. He and other workers from near-by offices were so pleased by the likeness that news of the picture spread rapidly—soon reaching the elder Hunt, who promptly complained to Holman's employer that his son apparently was suffering from too much free time. When the man obliged Mr Hunt by becoming a stricter disciplinarian, young Hunt, encouraged by the response to his portrait, made up his mind to leave his position and devote his time entirely to art.

His father remonstrated at length but to no avail; determined to become a painter, Holman threatened to enlist in the army if his intentions were frustrated. Mr Hunt finally yielded reluctantly, and by the end of 1841 the boy was preparing for the R.A. entrance examination. Not wishing to enrol in Sass's (where Gabriel Rossetti was then a first-year student), he studied independently and partly supported himself with all too infrequent portrait commissions. He copied pictures and statues in the British Museum, the National Gallery and the British Institution, and he received permission to attend lectures at the Academy. In June 1843, two years after he had begun his self-directed training programme, he took the qualifying examination and failed. Six months later he again undertook the test and again was unsuccessful. He explained his two failures by saying that 'in the schools there were fashions in drawing, as there are in all human affairs, and I had scarcely taken pains to consider the methods then in vogue'. Mr Hunt's patience had almost come to an end, and

Holman agreed that if he failed on his third try, he would re-enter the world of business. But this drastic step was never necessary; on the third attempt he was rewarded for his perseverance and, on 11 July 1844, was accepted as a probationer in the Antique School. Five months later, after passing the second examination, he became a regular student.

By shunning Sass's, Hunt probably delayed his entrance into the Antique School, but he left himself free to gain a store of knowledge and understanding that never could have come from Mr Cary and his junior instructors. His studies in the National Gallery and especially in the British Museum's Print Room gave him a familiarity with old masters that could have been deepened only by continental travel—and since he had not been taught the 'proper' ways to examine and evaluate pictures, he was able to judge these works of art freely and independently. When he enrolled in the Antique School he was an enlightened, discriminating youth full of ideas and theories quite different from those which had been implanted in the minds of the other probationers. He questioned some almost universally accepted artistic conventions and beliefs, and he was critical of the most highly esteemed contemporary English painters, not one of whom he thought worth emulating. Most of them, he felt, were 'trite and affected', substituted 'inane prettiness for beauty', and created pictures notable for 'hackneyed conventionality' and for 'pictured waxworks playing the part of human beings'. Hunt contrasted his own unorthodoxy with the blind conformity of most of his schoolfellows:

> We knew little of Michael Angelo. . . . while Tintoretto in his might was not known at all. Della Robbia, Donatello, Luini, and Angelico were mere names in books or, at the most, to be seen in the Print Room. In their places the decadents were honoured in all the painting schools, and sober discussion seemed unprofitable. When I put down my brush, which was not often, and was assailed for my opinions as monstrous, I preferred to joke, and to accept the railing accusation of 'flat blasphemy', until my outspoken irreverence towards the reigning gods became a byeword.[1]

If Hunt ever doubted the wisdom of his rebellious course, his uncertainty was probably dispelled by a powerful external stimulant whose force he felt while he was in the Antique School, a book written by 'A Graduate of Oxford', entitled *Modern Painters*. This volume, published in May 1843, marked the debut of another godfather-to-be of

[1] *Pre-Raphaelitism and the Pre-Raphaelite Brotherhood*, vol. I, pp. 52–53.

the P.R.B.—John Ruskin who, only twenty-four years old, had withheld his name from the title page because of his youth. Begun as a defence and vindication of J. M. W. Turner, who in recent years had suffered greatly at the hands of outraged and outrageous critics, the book became the starting point for, eventually, an exhaustive five-volume discourse on the fundamental principles of art. Ruskin criticized the seemingly uncensurable old masters, contending that their gradually increasing conventionality ultimately led to the ruination of men of talent. If a nineteenth-century painter wished to profit from his predecessors, Ruskin advised him to look back to the Italian artists who had lived *before* the birth of Raphael, whose works show 'no effort of any fanciful or ornamental modifications, but loving fidelity to the thing studied'. English painters who were not able to study the paintings of such artists as Cima da Conegliano, Fra Angelico, and Ghirlandajo nevertheless could learn from them what Ruskin considered to be the most valuable of all lessons: for the best source of inspiration an artist should go directly to nature. This was the main theme of *Modern Painters*, expressed on nearly every page—the earnest advice to 'go to nature'.[1] In a typical passage, selected almost at random, from the seventh chapter of Section I of Part II, Ruskin declared:

There is room enough for invention in the pictorial treatment of what exists. There is no more honourable exhibition of imaginative power, than in the selection of such place, choice of such treatment, introduction to such incident, as may produce a noble picture without deviation from one line of the actual truth. . . . I would have the artist take shame to himself in the exact degree in which he finds himself obliged in the production of his picture to lose any,

[1] John Ruskin was not the first Victorian to advise painters to turn (or return) to nature. In the July 1838 issue of *The Edinburgh Review* a writer digressed from his discussion of a recently published art book to complain about a trend that English art for many years had followed: 'English art long laboured under the fatal error, that the exact imitation of reality was inconsistent with the loftiest style of the art; and that to create an ideal, the artist must form an abstraction from nature, not a union of its finest points. The result was a series of conventional forms, faces, and attitudes, in composition; groups composed in the taste of theatrical tableaux; emptiness substituted for breadth; an indifference to all details, a general looseness and indistinctness of form. Our English artists totally forgot or despised the example of all their great Italian predecessors. From the foregrounds of Titian's landscapes, it has been said, and almost without exaggeration, that one might study botany. . . . But attention to details like these was, for a time, thought beneath the dignity of English art. The more the subject could be generalized, the more every thing could be deprived of individualty, so that the whole might be fused into a washy abstraction called the ideal . . . till at last the chief part of the compositions of the English school might have been justly characterized as pictures of *nothing*, and extremely like.' Waagen's Works of Arts and Artists in England, *Edinburgh Review*. Vol. 67. July 1838, pp. 393–4.

even of the smallest parts or most trivial hues which bear a part in the great impression made by the reality. . . . All artists should be ashamed of themselves when they find they have not the power of being true; the right wit of drawing is like the right wit of conversation, not hyperbole, not violence, not friviolity, only well expressed, laconic truth.

After spending six months in Italy, Ruskin in April 1846 brought out Volume II of *Modern Painters*. Under the spell of his recent trip, he lauded the then slighted Venetian school of painters, with whom he had become intimate in Venice, and again he lavishly praised the early Italians—Fra Angelico, Giotto, Orcagna, Benozzo Gozzoli, and Ghirlandajo. Because of its eloquent, persuasive language, wrote E. T. Cook, Ruskin's first important biographer, Volume II of *Modern Painters* 'turned the taste of the age to the primitives'. Ruskin also dealt at length with the question of how truthfully to paint various aspects of nature, such as vegetation, rocks, water, and clouds. A representative passage deals with the proper way to paint the foreground of a picture. Contrary to the prevailing conventions, Ruskin insisted that it was important to devote a great deal of care to all of the details, even those that might seem to be trivial and insignificant:

One lesson we are invariably taught by all [great artists] however approached or viewed—that the work of the Great Spirit of nature is as deep and unapproachable in the lowest as in the noblest objects—that the Divine mind is as visible in its full energy of operation on every lowly bank and mouldering stone, as in the lifting of the pillars of heaven, and settling the foundation of the earth; and that to the rightly perceiving mind, there is the same infinity, the same majesty, the same power, the same unity, and the same perfection, manifest in the casting of the clay as in the scattering of the cloud, in the mouldering of the dust as in the kindling of the day-star.

[Part II, Section IV, Chapter IV, 30]

I have discussed both volumes of *Modern Painters* because although Hunt apparently first read the second volume,[1] it seems certain that by 1848 he was also familiar with the earlier book.

Permitted to keep his borrowed copy for only twenty-four hours, the enthralled Hunt sat almost till dawn poring over Ruskin's 450 pages. It was to him 'an event of the greatest importance', and 'of all its readers none could have felt more strongly than myself that it was written for him'. He declared to a friend, 'By Jove! passages in it

[1] In the passage in *Pre-Raphaelitism and the Pre-Raphaelite Brotherhood* where Hunt tells of his first reading of Ruskin's book (vol. I, p. 90), he refers to several specific pictures, all of which are treated in vol. II of *Modern Painters*.

made my heart thrill. He feels the power and responsibility of art more than any author I have ever read . . . the men he describes were of such high purpose and vigour that they present a striking contrast to the uninspired men of today. This shows a need for us young artists to consider what course we should follow . . . the book I speak of helps one to see the difference between dead and living art at a critical juncture. . . . The determination to save one's self and art must be made in youth. I feel that is the only hope, at least for myself. One's thoughts must stir before the hands can do.' This book showed Hunt that he did not walk alone, that his ideas were not foolish or wrong-headed. His reading of Ruskin also lessened the likelihood of his remaining for long in the Academy Schools. He continued to work diligently—Hunt could never have sat idling or day-dreaming—and in due time was promoted to the School for the Living Model. But by the spring of 1848, when Rossetti praised his *Eve of St Agnes*, it was clear that he would gain little more from the Royal Academy.

4

Millais, the Reluctant Brother

When Rossetti called on Holman Hunt at his home in Holborn, two or three days after their conversation at the Exhibition, it was a meeting of two young rebels who were eager to challenge the powers that governed the world of art. Hunt brought out paintings, studies and sketches, all of which Rossetti praised to the skies; Hunt voiced some of his artistic ideas, all of which Rossetti enthusiastically endorsed. Pleased to learn that his former schoolmate was not as frivolous as he had once thought him to be, Hunt said of their discussion, 'My last designs and experiments I rejoiced to display before a man of his poetic instincts; and it was pleasant to hear him repeat my propositions and theories in his own richer phrase.' Because of the opposition of the other students to his ideas, Hunt was particularly delighted with Rossetti's emphatic responses—which, unknown to Hunt, had been conditioned by two months of listening to similar views in a studio on Clipstone Street. (Indeed, it would have been quite in character for Rossetti to have clothed the opinions of Ford Madox Brown in his own words and voice.) Now that a rapport had been established between them, Rossetti directed the conversation to his own principal problem. He described to Hunt, agonizedly, the boredom and dejection from which he suffered because of Brown's instructional programme. Was it really necessary, he asked, to return again and again to still life paintings? Eager to be accepted as a pupil and co-worker, Rossetti probably magnified his woes—as is indicated by the already quoted letter to Aunt Charlotte, written a month later. But his plight won Hunt's sympathy—helped, no doubt, by the flattering thought that a mere acquaintance should come to him for guidance. A man of tact, Hunt offered no criticism of Brown's teaching methods; in fact he admitted that he himself would have recommended a similar course of instruction in all 'ordinary cases'. But Rossetti surely was no ordinary case. And so Hunt suggested a line of action which did not run counter to Brown's procedure but was more likely to be stimulating to this particular unordinary case. He advised Rossetti to select one of the three designs he had submitted to the Cyclographic Society and to use it as the model for an original oil-painting. Rossetti would begin by filling in all of the still life that was called for by the composition. Thus he would be doing what Brown had counselled, but he would not become bored: Hunt rightly believed that, 'invested with vital interest as links in an idea to be welded together, he would find each day's labour interesting and instructive until he had acquired sufficient proficiency to paint the figures in the picture'. That Hunt probably would be more sympathetic than Brown towards Rossetti's desire to paint meaningful pictures is shown by this sentence from an early undated letter to Stephens: 'No great painter, good or bad, ever wasted his time and energies upon preparatory work longer than was necessary to give him a rude power of expressing his thoughts.'

Rossetti responded with predictable enthusiasm: he would begin work at once, and, furthermore, in order to profit fully from Hunt's instruction, he would work in Hunt's studio. But for once Rossetti failed, at least temporarily, to have his own way. Hunt had already agreed to instruct a pupil, and it would have been impossible for three to work in the small studio. Hunt assured Rossetti, however, that they would see each other often, and that if he worked in Hancock's studio he (Hunt) would pay frequent professional visits. Hunt was probably relieved to have an exuse for not inviting Rossetti to share his studio: never one to act impulsively, he would have wanted further proof of his former schoolmate's seriousness of purpose before joining forces with him under one roof.

This meeting with Hunt began the most important stage in Rossetti's artistic career—yet for a few weeks his life outwardly was not greatly changed. He sometimes visited Hunt, and occasionally they met in Hancock's studio, but he also continued to go periodically to Clipstone Street, where he apparently completed a portrait of Christina, his second finished oil-painting.

It was a little over a month after his first visit to Hunt's home that

Rossetti brought his new friend to Brown's studio. The first face-to-face encounter of Rossetti's two closest associates was cool but not unpleasant. Brown's 'deliberate manner of speech and the reserve of his demeanour', Hunt reported, 'suggested that he was offended at the manner of my intrusion between him and his former pupil.' Rossetti, Hunt rightly guessed, had not 'deemed it expedient to explain the new arrangement' to Brown, nor had he even mentioned Hunt's name to his former teacher. Not long afterwards Brown paid a courtesy call on Hunt, and the two men were cordial, although Brown was somewhat critical of the 'microscopic detail' of Hunt's paintings. Hunt on his part never came close to sharing Rossetti's admiration of Brown's work. He thought *The Execution of Mary Queen of Scots* 'had lugubrious elements of tragedy without stirring an emotion of pity', and of *Parisina*, he felt that 'the subject,[1] objectionable even in verse, was incalculably more so when realized on canvas'. Concerning *Wickliffe*, he said, 'I never spared the precious time to go to Hyde Park Corner to see it . . . when first I saw it in Brown's studio . . . it struck me as being harmonious and pleasant in a decorative sense but as to natural truth much wanting in solidity—the hues being those of gelatinous matter if not of stained glass, rather than of substances absorbing some rays and reflecting others'. The relationship between Gabriel's first and second private tutors, chilly from the beginning, never completely thawed.

As time passed, Gabriel saw gradually less of Brown and more of Hunt. He and his new friend painted and talked and enjoyed themselves. They took time off from painting to travel by steamboat down the Thames to Greenwich and Blackheath, where, observing Ruskin's injunction to 'let the details of the foreground be separately studied', they sketched landscapes for future pictures. Rossetti, who had always loved the great, vital city, now fell in love with its crowded waterway—and never lost his enthusiasm for either.

Wherever they were, Rossetti and Hunt were fine companions, despite their personal dissimilarities. Hunt's simple, retiring way of life had seldom included visits to oyster shops or coffee houses, or evening hours spent anywhere but at home reading or sleeping. He possessed a lively intellectual curiosity that was stimulated by such

[1] *Parisina's Sleep* had been turned down by the Salon in Paris because of the alleged impropriety of its subject, a furiously jealous husband in bed with his sleeping wife immediately after she has murmured endearments to her absent lover.

non-artistic topics, anathema to Rossetti, as economics, politics, astronomy, biology, and geology, which he felt could and should serve the cause of art. Yet Hunt was never withdrawn in Brown's bitter and cynical way; he enjoyed dancing, and was noted for his hearty, uncontrollable laughter, which, Gabriel once said, 'answers one's own like a grotto full of echoes'. If he had anything in common with Brown, it was his fervent, unswerving devotion to painting. Both men regarded their art as almost their only *raison d'être*; both earnestly believed in the high moral and social purpose of their vocation, and in the influence, for good or ill, that artists could exert on their society; and neither would have had any sympathy for or understanding of the doctrine of art for art's sake. Both, too, aspired to be creators of fresh, original compositions—and except that Hunt, a loyal Ruskinite, placed greater emphasis upon the artist's obligation to be reverently faithful to nature, they had reached similar conclusions concerning the principles of painting.

Of the two, only Hunt showed any desire to propagate his conclusions. Brown was too misanthropic to be concerned with spreading a gospel: but Hunt, quiet though he was, at times displayed the zeal of a missionary. Whereas Brown regarded Rossetti as merely a friend and fellow rebel, Hunt considered him a convert whom he began proselytizing during their first conversation in his home. Hunt had recently begun the painting he would exhibit in 1849, and, as he later recounted, he explained to Gabriel his current objectives:

I showed him my new picture of 'Rienzi', in the painting of which . . . I was putting in practice the principle of rejection of conventional dogma and pursuing that of direct application to Nature for each feature, however humble a part of the foreground or background this might be. I justified the doing of this thoroughly as the only sure means of eradicating the stereotyped tricks of decadent schools, and of any conventions not recommended by experienced judgment.

When Hunt spoke, or sermonized, on the importance of adhering to nature rather than man-made doctrines, he found a responsive listener in Gabriel, who frequently burst in to rhapsodize on *his* favourite subject—their approaching artistic and financial prosperity.

The comradeship might never have become a real alliance had it not been for an unexpected occurrence in July: Hunt sold his *Eve of St Agnes* for the asking price, seventy pounds. Now he was able to rent a conveniently located studio he had seen and liked—and because his other pupil was no longer to study with him, and he had himself fallen under the Rossettian spell, he accepted Gabriel's proposal that they share its use and expense. (Rossetti could confidently enter into this agreement because his father's friend Charles Lyell had paid him ten pounds for his still incomplete painting of old Gabriele.) So, early in August, when Hunt had finished the landscape foreground and background of *Rienzi*, and Rossetti had begun the still-life portions of a picture entitled *The Girlhood of Mary Virgin*, the two youths took possession of a studio and an upstairs bedroom where Hunt would live at 7 Cleveland Street,[1] at the south-west corner of Howland Street, two streets east of Brown's residence. Although it almost touched fashionable Fitzroy Square, Cleveland Street was as shabby and squalid as Clipstone Street; and, as F. G. Stephens described it, the first studio of Dante Gabriel Rossetti was in keeping with its surroundings:

Nothing could be more depressing than the large gaunt chamber where Rossetti executed two memorable pictures and from which posterity must perforce date the inception of Pre-Raphaelitism. . . . Except early in the morning, nothing like that fulness of light which painters now demand was obtainable where the dingy walls, distempered of a dark maroon, which dust and smoke stains had deepened, added a most undesirable gloom. One's approach to it was by a half-lighted staircase, up which the fuss and clatter of a boys' school kept by the landlord of the house, and too often dashed with sounds of chastisement and sorrow, frequently arose; add to these uncomely elements a dimly-lighted hall, surcharged by air of which the damp of the timber-yard was not the only source of its mustiness, and a shabby out-at-elbows doorway, giving access from the street that even then was rapidly 'going down in the world'—it was sliding, so to say, to its present [1894] zero of rag and bottle shops, penny barbers, pawn-brokers, and retailers of the smallest possible capital.[2]

Offended by Stephens's brutally realistic picture of his first home away from home, Hunt observed that 'it had been whitewashed and distempered thoroughly ere our entrance'.

But the house was not the least depressing to Hunt or Rossetti, whose state of exultation might have seemed more fitting to Park Lane than to Cleveland Street. How could these two youths feel dejected when one of them had at last become independent of his family and the other felt for the first time like a truly creative visual artist?

. . .

[1] Later in the century the house number was changed from 7 to 46.
[2] F. G. Stephens, *Dante Gabriel Rossetti*, pp. 37–38.

The move to Cleveland Street alone would have made August 1848 memorable for Rossetti, but the month became momentous for him a few days later when he began his friendship with John Everett Millais.

A youth of nineteen (thirteen months younger than Rossetti), Millais had already been widely acclaimed as the most promising young painter in Great Britain—and in fact was a minor legend. When he was only a child of six, living in St Helier (on the English Channel Island of Jersey), the precocity of his talents and the maturity of his craftsmanship astonished everyone, including the local art masters. The boy's formal education lasted for exactly two days; on the third day his teacher spanked him for disobedience, whereupon young Millais bit him and was forthwith expelled from school. His education was carried on by Mrs Millais, of whom her son often said, 'I owe everything to my mother.' He was indeed heavily indebted to her, and also to his father, a country gentleman who was moderately talented in art and music: both of them recognized their son's ability and did everything they could to foster its development. Holman Hunt said that when first he heard of Millais, 'what surprised me most was that his family were delighted at the prospect of his becoming an artist'. Since they were comfortably well off financially, they could provide their son with more than moral encouragement; they did no less than dedicate their lives to 'Johnny', who, they were sure, would one day be ranked among the world's greatest painters.

In 1838 the leading drawing teacher of St Helier confessed that the nine-year-old boy could learn nothing more from him, and so his parents took him to London. There they showed some of his sketches to the President of the Royal Academy, Sir Martin Shee, who praised them highly, and, believing them to be the work of a teen-aged boy, advised the mother and father to enrol their child in Sass's school of art. The family soon established a London residence, and in the winter of 1838–9, two and a half years before Rossetti began his art schooling, Millais entered the Bloomsbury academy.

The routine at Sass's, which was to prove almost intolerably tedious and wearisome to Rossetti, and was to discourage Hunt from entering the school, was an enjoyment to Millais, who was such an exceptional student that on 17 July 1840, only one month after his eleventh birthday, he became the youngest probationary student in the history of the Royal Academy. His brief, seemingly effortless career at Sass's typified Millais the artist. Whereas neither Rossetti nor Hunt could ever hope to attain artistic proficiency except after a long, laborious struggle marked by many difficulties and frequent failures, Millais would always wield a facile pencil and brush. His success continued at the Academy Schools, where he was admitted to regular studentship on 12 December 1840. In 1843, 'The Child', as he was called, was awarded the Antique School's top medal, which was only the first of his Academic honours.

In 1845, when he was sixteen, Millais could have been self-supporting—and did in fact help to defray his family expenses with the £100, later increased to £150, he received from a dealer annually in payment for painting small pictures and backgrounds for large works. On 4 May 1846, five weeks before his seventeenth birthday, his long and distinguished career as a Royal Academy exhibitor began with the showing of *Pizarro Seizing the Inca of Peru.* In 1847 he exhibited at the Academy *Elgiva Seized by the Soldiers of Odo*; but in the following year he had to be content with a favourably received picture at the British Institution. He was unrepresented at Trafalgar Square for, surprisingly, his *Cymon and Iphigenia* had been rejected—possibly because, as Hunt suggested, 'the work was incomplete'.

Millais's early paintings showed that he was a highly gifted youth, but revealed nothing revolutionary or even unconventional. They were historical pictures painted within the framework of Academic traditions, violating none of the cherished rules and conventions. Young Millais, like most of his schoolmates, seemed unquestioningly to accept these man-made laws; he differed from them only in the degree of his talent and success. A typical journalistic opinion of Millais's early work is included in the 19 February 1848 issue of *The Literary Gazette*, whose review of the British Institution exhibition contained these words:

The Tribe of Benjamin seizing the Daughters of Shiloh in the Vineyards (259), by J. E. Millais. By Jove, there are no Jewish Disabilities here. The Hebrews are having fine fun, and clutching the dark, the brown, and the fairest daughters of Shiloh about in a fine fashion. It is a busy time, and, as the lasses are somewhat nude, the exploit does not seem so difficult or dangerous as Ruben's [*sic*] 'Rape of the Sabine Women'. The colouring is in the style of Etty, and some of the figures and countenances remind us of Maclise. The artist could not copy higher in our school for such a picture.

'Etty' and 'Maclise' refer to William Etty, who had been a distinguished Royal Academician for twenty years, and Daniel Maclise, who had been an Academician for eight years.

Neither as a person nor as a painter did the young Millais appear to be a rebel. His parents raised him to be not only an artist but also a level-headed middle-class Englishman. As a student, Hunt recounted, Millais always 'dressed with exact conventionality so as to avoid in any degree courting attention as a genius'. During one conversation with Hunt, Millais condemned 'agitators'. When Hunt observed that Jesus had been denounced as an agitator, Millais replied, 'Yes, and He got stoned! And quite right, too, from the point of view of the people who saw nothing of His divinity—only His agitation. That's all I'd have seen if I had been there; I'm afraid I'd have thrown stones, too!'

In 1847 Millais, was a thin, curly-haired six-footer whose handsome, typically English face almost always wore a friendly smile. Unlike Rossetti and Hunt, he enjoyed outdoor physical activities. One of his youthful friends recalled that 'in his studio Millais was wont, when time did not allow of outdoor exercises, to perform surprising feats of agility and strength. . . . He was great in leaping, and I well remember how in the studio he was wont to clear my arm outstretched from the shoulder—that is, about five feet from the ground—at one spring. The studio measures nineteen feet six inches by twenty feet, thus giving him not more than fourteen feet run. Many similar feats attested the strength and energy of the artist.'[1] An ardent, somewhat compulsive conversationalist, he talked in a vivacious manner about his many interests and enthusiasms, and he did not hesitate to voice his candid, unwavering confidence in himself as an artist. Perhaps this confidence produced his constantly tranquil and stable temperament. One of his boyhood companions wrote that he was 'blessed with a most pleasing, good-tempered, and gentlemanly manner. During the many years I knew him I never recollect his losing his temper or saying an unkind word to anyone.'

Yet that same self-confidence never lulled Millais into self-satisfaction. He worked indefatigably, always seeking to improve himself. As Hunt declared, 'he was always more eager to hear in what he could go beyond the mark reached than to be content with his present

[1] Frederic George Stephens, quoted by John G. Millais in *The Life and Letters of Sir John Everett Millais*, p. 87.

achievement'. Hunt first met Millais in the British Museum in 1844, before Hunt had been accepted into the Antique School. Millais noticed a drawing that Hunt had been working on, and complimented him on it, saying that it surely qualified him to be an Academic student. Soon Hunt passed his R.A. entrance examination, and in the ensuing months he and Millais frequently conversed together at school. Hunt noted with interest that though Millais worked within the accepted traditions, unlike most of the other students he had never copied old masters or the works of any of his predecessors. For several years their friendship was confined to Trafalgar Square, and then late in 1847 Hunt was invited to visit the Millais home at 83 Gower Street, where he was introduced to Mrs Millais as 'the student who draws so well'. Millais brought out his studio work, and, said Hunt, 'he was unaffectedly eager to hear my appreciation, and led me on to the points with which he was himself best content; yet he invariably challenged candour, and ended with, "you'll see I'll make my next much better!" ' Millais returned Hunt's call, and they then became close friends who constantly visited each other's studios.

Hunt happily found that Millais was by no means 'bound to dogmas . . . that had gained general acceptance, but quite ready to re-examine settled views, even though they seemed to him at first above question'. Thus when Hunt spoke of the harmful influence that Reynolds's teaching had had on English art, Millais replied, 'I quite agree with what you say.' Hunt then told Millais that his current work in progress, *Cymon and Iphigenia,* showed that he actually was far from being a die-hard conservative: 'You see what a dangerous rebel I am, but you are every bit as bad as myself! Here you are painting a poetic subject in which you know all authorities would insist upon conventional treatment, and you cannot pretend that this work of yours is academic. If Howard or Frost undertook the subject, you know perfectly well that while they would certainly have made some of the nymphs fair, and some dark to give contrast, there would be no kind of variety in the shape of the faces, not one would be out of the oval in any degree, none would have nose, eyes, or mouth a bit different in any shape from the other; all their limbs, too, would be of the same pattern; in fact, every care would be taken that they should be waxen effigies than living creatures. . . . Now what have you done? You've made beings of varied form as you see them in Nature. You've made living persons, not tinted effigies. Oh, that'll never do! it is too revolutionary.'

Millais's answer certainly must have pleased Hunt: 'I know, but the more attentively I look at Nature the more I detect in it unexpected delights: it's so infinitely better than anything I could compose, that I can't help following it whatever the consequences may be.'

Hunt then concluded that neither of them was 'sophisticated enough to appreciate the system in vogue, not to feel that it ends in an insufferable mannerism and sameness of feature that soon pall upon the senses beyond toleration'.

At this stage in their friendship the dominant partner was Hunt. He freely offered his opinions and theories, analysed styles of painting, commented on the work of past and present painters. He talked enthusiastically about Ruskin and *Modern Painters*—which his unscholarly companion refused to read. He even tried to introduce the poetry of Keats to Millais, who at first responded unappreciatively, putting a stop to Hunt's reading of 'The Eve of St Agnes' by saying deprecatingly, 'It's like a parson.'

Although he could not read Ruskin or relish Keats, Millais was a receptive and impressionable listener, who was so forcibly impressed by Hunt's words that he seemed very quickly on artistic matters to be of one mind with his friend, who now embraced him as a fellow insurgent. Together they began systematically to re-examine the accepted ideas of painting. They came to view in a new light many highly regarded works of art, including those of the Academic idol, Raphael whose *Transfiguration* they condemned 'for its grandiose disregard of the simplicity of truth, the pompous posturing of the Apostles, and the unspiritual attitudinizing of the Saviour'. They agreed that as soon as they had completed their current pictures, neither of which was unconventional, they would put to the test these concepts which had been dominating their discussions. Millais now was as eager as Hunt to depart from the conventions, and he declared, 'You shall see in my next picture if I won't paint something much better than "Cymon and Iphigenia"; it is too late now to treat this more naturally; indeed I have misgivings whether there is time to finish it as it is begun.'

Of the two paintings, only *The Eve of St Agnes* was exhibited, and while Millais spent the summer sketching in Oxford, Hunt painted the foreground and background of *Rienzi* and took possession of the studio in Cleveland Street. Shortly after he and Rossetti had become established in their workshop, Millais returned to London, and Hunt invited his co-tenant to accompany him to 83 Gower Street. Since

Millais had almost completed his work in the School for the Living Model when Rossetti had entered the Antique School, they were barely acquainted with each other, and it was with great anticipation that Gabriel walked with Hunt to the street Tennyson once called 'long and unlovely', to meet John Everett Millais.

They found Millais in a long, shed-like room, converted into a studio, at the rear of the house; it contained a window covered with painted Gothic figures so as to resemble stained glass, a mantelpiece holding statuettes of a cow and a calf, and a lady's work-table upon which rested a nearly empty canvas. In this studio in August 1848 three young men engaged in their first conversation together: a twenty-one-year-old thinker, a twenty-year-old dreamer, and a nineteen-year-old doer. In the words of the noted French art critic, Robert de la Sizeranne,

> The trio made a perfect whole. Hunt had faith, Rossetti had eloquence, and Millais had talent. Rossetti was more of a poet, Millais more of a painter, Hunt more of a Christian. Rossetti, restless and excitable, wanted to prophesy something, it mattered not what it might be, to every newcomer. The excellent, conscientious Hunt wanted to believe, and devote himself to some great work. The practical and ambitious Millais wanted a theory to raise him above the intelligent crowd, and thought nothing about prophecy or belief.[1]

Less than thirty days after their initial meeting this striking threesome founded an organization which would become the most notorious and most controversial artistic coterie in the English-speaking world of the nineteenth century—an organization which called itself The Pre-Raphaelite Brotherhood.

[1] *English Contemporary Art*, pp. 32–33.

5

The Formation of the Brotherhood

The three young artists continued to work by day in their studios, and after sunset almost invariably met in Millais's home, where for hours they talked about art. One evening in August, a few days after their first conversation, Hunt and Rossetti saw lying on a table a volume of Carlo Lasinio's engravings of the famous frescoes at the Campo Santo. Most visitors to Pisa have seen the Burial Ground, known as the Campo Santo, which is situated on Piazza del Duomo alongside the Cathedral and the Baptistery, a little over a hundred yards from the Leaning Tower; it was established in the twelfth-century and is surrounded by a thirteenth-century building whose interior is decorated by fourteenth- and early fifteenth-century frescoes. The paintings depict scenes inspired by the Bible, legends of the saints, and other religious material; and although the artists cannot be reliably identified, the Lasinio book attributes half the pictures to Benozzo Gozzoli and the rest to Giotto, Spinello Aretino, Simone Memmi, Veneziano, Pietro Laurati, Buffalmacco, and Andrea Orcagna. Ruskin visited the Campo Santo in 1845 and, though they were badly preserved, he proclaimed the frescoes to be 'eternally and unalterably true . . . a veritable Palestine'. A letter to his father, dated 18 May 1845, shows how these works had affected Ruskin:

I never believed the patriarchal history before, but I do now, for I have seen it. You cannot conceive the vividness and fullness of conception of these great old men. In spite of every violation of the common confounded rules of art, of anachronisms and fancies . . . Abraham and Adam, and Cain, Rachel and Rebekah, all are there, real, visible, created, substantial, such as they were, as they must have been; one cannot look at them without being certain that they have lived . . .

But Ruskin was less complimentary about Lasinio's engravings, which he called 'execrable'. Anyone who has seen both the Campo Santo and Lasinio might agree with him, but Holman Hunt had never been to Italy, and so was exhilarated: for the first time he and his two friends could inspect a book of reproductions of early Italian paintings.[1] They turned its pages and looked at the Pre-Raphaelite images—the creation of man, the expulsion from Paradise, the building of the Ark, the construction of the Tower of Babel, the sacrifice of Isaac, the destruction of Jericho, the meeting of Solomon and Sheba, the suffering of Job, and so on—and Hunt remarked on the artists' obvious sincerity and seriousness of purpose and on the originality of the treatment, untrammelled by conventions; and, as he later related, he noted 'that the Campo Santo designs were remarkable for incident derived from attentive observation of inexhaustible Nature'.

To illustrate Hunt's comments, I have selected from the designs, two paintings that portray events in the life of Abraham, *The Departure of Hagar from the House of Abraham* and *The Sacrifice of Isaac*. Both pictures surely reveal an 'inexhaustible Nature'. In the former work one may see in addition to the principal figures—Abraham, Sarah, Hagar, and Ishmael—twenty-eight other human beings, four angels, two donkeys, three birds, portions of three buildings, five tents, eleven trees, and assorted foliage, clouds, cliffs, and mountains. The latter painting naturally includes Abraham, Isaac, and the rescuing angel, but it also exhibits nearly thirty other people, one donkey, one cow, more than two dozen assorted trees, and an abundance of shrubbery, and hills and mountains. Each picture is overbrimming with vitality, and each shows a fine feeling for nature, in everything from the expressions and gestures of the human and angelic beings to the garments, buildings, and trees. Neither scene contains one centre of interest, and it does not appear that more attention was devoted to the principal figures than to secondary details. In *The Sacrifice of Isaac*, the two children in the left foreground who seem to be shadow boxing,

[1] Among the 214 paintings owned by the National Gallery at this time were eight works by Rubens, eight by Claude, seven by Rembrandt, four by van Dyck, three each by Correggio, Titian, Murillo and Poussin, two each by Raphael, Veronese and Canaletto, and one each by Andrea del Sarto, Bellini, Tintoretto, Cuyp, Ruisdael and Velasquez. The collection contained nothing by an Italian who ante-dated Raphael; the only 'Pre-Raphaelite' picture, chronologically speaking, was van Eyck's famous *Portrait of Jan Arnolfini and His Wife*.

Courtesy of Walker Art Gallery, Liverpool.

The Eve of St Agnes by Holman Hunt.

Courtesy the Trustees of the British Museum.

The Departure of Hagar from the House of Abraham from Lasinio's Campo Santi Engravings.

Courtesy the Trustees of the British Museum.

The Sacrifice of Isaac from Lasinio's Campo Santi Engravings.

Courtesy National Portrait Gallery, London.
Ford Madox Brown by Rossetti.

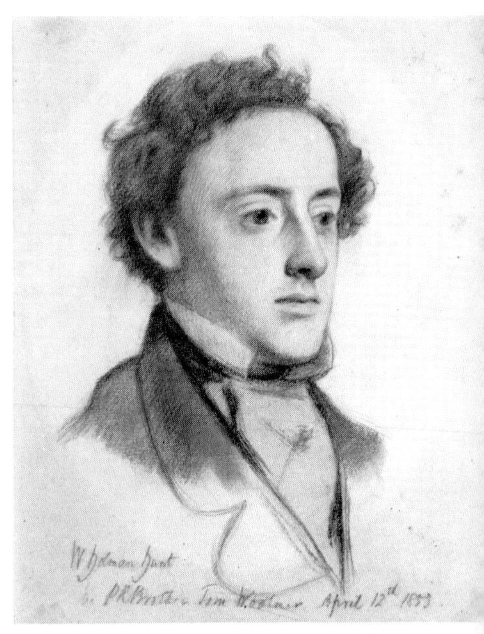

Courtesy National Portrait Gallery, Londc
John Everett Millais by Holman Hunt.

Courtesy National Portrait Gallery, London.
Dante Gabriel Rossetti, by Himself.

By permission of the Museum and
Gallery, Birmingh
William Holman Hunt, by Himself.

Reproduced by courtesy of the Trustees of the Tate Gallery, London.

Cordelia Watching at the Bedside of Lear by Ford Madox Brown.

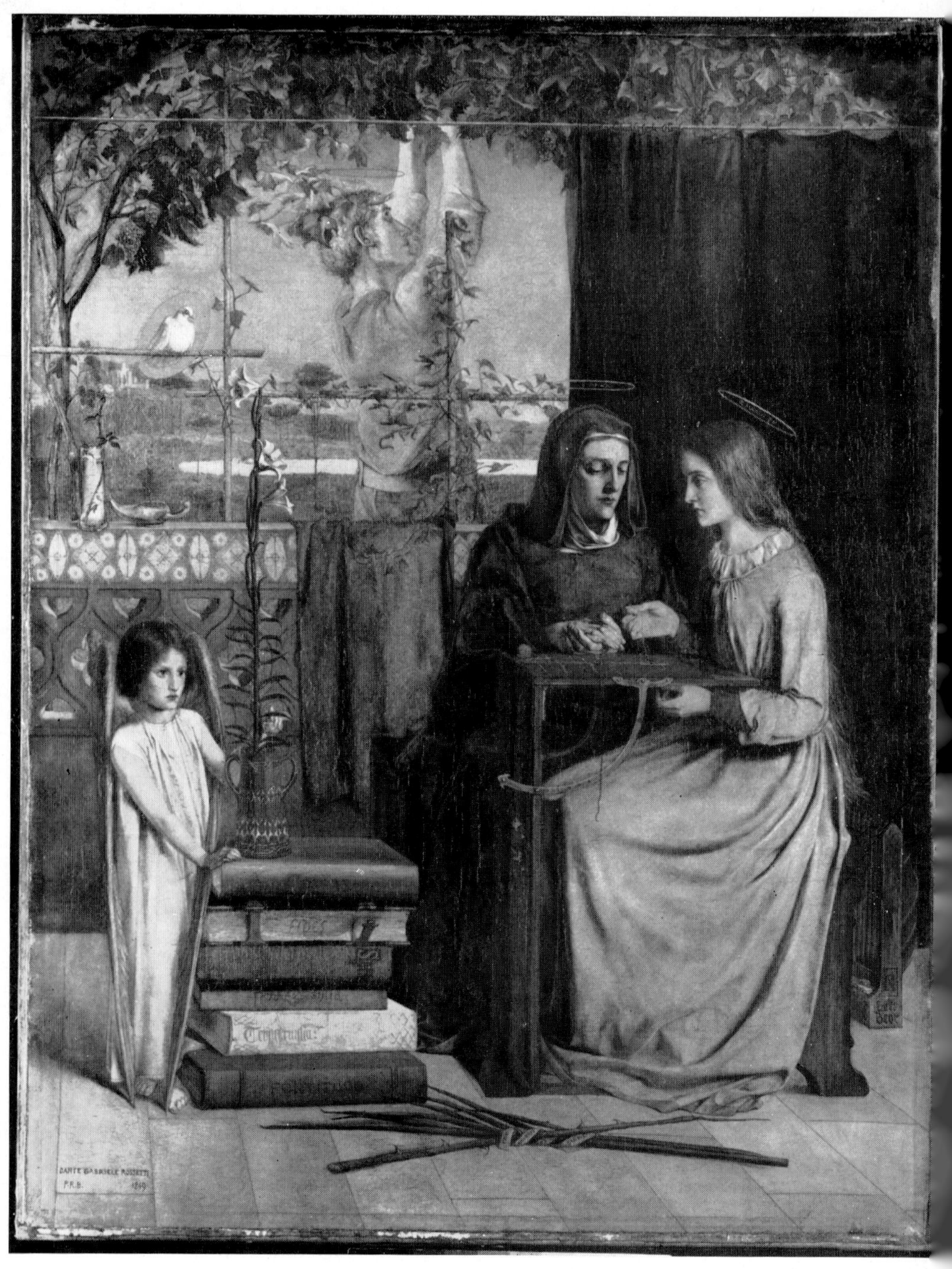

Reproduced by courtesy of the Trustees of the Tate Gallery, Lond

The Girlhood of Mary Virgin by Rossetti.

Courtesy of Walker Art Gallery, Liverpool.

Lorenzo and Isabella by Millais.

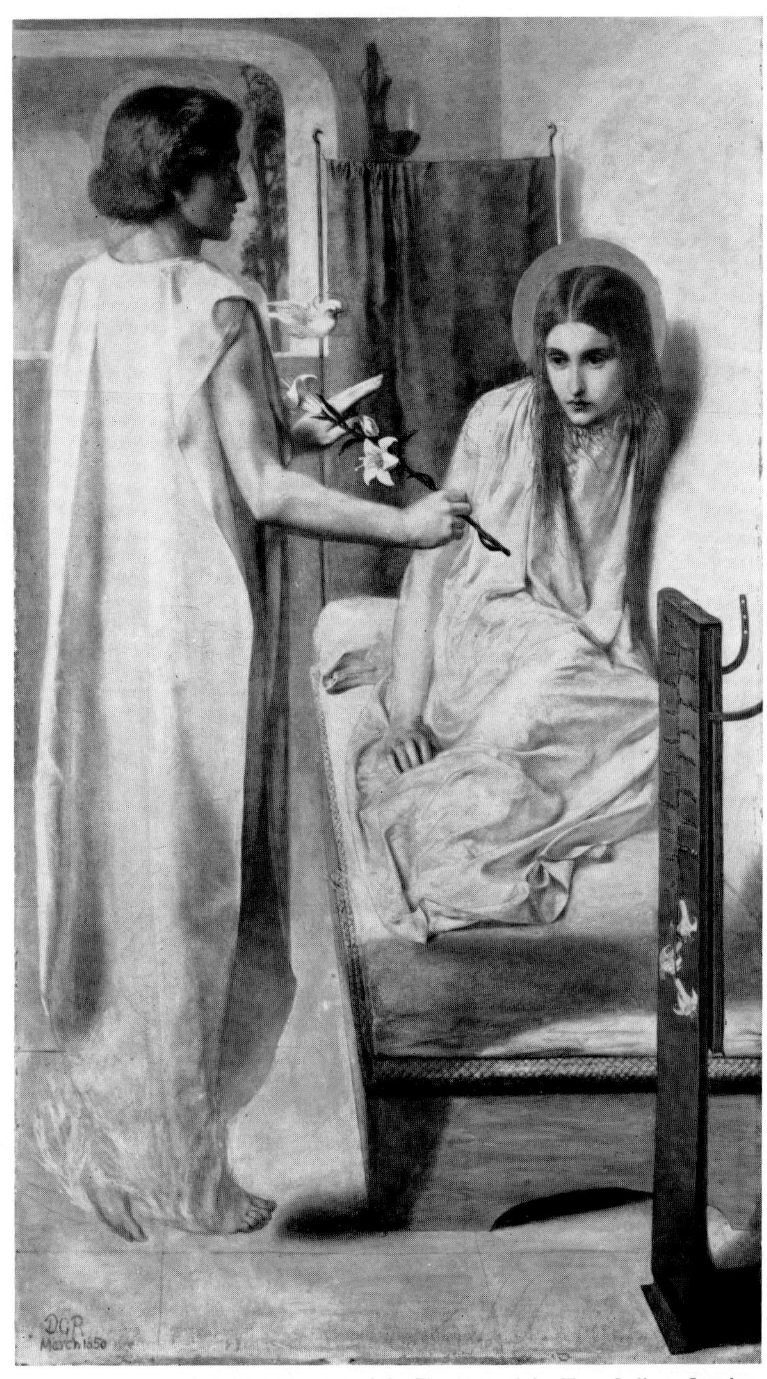

Reproduced by courtesy of the Trustees of the Tate Gallery, London.

Ecce Ancilla Domini by Rossetti.

the partially loaded donkey standing alongside them, the four men seated to the right of the donkey, the cow grazing to the right of them, the large tree in the centre of the picture, and all the rest of the foreground and background have been delineated as carefully and prominently as the group of three who appear (not conspicuously) to the far right, the angel staying the hand of Abraham as he is about to take his son's life. Both pictures present universally familiar incidents in a fresh and unaffected way.

It has long been accepted that Lasinio's engravings motivated the formation of the Pre-Raphaelite Brotherhood. But the August evening when Hunt, Millais and Rossetti first saw the book did not seem to be destined for immortality. Millais was not excited by the volume, and Rossetti was amused by the naïve simplicity of the pictures. On the following day, Brown reported, 'Rossetti came to me laughing, or at least more or less joking about some discovery of Hunt's . . . I told him it was nonsense to laugh at them, they were the finest things in the world, and he would far better go and look at them again.'

Chastened by Brown's remarks, Rossetti looked again—and reversed his opinion. As Brown put it, 'Of course he said just what I did after he had thought about it.'

So Hunt's enthusiasm for these mediocre engravings became contagious. As F. G. Stephens later said, Lasinio's pictures became 'points of crystallization or nuclei of enthusiasm for their till then somewhat nebulous ideals in art'. Hunt had been looking for something to serve as the focal point of their rebellion, and when he came upon this book he knew his search had ended. Their manual of instruction, the embodiment of their ideals, the shining example to be held before their eyes, would be the frescoes at the Campo Santo. For the mercurial Rossetti and the highly impressionable Millais, as well as for the zealous Hunt, this oversize book of engravings would be the touchstone.

In view of the many misconceptions that exist concerning the relationship between the Italian Pre-Raphaelites and their English descendants, it must be stressed that it was no antiquarian impulse that drew the three young men to these paintings. The imperfections, as Hunt pointed out, did not escape them:

. . . we did not curb our amusement at the immature perspective, the undeveloped power of drawing, the feebleness of light and shade, the ignorance of any but mere black and white differences of racial geometrical forms in the landscape; these simplicities, already out of date in the painter's day, we noted as belonging altogether to the past and to the dead revivalists, with whom we had determined to have neither part nor lot.[1]

Hunt, Millais and Rossetti intended to be *guided* by the Campo Santo frescoes—not to imitate or copy them.

The development from this 'point of crystallization' to the actual formation of the Pre-Raphaelite Brotherhood was relatively quick—and the motivating force behind it was the personality of Dante Gabriel Rossetti. As Hunt admitted, it was he who originated the 'idea of extending our numbers'. Hunt and Millais had no thought of asking anyone to join them; indeed Millais was lukewarm even about associating himself with the inexperienced Rossetti. Gabriel himself, however, whose 'enthusiasm for our principles', Hunt said, 'grew with greater familiarity', was eager to bring in others to share this enthusiasm. His desire to augment the informal trio grew from his inborn love of fellowship, his keen interest in the idea of an organized attack upon the art establishment, and perhaps also his feelings of insecurity. Rossetti was accustomed to dominate those with whom he was associated; but how could a mere tyro dominate two such talented and experienced young men as Holman Hunt and John Millais? Only, perhaps, if he was emboldened by the presence of other less glittering confederates. So he raised the question of expanding their alliance.

Rossetti's companions responded with a marked lack of enthusiasm. Millais was too single-minded about his own work to take much interest in forming an organization; and Hunt worried about a possible distortion of his principles and ideals if they brought in fresh associates. But the resistance was neither strong nor enduring. After assuring him that they would select discriminatingly, Rossetti won a qualified stamp of approval from Hunt, always the proselytizer, who came to recognize that their cause in fact might be pushed forward by a small number of judiciously chosen converts. Hunt then won Millais over to subscribing in principle to Rossetti's plan: 'If they fail, I don't see how they can interfere with us; and if they are made truly good artists, our Body will become the stronger, and we may more perfectly revolutionize good taste.' Millais remained cool to the idea (he

[1] *Pre-Raphaelitism and the Pre-Raphaelite Brotherhood*, vol. I, p. 133.

was one of the few who could withstand Rossetti's spellbinding); but he agreed to keep an open mind—partly because he respected Hunt's judgment, and partly, perhaps, because he was attracted to the idea of a united onslaught upon the society which, though it had rendered him many honours, had also humiliated him recently by rejecting his latest offering.

Many years later Brown said, concerning the Pre-Raphaelite Brotherhood, 'Rossetti talked them into founding it.' Gabriel, to be sure, was the prime mover behind its formation, but Hunt's generative importance is self-evident. He was the philosopher of Pre-Raphaelitism, the man who had formulated the ideas which gave impetus to the organizational zeal of Rossetti. Millais, too, was indispensable, simply because he was the best known young painter in the country: his mere presence would be a stabilizing and unifying force, and his unhesitating self-reliance and self-confidence could not but be an inspiration to his comrades. When William Rossetti took up the question of who had been responsible for establishing the Pre-Raphaelite Brotherhood, he rightfully deemed the 'just claims of Hunt and Millais . . . as co-equal with Gabriel's . . . Not one of the three could have done much as innovator without the other two. The bond of mutual support was essential . . .'

Now the three youths' principal concern was the composition of their organization-to-be. It might seem as if the first person to be extended a membership invitation should have been Ford Madox Brown, who was talented and diligent and obviously in accord with them on major questions of principle. But Brown never formally joined the group. According to his grandson, he said, 'I don't know, for one thing, whether they ever asked me to become a Pre-Raphaelite Brother; I suppose they did; but I never would have to do with societies—they are bound in cliquishness; besides I was a good deal older than they.'[1] F. G. Stephens agreed that Brown had been solicited, but gave a different reason for his not becoming a member:

> . . . he, chiefly because of a crude principle which for a time was adopted by the others, declined to join. This principle was to the effect that when a member had found a model whose aspect answered his ideas of what his subject required, that model should be painted exactly, and so to say, to a hair.[2]

[1] Ford Madox Ford, *The Life of Ford Madox Brown*, p. 63.
[2] F. G. Stephens, *Dante Gabriel Rossetti*, p. 49.

Holman Hunt, on the other hand, denied that Brown had ever been asked to join the Brotherhood:

I do indeed remember some talk by Gabriel about the desirability of electing him, but at once felt that the act would be beset with misunderstanding of the most damaging kind . . . We were intending to stand or fall by the determination to cut away all conventions not endorsed by further appeal to unsophisticated Nature. German antiquarianism, which was Brown's last form of allegiance to Continental dogma, was one of the principal enemies which we originally committed ourselves to destroy. Moreover, there was always his grim grotesqueness of invention; and there was no knowing when he would not fly some startling crotchet in his head before the eyes of the essentially mild-minded public. Why should we increase the unavoidable prejudice against our originality by adding Brown's gratuitous peculiarity to our first measure of offence to the world? If after three years' struggle we had taken into our boyish ranks one seven or eight years our senior, it would have looked like an admission of weakness such as we had no mind whatever to make. I knew perfectly well that Millais would agree with me, so if I heard that Rossetti had put the question to Brown, I took good care not to propose to have it repeated officially, nor to promise any attempt to gain Millais's consent.[1]

Although his memory was not always trustworthy, Hunt's recollections on this matter were probably substantially true. Rossetti undoubtedly told Brown of their scheme, and must have suggested to Hunt and Millais that they invite him to join. Hunt just as surely must have unhesitatingly vetoed this proposal. Not only was he cool towards Gabriel's former teacher (and perhaps a little jealous of him), but he could not have failed to recognize that because of his age Brown probably would have assumed leadership of the group, with Rossetti seated at his right hand. Rossetti, on his part, knowing that his two companions had only tentatively assented to his original idea, would not have jeopardized the existence of the embryonic organization by insisting on Brown's candidacy.

But even if he had been asked to join the three young men, it is almost certain that Brown would have declined the invitation, though not because of the 'crude principle' cited by Stephens—for although the Pre-Raphaelites talked about literally copying a model, they never insisted on or even recommended this practice. Brown would have refused to ally himself with the youths because, as he told his grandson, he had no taste for coteries, and he was six years older than the

[1] *Pre-Raphaelitism and the Pre-Raphaelite Brotherhood*, vol. I, pp. 226–7.

eldest of them at a time in life when a seniority of six years has real meaning; and also because he was too proud to join hands with one youngster who had recently been his elementary pupil and two others who had received considerably more public recognition than he; and finally because in 1848 he was too misanthropic to enter into the camaraderie which would inevitably be part of any group that included Gabriel Rossetti.

When it was clear that Brown was unacceptable to Hunt, Rossetti put forward the name of another friend, a twenty-three-year-old sculptural student at the Royal Academy, Thomas Woolner. The son of a Post Office letter-sorter, Woolner as a child had demonstrated exceptional skill in drawing and modelling, and when he was twelve he became a pupil of England's leading academic sculptor, William Behnes. Behnes took no payment for instructing the youth; in return, Woolner agreed that later he would assist his master for less than the customary compensation. In December 1842, on the day before his seventeenth birthday, he was enrolled in the Antique School of the Royal Academy; while he was a student he continued to spend his spare hours in Behnes's studio. In 1843, two years before Rossetti left Sass's, one of Woolner's 'groups' was displayed at the Royal Academy Exhibition. By August 1848, his artistic record of performance was nearly as imposing as that of John Everett Millais: he had had four works shown at the Academy and two at the British Institution, and in 1845 had won the silver medal of the Society of Art for an original design.

Sculpture had little appeal for Rossetti: he was attracted less to the artistry than to the personality of Woolner, who in 1848, a companion later recollected, was 'broad-chested, square-shouldered, rather more set in form than usual at that time of a man's life, robust, active, muscular, and with remarkably fine hands; his square-featured and noble face was set in roughly-cut, thick masses of brownish hair, and under his full eyebrows vigorous, resolute, and penetrating eyes glowed steadfastly while he looked at you'.[1] Poorly educated, and somewhat uncouth, Woolner nevertheless had a broad range of interests, including English literature and especially poetry, of which he had been an extensive reader and a modestly gifted amateur writer. And he was a spirited and stimulating conversationalist. He had spent

[1] Frederic George Stephens's obituary notice 'Thomas Woolner, R.A.', *Art Journal*, March, 1894, p. 82.

many hours talking with Rossetti, before whom he emerged as a man who, like Brown, was warm-hearted and generous, but whose kindliness, like Brown's, lay concealed under a veneer of self-assertiveness and irascibility. He was candid, free-thinking, and outspoken; he was also embittered because of the current low standing of sculpture. *The Athenaeum* noted in May 1848, that 'So far as the Academy is concerned, Sculpture may be said to be at a very low ebb in England. The painters are the privileged body in Trafalgar Square . . .'. The painters were also the privileged body with the patrons of art; although Woolner was a seasoned exhibitor, he had received few commissions, and was still forced to earn his livelihood by working for Behnes.

Hunt, the nonconformist within the confines of his own medium, conformed closely to the prevailing opinion of sculptors; he responded half-heartedly to Rossetti's nomination of Woolner, observing that his artistic principles were intended for painters. Gabriel stated that he had spoken to Woolner of their conviction that artistic inspiration should come from nature, and Woolner, a nature lover since early childhood, had enthusiastically endorsed the idea, saying that it provided the only basis for a reformation not only of painting but also sculpture. This helped Hunt to modify his opinion of sculptors—but he still had to be satisfied that a young man who for years had worked in the studio of a well-known Academician could actually be favourably disposed to their creed.

So Rossetti took him to Stanhope Street to Woolner's studio. After he had been through the studio, Hunt concluded that 'the many indications of Woolner's energy and his burning ambition to do work of excelling truthfulness and strong poetic spirit expressed in his energetic talk were enough to persuade me that Rossetti's suggesting that he should be made one of our number was a reasonable one'. A conference with Millais drew no objection, and Woolner's candidacy was approved. And now there were four.

Encouraged by the acceptance of Woolner, Rossetti immediately nominated another twenty-three-year-old friend, James Collinson. The son of a well-to-do Nottinghamshire bookseller, Collinson lived comfortably in the Polygon, in Clarendon Square, and for several years had been an R.A. student. He had painted a few timidly conceived, unexciting domestic-genre pictures which had gone unnoticed by almost everyone and then, in May 1847, he had emerged from obscurity with a highly praised picture exhibited at the Royal Academy Exhibition, *The Charity Boy's Debut*, which *The Athenaeum* said 'augurs great future excellence'. Among those who had taken note of the picture were Holman Hunt and Gabriel Rossetti. In his memoir Hunt said that he had felt that it embodied an 'honest idea, and although the invention did not go far beyond the initial conception, the pencilling was phenomenally painstaking throughout'. Collinson, he said, 'with higher inspiration might do something good'. Rossetti, naturally, had been less restrained. He had enthusiastically congratulated the artist, to whom he extended his highest compliment by calling him 'a born stunner', and they had struck up a friendship which had continued uninterruptedly for fifteen months. (In 1848 Collinson again was represented at the R.A. Exhibition, but his picture, *The Rivals*, was passed over by most spectators.)

Collinson's association with the Rossetti family however went beyond his companionship with Gabriel. He had been a regular worshipper at Christ's Church, in Albany Street, where the congregation included the female Rossettis; and at some time in 1847 he was captivated by the sight of Christina, who in turn showed an interest in this devout young man. Gabriel introduced them to each other, and they very quickly fell in love. But after coming under Cardinal Wiseman's influence, Collinson suddenly joined the Roman Catholic Church, causing a severance with Christina—who could not contemplate a relationship with a member of a church other than her own. When Collinson learned of her feelings, he returned to the Anglican Church, and in mid-1848 it seemed possible that one day Christina would become Mrs James Collinson.

Collinson as a person, in the words of William Rossetti, 'was not the sort of man to excite ardent emotions of friendship'. Hunt observed that he had been 'amiable', but 'tame and sleepy', and he said that 'no one years later could have trusted his memory to say whether our quiet friend had or had not been in the schools, so successfully had he avoided disturbing anyone in any way'. He seems to have been remembered primarily for his sleepiness, and of all of Rossetti's friends he has been the most disparaged. One of Gabriel's later acquaintances, his early biographer, Joseph Knight, for example, called him 'the one weakling' among Rossetti's associates, and a twentieth-century commentator, Rodolphe Mégroz referred to him as the 'dullest member' of Gabriel's entourage. And yet, one wonders

—could a downright dullard have been liked by Gabriel and loved by Christina?

Hunt was dubious about Collinson, principally because he seemed to be a thoroughgoing disciple of the highly popular and conventional genre painter David Wilkie; but Rossetti insisted that he had been converted to their way of thinking and now required only their moral support to become a truly great painter. So Hunt agreed to accept Collinson and to present his name for approval to Millais. And now there were five.

If it had been a descent from Woolner to Collinson, it was a headlong plunge from Collinson to Gabriel's third nominee, his brother William. William's only qualification for membership in a society of artists was his current enrolment in the Maddox Street drawing school (where Gabriel was still an occasional student). Hunt was assured, however, that William was exerting himself diligently and would quickly make up for lost time; soon he would resign from his government job and become a professional painter. Hunt knew that William would never be an artist; but because he liked him, and because he saw the futility of objecting to Rossetti's brother, he did not oppose William's candidacy. And now there were six.

At about this time Hunt, who had never entirely lost his misgivings concerning the incipient society, became more apprehensive. Their three provisional colleagues were, respectively, a close friend, a potential brother-in-law, and the brother of Gabriel Rossetti. Alarmed by the thought of the organization coming wholly under the control of Rossetti, Hunt almost impulsively proposed *his* first candidate—his friend Frederic George Stephens.

The nineteen-year-old Stephens, whose father was a poorly paid minor functionary in the Tower of London, lived with his family across the river in Lambeth. In his art studies he had not advanced beyond the Antique School, and he had never painted a complete picture; but he had taken a few painting lessons from Hunt. He provided a contrast to both Woolner and Collinson; William Rossetti pictured him as a 'man of firm and settled opinions and of a character far from supple—even rather unbending—but none the less the kindliest and most persistent of friends'.

In defence of his choice of a youth with no artistic accomplishments behind him, Hunt wrote that 'when the enthusiastic desire of these fellow students was declared to be a sure earnest of future zeal and power, I urged that he also, with the whirl of enthusiasm in operation and under a seal of promise to us, might become an active artist'. No one had to urge Rossetti to endorse the latest selection; he was elated by Hunt's action, which put the seal of acceptance on his idea of a society of young artists. Since Millais would go along with Hunt, Gabriel now saw his brain child existing in actuality. He enthusiastically seconded the nomination of Frederic George Stephens.

And now there were seven.

Seven they were, and seven they would remain. Hunt firmly made it clear that since the proposed group was already large enough to attain its objectives, the naming of Stephens had completed their roster. Rossetti did not protest; not only was he now not disposed to remonstrate against anything, but he probably felt that the number seven was perfectly fitting. The most sacred number among the Babylonians, Egyptians, and Hebrews had been seven, the cardinal virtues were seven, the Wonders of the World were seven, the Wise Men of Greece and the Champions of Christendom had been seven, and stars in the hair of the Blessed Damsel were seven. Was it not appropriate that the members of what surely would become the world's greatest brotherhood of artists should also number seven?

Although Hunt had been won over by Rossetti, Millais, having the most to lose from an indiscriminate affiliation with untested artists, was sceptical and even derisive of their new allies. 'Where's your flock?' he tauntingly asked when Hunt entered the Gower Street studio after the last man had been chosen. 'I expected to see them behind you. Tell me all about it. I can't understand so far what you are after. Are you getting up a regiment to take the Academy by storm? I can quite see why Gabriel Rossetti, if he can paint, should join us, but I didn't know his brother was a painter. Tell me. And then there's Woolner. Collinson'll certainly make a stalwart leader of a forlorn hope, won't he? And Stephens, too! Does he paint? Is the notion really to be put in practice?'[1]

Millais held out little hope for Stephens and William Rossetti, and, like Hunt, had his doubts about Woolner's medium and Collinson's discipleship to Wilkie. But when he realized that Hunt and Rossetti did indeed plan to put their notion in practice, he suggested that they

[1] *Pre-Raphaelitism and the Pre-Raphaelite Brotherhood*, vol. I, pp. 128–9.

all assemble in his studio to talk over the principles by which they would be governed; if he were then satisfied that the four nominees understood and would comply with these precepts, he would not oppose the formal establishment of an alliance. And so it was decided that within a few days the seven would gather in a body at 83 Gower Street.

Before this meeting, and thus before the organization even existed, the three founders had chosen a name for it. They would call it The Pre-Raphaelite Brotherhood.

Much has been said and written about the origin of this name. No one argues about the source of 'Brotherhood': it was indisputably contributed by Rossetti, who would have characteristically been disappointed without some element of secrecy and romance about the venture. But there is considerably less unanimity concerning the origin of 'Pre-Raphaelite'. According to A. C. Benson, the name grew out of Rossetti's reading in August 1848 of Lord Houghton's lately published *Life and Letters of Keats*: he wrote to his vacationing brother that Keats 'seems to have been a glorious fellow, and says in one place (to my great delight) that, having just looked over a folio of the first and second schools of Italian painting, he has come to the conclusion that the early men surpassed even Raphael himself!' Ford Madox Brown, on the other hand, maintained that Rossetti and his friends had acquired the name from him: 'As to the name Pre-Raphaelite, when they began talking about the early Italian masters, I naturally told them of the German Pre-Raphaelites (the name at that time was fairly familiar to the art world), and either it pleased them or not, I don't know, but they took it.'

The 'German Pre-Raphaelites' alluded to by Brown were Peter Cornelius, Johann Friedrich Overbeck, and several other painters, who in 1810 had founded a society in Rome which they called The Pre-Raphaelite Brethren. These men were protesting against what they considered to be the irreligion of contemporary art and artists, and proclaimed that only morally pure individuals can produce spiritually great art; some of the Brethren even wore cassocks and rope girdles and lived in monastic seclusion. They designated themselves Pre-Raphaelites because they considered Raphael's predecessors to be pious, ascetic men who had consecrated their lives to the beautification of monasteries and churches. The relationship between the German and English Pre-Raphaelites was clearly little more than nominal:

the latter were mostly unconcerned with religion (of the seven only Hunt and Collinson were religious), and the artistic principles of the two groups had very little in common. In 1845 Brown had visited the German Pre-Raphaelite studio and recorded his impressions of the five or six cartoons he saw: 'I noted that where any naked flesh was shown it looked exactly like wooden dolls' or lay figures'. I heard Overbeck explain that he never drew these parts from nature, on the principle of avoiding the sensuous in religious art.' But even though they shunned nature, Brown was attracted to and fascinated by the art of these German recluses: '. . . the sentiment—as depicted in the faces—was so vivid, so unlike most other art, that one felt a disinclination to go away. One could not see enough of it. . . . Full of action and strange character, it was everything the reverse of that dreadful commonplace into which the Art on the Continent seems to be hurrying back.'[1] (It was partly this interest in the German Pre-Raphaelites, whose work frequently was called 'Early Christian' or 'Catholic' art, that led Hunt to regard Brown as an unacceptable potential associate.)

Hunt maintained that the adoption of the name 'Pre-Raphaelite' was attributable neither to Brown nor to Rossetti, but to an incident which had occurred in 1847 in the Royal Academy Schools. He and Millais had voiced criticism of Raphael's *Transfiguration* before several fellow students, who, according to Hunt, retorted, ' "Then you are Pre-Raphaelite." Referring to this as we worked side by side, Millais and I laughingly agreed that the designation must be accepted.'[2]

But, reading these words, we must remember that they were written late in life and that for many years Hunt had been extremely touchy about statements that the real founder and guiding light of the Pre-Raphaelite Brotherhood had been Dante Gabriel Rossetti. The incident may have occurred as he described it, but it is certain that Brown had spoken of the German Pre-Raphaelites to Rossetti; and although nothing substantiates Brown's account of his unlikely conversation with Rossetti and his friends in August 1848, his earlier reflections may have been recalled and put forward at this time by his former pupil. It seems, then, that the most plausible explanation of the origin of 'Pre-Raphaelite' is that it was offered by

[1] *The Life of Ford Madox Brown*, p. 45.
[2] *Pre-Raphaelitism and the Pre-Raphaelite Brotherhood*, vol. I, pp. 100–1.

Rossetti and that Hunt, remembering its earlier use in the Academy, agreed that they should be named The Pre-Raphaelite Brotherhood.

The Brotherhood held its first meeting on an evening early in September in Millais's studio, where the four recruits looked at the Campo Santo engravings and listened to Hunt describe the basic principles of the society—principles which for more than a century have been consistently misunderstood and misinterpreted. Hunt explained that, despite their name, they were not antiquarians or mediaevalists, and they would not copy or even follow the works of any artists who had lived before Raphael. They would recognize only a spiritual bond between themselves and the Italian Pre-Raphaelites—a bond of simplicity, integrity, sincerity, and imaginative originality. They were not, he continued, taking issue with Raphael himself, whose greatness is incontestable, but rather with his baneful influence on his followers and imitators, which led to the ruination of whatever originality and inventiveness they might otherwise have demonstrated. As Hunt later wrote:

> Raphael in his prime was an artist of the most independent and daring course as to conventions . . . but the prodigality of his productiveness, and his training of many assistants, compelled him to lay down rules and manners of work; and his followers, even before they were left alone, accentuated his poses into postures. They caricatured the turns of his heads and the lines of his limbs, so that figures were drawn in patterns; they twisted companies of men into pyramids, and placed them like pieces on the chess-board of the foreground. The master himself, at the last, was not exempt from furnishing examples of such conventionalities.[1]

Furthermore, Hunt announced, in their painting and sculpting the Brotherhood would disregard and indeed fly in the face of all lifeless, outworn rules, conventions and traditions. Instead of the works of other artists, they would take their inspiration directly from nature, from the bright, glowing colours of skies, hills, landscapes, and vegetation to the lifelike expressions, gestures, and movements of human beings, all of which they would study painstakingly and endeavour to

[1] Ibid., pp. 135–6. In 1933 Laurence Housman declared that Raphael's name was selected 'because he was the 300-year-old godfather of a dead school of painting—so dead that it had begun to stink. Raphael, that great creator of form, had been reduced to a recipe, and had become accountable for painters like Benjamin West, and Eastlake, and Ary Schafer; and what they made him stand for had become an embedded code.' 'Pre-Raphaelitism in Art and Poetry', *Essays by Divers Hands*, p. 3.

reproduce faithfully.[1] But this precept was qualified: since all art must entail selection and interpretation, they would not in their fidelity to nature become literal copyists refusing to change or omit details. (The mistaken notion that Pre-Raphaelites insisted on exact, undeviating likenesses of everything they painted was partly the result of Ruskin's famous injunction, probably the most often quoted sentence in *Modern Painters*: 'Go to nature in all singleness of heart, selecting nothing, rejecting nothing.' Anyone who has read ten pages of *Modern Painters* knows that Ruskin was urging not non-selectivity but fidelity—as opposed to distorted representations of Nature. As Hunt put it, 'Pre-Raphaelitism in its purity was the frank worship of Nature, kept in check by selection and directed by the spirit of imaginative purpose.')

Finally, Hunt proclaimed that in all their work they would abide by the principle of *sincerity*: that they would select for their paintings and statues meaningful subjects; that they imbue their works with a lofty purpose and, as Hunt later said, would make 'art handmaid in the cause of justice and truth'.

On this last point—whether or not their works had to be impregnated with a high moral purpose—the Pre-Raphaelites themselves did not always agree. (We have already noted that most of them were by no means deeply religious men.) The following was Hunt's unvarying stand on this point: 'It stirred us to proclaim that art should interpret to men how much more beautiful the world is, not only in every natural form, but in every pure principle of human life, than they would without her aid deem it to be. If artists' work misguides men, making them believe that there is no order in creation, no

[1] A connecting link joining the Italian and English Pre-Raphaelites appears in a passage from Browning's 'Fra Lippo Lippi', wherein the speaker, one of the best early Italian painters, tells of how he is inspired by nature:

> . . . you've seen the world
> —The beauty and the wonder and the power,
> The shapes of things, their colours, lights and shades,
> Changes, surprises,—and God made it all!
> —For what? Do you feel thankful, ay or no,
> For this fair town's face, yonder river's line,
> The mountain round it and the sky above,
> Much more the figures of man, woman, child,
> These are the frames to? What's it all about?
> To be passed over, despised? or dwelt upon,
> Wondered at? this last course!—you say,
> But why not do as well as say,—paint these
> Just as they are, careless what comes of it?
> God's works—paint anyone, and count it crime
> To let a truth slip.

wisdom in evolution, decrying the sublime influences as purposeless, we shall indeed be a sorry brood of men.' Millais apparently agreed with Hunt, for in a letter of 28 May 1851, he wrote concerning a painter-friend, Charles Collins, that 'there are few so devotedly directed to the one thought of some day (through the medium of his art) turning the minds of men to good reflections and so heightening the profession as one of unworldly unusefulness to mankind. *This is our great object in painting*, for the thought of simply pleasing the senses would drive us to other pursuits requiring less of that unceasing attention so necessary to the completion of a perfect work.' Stephens, on the other hand, said, 'Nothing like a didactic, religious, or moral purpose was insisted on by anyone.' William Rossetti's middle-of-the-road position probably accurately reflected that of most of his colleagues: 'Had the Pre-Raphaelite Brotherhood any ulterior aim beyond producing good works of art? Yes and no. Assuredly it had the aim of developing such *ideas* as are suited to the medium of fine art, and of bringing the arts of form into general unison with what is highest in other arts especially poetry. . . . That the Pre-Raphaelites valued moral and spiritual ideas as an important section of ideas germane to fine art is most true, and not one of them was in the least inclined to do any work of gross, lascivious, or sensual descriptions; but neither did they limit the province of art to the spiritual or moral.'

It is doubtful if the seven young men engaged in a prolonged discussion of these principles, for there is no record of any such conversation in the works of the three Brothers who wrote memoirs of their movement—Stephens, Hunt and William Rossetti. We do know, however, that by enthusiastically promising to live up to these articles of faith, the four nominees overcame Millais's remaining doubts. They were then told the name of their society and also told that, to symbolize their unity and solidarity, each should inscribe beside his signature on works of art the initials 'P.R.B.' They then all swore a solemn oath that under no circumstances would they ever divulge the meaning of these initials.

Rossetti now brought forth a document which he and Hunt had lately drawn up, and which all of them would sign: the famous List of Immortals. The list was preceded by a one-sentence preamble: 'We, the undersigned, declare that the following list of Immortals constitutes the whole of our Creed, and there exists no other Immortality than what is centred in their names and in the names of their contemporaries, in whom this list is reflected.' This prefatory statement was followed by the list, which in a descending order of greatness was divided into five groups. The topmost category contained only one name, that of Jesus Christ, and immediately below him were Shakespeare and The Author of Job. (Rossetti had at first placed Shakespeare in the highest classification, but Hunt insisted that Jesus stand alone at the top.) The third group comprised twelve names: Homer, Dante, Chaucer, Leonardo da Vinci, Goethe, Keats, Shelley, King Alfred, Landor, Thackeray, Washington, and Browning. The fourth subdivision included Boccaccio, Fra Angelico, Mrs Browning, Patmore, Raphael, Longfellow, the Author of *Stories after Nature*, and Tennyson. The fifth order of 'immortality' was the largest: Isaiah, Phidias, the Early Gothic Architects, Cavalier Pugliesi, Rienzi, Ghiberti, Spenser, Hogarth, Flaxman, Hilton, Kosciusko, Byron, Wordsworth, Haydon, Cervantes, Joan of Arc, Michelangelo, the Early English Balladists, Giovanni Bellini, Giorgione, Titian, Tintoretto, Poussin, Milton, Cromwell, Hampden, Bacon, Newton, Poe, Hood, Emerson, Leigh Hunt, Wilkie, and Columbus.

This document, not surprisingly, has been the source of much merriment, for it is easy to smile at a list of 'immortals' that includes Cavalier Pugliesi, William Hilton, and Leigh Hunt, but not Socrates, Plato and Aristotle; that gives Benjamin Robert Haydon and John Flaxman equal greatness with Titian and Michelangelo; that rates Walter Savage Landor on even terms with Homer, Dante, Chaucer, and Goethe; and that attributes greater excellence to Coventry Patmore, Henry Wadsworth Longfellow, and Elizabeth Barrett Browning than to Spenser and Milton. It also may seem strange that the English Pre-Raphaelites passed over the greatest of their Italian counterparts, Giotto. (Less surprising is the absence from the list of musical composers, for of the seven Pre-Raphaelites only Millais, the son of an accomplished amateur musician, had any knowledge or love of music.)

In defence of Hunt and Rossetti, however, it should be added that they were remarkably far-seeing when they raised the neglected Keats and Shelley to prominence; when they favoured the obscure Browning over the renowned Tennyson; when only two months after the completion of his first novel they recognized the merits of Thackeray (although rather over-stating them); and when, five years before the appearance of Ruskin's influential 'On the Nature of Gothic', they paid tribute to the underestimated and generally slighted Gothic architects. Note also that they did not repudiate Raphael and his two most eminent contemporaries, Michelangelo and Leonardo da Vinci, nor did they overlook the three leading Raphaelite and post-Raphaelite Venetians, Giorgione, Titian, and Tintoretto. The document becomes less preposterous if we view it from the standpoint of 1848, and if we remember that it was drafted by two young men in one short sitting.

Everyone readily signed the paper, and their endorsements marked the birth of the Pre-Raphaelite Brotherhood. Because of the frequently far-ranging application of the term 'Pre-Raphaelite', it should be emphasized that nobody other than the original seven was to have the right to affix the initials P.R.B. to his works, or would be considered by the Brothers to be a fellow Pre-Raphaelite. The only persons whom we can rightfully call Pre-Raphaelites are the seven signers of the List of Immortals: James Collinson, William Holman Hunt, John Everett Millais, Dante Gabriel Rossetti, William Michael Rossetti, Frederic George Stephens, and Thomas Woolner.

Many commentators have suggested, remembering the year in which the P.R.B. was born—the year of a major continental uprising—that Pre-Raphaelitism was another manifestation of the wide-ranging, all-embracing revolutionary spirit of 1848. And, to be sure, the Pre-Raphaelites, like all of their countrymen, could not avoid being conscious of and somehow affected by events that had convulsed the entire civilized world. 'Like most young men', Holman Hunt wrote, 'I was stirred by the spirit of freedom of the passing revolutionary time.' That spirit found its way into his first P.R.B. painting, *Rienzi*. The current happenings also excited three of Hunt's colleagues—William Rossetti, Stephens, and Woolner. It is difficult, however, to discern any causal connection between their excitement and the formation of the Brotherhood, since the latter three took no part in the creation of the society, and Hunt had worked out most of his ideas before 1948. Significantly, of the three comparatively unaffected Pre-Raphaelites, two were founders of the organization. Millais, as might be expected, showed no great sympathy for those engaged in rebellious activities, and the person least of all influenced by news from abroad was the one most responsible for the establishment of the Brotherhood. Gabriel Rossetti.

Rossetti took no more interest in politics than his father had forty-four years earlier upon arriving in Naples. His rebelliousness was a strictly personal matter, and if a greater insurgence rose within him in 1848 than, say, 1846, it was only because the intervening months had intensified his general restlessness. During the last week of February 1848, revolution suddenly erupted in Paris: the Palais Royal was sacked and burned; the Tuileries was successfully assaulted; the detested King Louis Philippe, along with his Queen, was forced to flee for his life across the English Channel; and, on 27 February, a formal proclamation was issued heralding the establishment of a new Republic. While these earth-shaking, long-awaited events were taking place, when the exhilaration within the parlour of 50 Charlotte Street was indescribable, Gabriel Rossetti was preoccupied with a different matter of urgency: how to find the money he needed to leave the Academy Schools and begin his apprenticeship under Ford Madox Brown. In March the revolutionary spirit spread all over Europe: insurrections and riots burst out in Italy, Austria, Prussia, the German States, Poland, and even Belgium and Denmark. And during March, Gabriel Rossetti remained insensible to the events on the Continent as he joyfully learned, at Clipstone Street, how to use a paint brush.

As the weeks passed, Gabriel continued as always to devote his thoughts to his personal affairs. Nowhere in Europe could one more easily mind one's own business than in England, where there was nothing extraordinary about the year 1848. No one suggested rebelling against Queen Victoria; the current of reform which had been set in motion in 1832 was flowing along smoothly, but no more rapidly than in 1847 or 1849. Chartism, England's ten-year-old revolutionary democratic political movement, had passed its moment of greatest strength, and 1848 was the year of its most ignominious failure, when a monumental demonstration planned for 300,000 attracted only 15,000, few of whom raised a voice in anger.[1]

The political events of 1848, therefore, had only the most remote bearing upon the establishment of the Pre-Raphaelite Brotherhood. The defiant youths who sat in the studio at 83 Gower Street on that September evening were primarily concerned with their own impending rebellion, not against Europe's crowned heads but against the

[1] Gabriel Rossetti's attitude toward the Chartist Movement is illustrated by his poem 'The English Revolution of 1848', which begins, 'Ho ye that nothing have to lose! ho rouse ye, one and all!' and ends with the arrest of a Chartist speaker, who pleads, 'Oh please, sir don't! It isn't me. It's him. Oh, don't, please, sir, please!'

unanointed rulers of the British art world. They expected to be subjected to merciless attacks, for, as William Rossetti said, the mere formation of the organization was 'a *carte-blanche* for abuse'. But they looked forward with anticipation to the first battle, which would begin on 7 May 1849—the opening day of the eighty-first Exhibition of the Royal Academy of Arts.

6

The Fruits of a Year

Any battles to be fought on behalf of the P.R.B. would, of course, be led and dominated by the 'big three', Millais, Hunt, and Rossetti. Thomas Woolner, to be sure, was eventually recognized as one of his century's leading sculptors and elected a Royal Academician, but despite his fine modelling technique and his acute powers of character discernment, he was never considered a 'Pre-Raphaelite' artist. During the late 40's and early 50's he lived by commissions for such routine work as portrait medallions; and when he did have time to carve an original statue, it was never more than incidentally related to Pre-Raphaelitism. In fact, Woolner's work to some extent vindicates Hunt's and Millais's belief that their ideals could be fully realized only through the application of colour onto a plane surface. As for the other Brothers, Collinson exhibited very few pictures, Stephens even fewer, and William Rossetti none at all. Although eventually he painted one tolerably good Pre-Raphaelite picture, the lazy, indecisive Collinson never came close to fulfilling the hopes his colleagues had held out for him; of the seven he was the least active and least productive. Stephens, who had some artistic talent, executed a few paintings, two of which, portraits of his parents, were exhibited at the Academy, but he kept most of them hidden from his friends and they were not discovered until many years later. William was too old to be an elementary student, and before he had drawn or painted any pictures he gave up the idea of becoming an artist. But, though they were unproductive painters, Stephens and William Rossetti were valuable to the Brotherhood in other ways. Both took a spirited part in the social and other non-artistic activities which helped to keep the group together, and both became critics who advanced the aims of Pre-Raphaelitism by the pen. William, additionally, was chosen early in 1849 to be the brotherhood secretary, and in this capacity for four years he kept a journal of his colleagues' activities, providing us with the best contemporary source of information concerning the P.R.B.

So it soon became clear that the three leaders would generate whatever excitement the Brotherhood might arouse in the world of art. Since he had a commission to complete, Millais could not immediately begin his first Pre-Raphaelite picture, but Hunt and Rossetti turned exhilarated to their works in progress. In order to emphasize their unity of purpose, Rossetti, Hunt, and Millais had all originally intended to depict scenes from Keats's 'Isabella' as their first P.R.B. works. But the only one to carry out the plan was Millais —who of the three least understood and appreciated the poetry of Keats. Hunt and Rossetti looked elsewhere for their subjects, though each resolved to paint a picture that would tell a meaningful story and that, in Ruskin's words, would delineate a 'motivating idea'.

After Hunt had completed his conventionalized *Eve of St Agnes*, he had decided to venture on a more challenging 'out-of-door picture, with a foreground and background, abjuring altogether brown foliage, smoky clouds, and dark corners, painting the whole out of doors, direct on the canvas itself, with every detail I can see, and with the sunlight brightness of the day itself'. He had found his subject in Bulwer-Lytton's popular historical novel of 1835, *Rienzi*, the story of a heroic fourteenth-century Roman warrior-statesman who attempted to re-establish the glory of Rome and after a bitter struggle with the papacy met death by assassination. Hunt chose a crucial scene from the first chapter, when Rienzi, just after coming upon the body of his murdered brother, 'turned the boy's face from the grass, and strove wildly to feel the pulse of his heart; he drew back his hand hastily; for it was crimsoned with blood, and lifting that hand on high, shrieked out again, "Justice! justice!" ' Hunt intended to portray the kneeling Rienzi holding up his brother's body and crying out for justice. Beside him, also kneeling, would be two armed soldiers and a boy scarcely older than the dead youth; behind them a group of soldiers would be seated on horses facing rearward. The foreground would contain foliage, while the background, reminiscent of early Italian paintings, would be well filled with several buildings, an arboreal hillside, and a cloud-covered sky.

Of the three leaders only Rossetti did not select his subject from literature. He had chosen to represent a scene from the home life of the seventeen-year-old Virgin Mary, *The Girlhood of Mary Virgin*. Supervised by her mother, St Anne, Mary would be embroidering a lily (a symbol of purity), copying from a flower in a vase atop six massive books, each bearing the label of a cardinal virtue. Watering the lily would be a child angel. The immediate foreground would show several slips of thorn, obviously symbolic of the future suffering of Jesus, while behind the women a drawn curtain would disclose a carved balcony with an overhanging, fruit-laden vine, and, in the distance, a landscape background. Mary's father, St Joachim, would be standing on the balcony, pruning the vine, on one of whose supports would rest a dove, symbolic of the Holy Spirit.

Like Hunt, Rossetti was endeavouring to portray the incident just as it might actually have taken place;[1] but unlike Hunt, who could not disregard the moral purpose underlying a work of art, and who had been inspired by what he called the current 'spirit of freedom' to paint *Rienzi*,[2] Rossetti was unmindful of any didactic intention—even though he said his picture 'belongs to a religious class which has always appeared to me the most adapted and most worthy to interest members of a Christian community'. That *The Girlhood of Mary Virgin* 'belongs to a religious class' of paintings means only that Rossetti thought its subject would have popular appeal and would be appropriate for a 'Pre-Raphaelite' painting. (How many non-religious pictures, he might have asked, had been painted by the early Italians?)

Both youths had made their designs and started the actual painting prior to the establishment of the Brotherhood, and the technique they were employing was as unorthodox and unconventional as any other aspect of Pre-Raphaelitism. Hunt described their *modus operandi*,

[1] On 11 November 1848, Rossetti described his intention in a letter to his father's friend, Charles Lyell: 'The subject is the education of the Blessed Virgin, one which has been treated at various times by Murillo and other painters—but, as I cannot but think, in a very inadequate manner, since they have invariably represented her as reading from a book under the superintendence of her Mother, St Anne, an occupation obviously incompatible with these times, and which could only pass muster if treated in a purely symbolical manner. In order, therefore, to attempt something more probable and at the same time less commonplace, I have represented the future Mother of Our Lord as occupied in embroidering a lily . . .'

[2] Hunt asserted, 'The appeal of Heaven against tyranny exercised over the poor and helpless seemed well fitted for pictorial treatment. "How long, O Lord!" many bleeding souls were crying at that time.' The full title of the picture, incidentally, is *Rienzi Vowing to Obtain Justice for the Death of His Young Brother Slain in a Skirmish Between the Colonna and the Orsini Factions.*

which he and Millais had developed earlier but, except experimentally, had not yet used:

> Select a prepared ground originally for its brightness, and renovate it, if necessary, with fresh white when first it comes into the studio, white to be mixed with a very little amber or copal varnish. Upon this surface, complete with exactness the outline of the part in hand. On the morning for the painting, with fresh white . . . spread a further coat very evenly with a palette knife over the part for the day's work, of such consistency that the drawing should faintly show through. In some cases the thickened white may be applied to the forms needing brilliancy with a brush, by the aid of rectified spirits. Over this wet ground, the colour (transparent and semi-transparent) should be laid with light sable brushes, and the touches must be made so tenderly that the ground below shall not be worked up, yet so far enticed to blend with the superimposed tints as to correct the qualities of thinness and staininess, which over a dry ground transparent colours used would inevitably exhibit.

The Pre-Raphaelites avoided using asphaltum, that tarry, liquid, neutral brown compound which was universally and copiously used as a ground and as a glazing material, and was a principal cause of the subdued, toned down colours and 'brownness' to which the young rebels objected in contemporary paintings.

Their technique was revolutionary but not unprecedented; it was a revival of the practice of early Italian fresco painters, who worked on freshly spread, moist plaster and prepared only so much of the surface as could be covered in one sitting. But this revival was not mere antiquarian copying on Hunt's and Millais's part. They saw how the process would bring out colours vividly and brilliantly—for as the white ground reflects light shining through pigments, it illuminates a picture and gives its colours clarity and splendour. Also, because of the difficulty of making corrections, this procedure demanded high discipline and their most careful, painstaking efforts. The fresco technique leaves nothing to chance: before he lifts his brush the artist must know precisely what he intends to do, and while working he cannot afford even one faulty stroke. It was a mode of painting that harmonized with the character of Hunt, but severely tried the patience of Rossetti.

Hunt was still a student in the Academy's Life School, but in his free time he toiled laboriously and methodically on *Rienzi*, patiently constructing the picture piece by piece. The foreground and background, as we have noted, were completed by summer's end. The leaves and branches, Hunt explained, were painted not, in accordance with Reynolds's prescription, as 'ideal' leaves and branches, but 'in full sunlight with what was then unprecedented exactness', and in the foreground, instead of the usual 'meaningless spread of whitey brown', he depicted 'gravelly variations and pebbles, all diverse in tints and shapes as found in Nature'. When the landscape was finished, he turned to the costumes, the battle equipment, and the architecture of distant buildings, and, obsessed as he was with microscopic chronological accuracy, he spent hours in the British Museum and the Tower, making careful studies of spears, shields, and armour. Next he visited a friend's stables, where he meticulously drew the hind quarters of horses.

During these weeks, when Hunt was seeking such verisimilitude in his details, he was also supervising the work of his immediate companion. Rossetti closely followed Hunt's instructions as he proceeded step by step with his *Girlhood of Mary Virgin.* After making studies from the nude of all the figures and transferring them to his 33 by 25 inch panel, he painted, in order, the floor, the balcony, and the books (using as models six ponderous volumes taken from his father's study). By now it was early autumn, and so Hunt advised Rossetti to visit a conservatory and paint the overhanging vine. For about a week Gabriel was absent from the studio; when he returned, Hunt, never one to flinch easily before strong colours, was startled by the 'too crudely emerald green' vine. It was nevertheless left unchanged.

For a time Rossetti worked hard at reproducing the 'Pre-Raphaelite' details of what he saw; but before long he began to show his independence (or his impatience) by refusing to give much heed to absolute historical accuracy. He announced, as Hunt related, that 'attention to chronological costume, to the types of different races of men, to climatic features and influences, were of no value in any painter's work, and that therefore oriental proprieties in the treatment of Scriptural subjects were calculated to destroy the poetic nature of a design'.[1] Adhering to this Huntian doctrine might well have shackled Rossetti's poetic imagination, but it also would have

[1] On this point Rossetti probably had been influenced by Blake, who in his 'Annotations to Sir Joshua Reynolds' Discourses' had written 'Excellent Remarks!' after this sentence from Discourse IV: 'In the same manner as the historical Painter never enters into the details of colours, so neither does he debase his conceptions with minute attention to the discrimination of Drapery.'

called for rather more perseverance than Rossetti had ever before demonstrated. Whatever its motivation, Gabriel's position on this question demonstrated his consistent individualism, which he continued to display even though, throughout the progress of his picture, he needed the advice and close surveillance of Hunt—who patiently and tactfully shepherded his charge, watching and instructing him, even guiding the hand that held the brush. From time to time Rossetti also received help from Brown, with whom he continued his close friendship. (This was a source of anxiety to Hunt, who professed to fear what he called Brown's 'Overbeckian' or 'Early Christian' mannerisms, which, he contended, might lead Rossetti to distort the principles of Pre-Raphaelitism. Hunt also may have been jealous of the hold still retained on Rossetti by his former teacher.)

Although he was helped constantly by Hunt, frequently by Brown, and occasionally by others, and although he was painting a comparatively simple picture, Rossetti was exasperated almost to distraction by *The Girlhood of Mary Virgin*. Most of his troubles stemmed from his still glaring technical deficiencies, some of which he remained stubbornly unwilling to correct—as, for instance, his attitude to perspective. When he began his picture, he was wholly ignorant of the rules of perspective, and found them unintelligible. Hunt tried to teach him these principles, but Gabriel superciliously declared that the rules were worthless and dismissed the subject from his thoughts. Nor did he change his attitude throughout his life: William later wrote that 'Gabriel never paid any attention, worth speaking of, to perspective, and indeed—so far as his own interest in matters of art was concerned—was at all times almost indifferent to the question of whether his works were in perspective or out of it.'

These views on perspective were typical of Rossetti, still and always a creature of extremes. Sometimes he worked uninterruptedly for hours or even days, oblivious of the world beyond his easel, and on these occasions his achievement, said Stephens, was 'astounding'. Hunt described his studio mate in this state of mind:

> When he had fairly got entangled in a new design he would refuse the attraction of home, meals, out-of-door engagements, or bed, and sit through the night, sleeping where he sat for hours at the time, recommencing his work when he woke. He ate whatever was at hand when hunger suggested, and when time came for bed on the second night he would ask me to leave him; in the morning I would find him still at his engrossing task.

His lassitude, at other times, was equally striking: he might, for example, spend hours simply sitting in a rocking chair.

Rossetti's moody, temperamental behaviour was disturbing to the systematic and even-tempered Hunt. But, at least for the present, Hunt was willing to put up with his companion's idiosyncrasies because of his faith that eventually Gabriel would develop into a mature artist—although he acknowledged that 'it needed the bold gift of prophecy to decide that he would ever discipline himself enough to become a real painter'. So Rossetti, encouraged by Hunt's confidence in him and goaded by his eagerness for success, struggled on. As autumn passed into winter his picture slowly but perceptibly took shape.

But the Pre-Raphaelite Brotherhood was a social as well as an artistic society, and in its first year the members devoted themselves to pleasure as well as work. Once each month they met formally in the home of one of the Brothers: when the Rossettis were hosts, they gathered in a small fourth-floor room which had been the professor's dressing chamber but now was Gabriel's work-room and study, and William noted that although the furniture consisted of a shabby table and two or three well-worn chairs, 'we managed to make ourselves quite comfortable according to our unexacting standards of those days'. During the meetings they discussed serious artistic questions but as often talked such nonsense as Gabriel's proposal that they form a suicide club; they read poetry aloud, their own and that of established poets; and they sang and joked and thoroughly enjoyed themselves.

Rossetti, spirited and witty, may have dominated the conversation; but Hunt, in his judicious way, and Stephens (bolstered by a fair knowledge of early Italian art) in his argumentative way, contributed their share. Woolner, always a provocative talker, sometimes recounted tales of famous artists he had encountered in Behnes's studio, but more often lashed out at the obsessive materialism of his contemporaries. As for the others, Millais had a loud voice but seems to have said little that was memorable; William Rossetti was reluctant to speak at length because of shyness and the self-consciousness he felt as the group's only non-artist; and the lethargic Collinson sometimes slept while the others were shouting, and often had to be awakened at the close of a meeting. (For that matter he was more than once discovered slumbering in his studio while a model sat idly earning a shilling an hour.)

During the readings the predominant voice was Rossetti's, who resonantly read from his own poems and those of his favourite (usually unheralded) contemporary poets, such as Edgar Allan Poe, Coventry Patmore, William Bell Scott, and, most notably, Robert Browning. He also often demonstrated his prodigious memory for poetry he liked by reciting as many as twenty pages of Browning's *Sordello* or *Paracelsus*. 'Rossetti was at all times a magnificent reader of poetry,' Stephens later reminisced, 'and no tax exhausted his ever-copious and exact memory of poetic texts. . . . He would sit for hours surrounded by friends. . . . I have seen youths' tears flow rapidly on hearing "A Blot on the 'Scutcheon" read aloud by Gabriel Rossetti.'[1] Stimulated by Gabriel's love of poetry, at least four of the others—Hunt, Woolner, Stephens, and William—read, discussed, and even wrote poems. None of their verse was outstanding; the least objectionable was composed by Woolner, who, if not in his statuary, at least in his poetry was a 'Pre-Raphaelite' artist.

The formal monthly readings were a source of fun and fellowship, but were only a small part of the Pre-Raphaelite camaraderie. During their first organizational year, rare was the day when two or more Brothers did not see or at least contact each other (when they corresponded with each other they replaced 'Esq.' with 'P.R.B.'). This bond of comradeship was perhaps the strongest of the ties that held the body together. Their favourite diversion was to walk in the moonlight and, led by Gabriel, to sing stirring songs like the *Marseillaise* and *Mourir pour la Patrie*; they might stroll for an hour or two along the Thames, or they might take an extended hike to a neighbouring village such as Hampstead. Often other art-loving, fun-loving youths, not Pre-Raphaelites, joined these jaunts, substituting for the two Brothers who seldom went for an evening outing, Collinson and Millais. The group often stopped by the sleeping Collinson's house, where their clamour would succeed in arousing only his ugly six-foot-tall landlady; if admitted, they would drag their dormant Brother out of bed. Collinson, lacking a sense of humour, was seldom amused by these or other revels—and so contributed even less to Pre-Raphaelite camaraderie than to Pre-Raphaelite artistry. As for Millais, he enjoyed outdoor exercise and was habitually cheerful and outgoing, but this decorous, un-Bohemian young Englishman would have felt foolish striding down a street in the middle of the night singing the

[1] 'Earlier Works of Dante Gabriel Rossetti', *Portfolio*, June 1883, p. 116.

Marseillaise. He was also a thoroughly practical youth who once told a friend that because of his painting 'I give up all invitations and scarcely ever see anyone', and politely but firmly declined to do anything that might seriously interfere with his life's work. So he was not ready to take part in escapades that might end at dawn. Millais also probably avoided some of the informal Pre-Raphaelite activities because of his never warm relationship with the uncontested master of the revels, Gabriel Rossetti.

As the non-artistic leader of the Brotherhood, Rossetti was as responsible for its life as he had been for its birth. The Pre-Raphaelites' social affairs had to be tailored to their money shortages—for only the two irregular participants, Collinson and Millais, lived in fairly comfortable circumstances. But though short on cash, they were long on enthusiasm, whether talking in their studios or walking in the moonlight or visiting inexpensive oyster bars or coffee houses where for hours they could nurse along one cup of coffee or tea. During these days Gabriel was surprisingly frugal; his only self-indulgence, permitted by his brother's generosity, was his still frequent attendance at the theatre.

Unlike most contemporary bohemians, the Pre-Raphaelites lived remarkably unsullied lives. They used much slang but little profanity; they drank sparingly or not at all; only Woolner among them smoked; and if they copulated, they did not publicize it. Their purity may have been partly due to their poverty, but certainly not to a shortage of opportunities. In this second decade of the reign of Queen Victoria, dozens of pubs, taverns, gin-shops, and underground cider cellars flourished in the West End of London, and for a shilling or two a patron could remain all night in any of them, hear performers sing salacious songs and tell unprintable jokes, join with other customers in singing bawdy ballads, and consume enough gin to send him under a table. And for only two shillings or half a crown he could procure a prostitute to share and complete the evening's pleasure.

But the Pre-Raphaelites kept clear of these dens—even though, as A. C. Benson observes, 'they probably had little respect for purely conventional morality'. They just instinctively recoiled from vulgarity; and their temperateness was encouraged by their leader, whose life, Holman Hunt said, 'with all his headstrongness and a certain want of consideration . . . was untainted to an exemplary degree'. Rossetti did not smoke; he avoided beer, which he found distasteful; he drank wine in moderation; and curiously, considering his adult life, until he was nearly twenty-one he showed no strong interest in the opposite sex. William said that his brother, 'though there was nothing of the Puritan in his feelings, nor in his demeanour or conversation—had no juvenile amours, *liaisons*, or flirtations'. Although soon his powerful sexual drive would reveal itself, it is almost certain that when he reached manhood Gabriel was a virgin—partly because of his refusal to think of women as creatures to gratify men's bodily appetites. His sympathetic study of a streetwalker, 'Jenny', was begun in 1847; he wrote only a few of its lines then, but fixed in his mind its main idea—that the responsibility for Jenny's life must be attributed not to the girl herself but to

> . . . the hatefulness of man,
> Who spares not to end what he began,
> Whose acts are ill and his speech ill,
> Who, having used you at his will,
> Thrusts you aside, as when I dine
> I serve the dishes and the wine.

'How atone, Great God,' Rossetti asked, 'for this which man has done?' Selfish though he was in many ways, Gabriel would not consider 'using at his will' any young Jenny. He had formed a mental image of his blessed damozel, who if not easily described surely would be readily recognized; but until then he had not seen her embodiment in reality.

Not that he was diligently searching for the girl of his dreams. His physical and emotional desires were being satisfactorily sublimated in the activities of the Pre-Raphaelite Brotherhood. These early Pre-Raphaelite days were his happiest: his worries concerned only his painting, and except when *The Girlhood of Mary Virgin* was troubling him, he was genial and affable. A. C. Benson picturesquely described the enchantment of this stage in Rossetti's life:

> The Pre-Raphaelite period has an intrinsic beauty of its own. It has the eternal charm of generous and enthusiastic youth. To read of these days is like listening to young and careless voices breaking the stillness of the morning air in some enchanted landscape of falling streams and dewy thickets. It is like a draught of fresh springwater to recall the life of so gifted and hopeful a circle, and to revive the ardent dreams of youth in their incomparable brightness and strength.[1]

[1] Arthur C. Benson, *Rossetti*, pp. 26–27.

No one attached more importance to the Brotherhood than Rossetti; in some ways it had supplanted his family. During the autumn and and winter of 1848–9 he grew, as his niece Mrs Helen Angeli wrote, 'somewhat alien to the atmosphere of mild *patria podestà* natural in an Italian home of that period. He was from this time on more noticeably English in attitude and tastes than his brother became at any period in his life.[1]

Old Gabriele Rossetti was now incapacitated for any professional work except writing prose and verse, which he continued to do without hope of publication. Friction had developed between him and Gabriel; more and more often he rebuked his elder son for indolence, irregular habits, and unproductiveness. The old man's annoyance was to some extent justifiable, but his conclusions were based solely on Gabriel's doings at home—conversing loudly in his room, coming home in the early morning, getting up at noon. William rightly said of the conflict, 'Gabriel more than his father, was in the wrong; yet not so much in the wrong as at first sight he seemed.'

William now provided the main financial support for his family, even though his annual salary was only ninety pounds. He did not especially enjoy his employment, but never grumbled, and was a faithful, capable civil servant. Although he was only nineteen in the autumn of 1848, his hair was rapidly thinning, and a little over a year later he was nearly bald. 'This, in youth,' said the shy, sensitive William, 'was anything but pleasant to me. In particular I used to dislike entering a theatre or other public place with my hat on, looking, as I was, quite juvenile, and then, on taking off my hat, presenting the appearance more like a used-up man of forty.' Ironically, several people attributed his premature baldness to dissipation!

Both the Rossetti sisters continued to live at home, Maria was earning a small sum from her work, while Christina, still ailing, seldom went out of doors. In late 1848 and early 1849 she wrote more than a dozen poems, several of which are excellent; and she continued to see and (inexplicably to many people) to love Collinson, who when he visited Charlotte Street managed to stay awake. Because she was also friendly with the other Pre-Raphaelites and was one of only two women whose names were associated with the Brotherhood, in later years it was often said that she had been known as the 'Queen of the Pre-Raphaelites'. William Rossetti and Stephens could not

[1] Helen Angeli, *Dante Gabriel Rossetti*, pp. 15–16.

recall ever hearing this title applied to Christina, although William acknowledged that 'certain it is that she might without much unreason have been so called'.

Gabriel now spent most of his time at Cleveland Street, where increasingly he was a trial to his usually patient, uncomplaining studio mate. Holman Hunt enjoyed most of the proceedings of the Pre-Raphaelite Brotherhood, but for both temperamental and financial reasons he lived very simply—his meals, for example, did not include meat, partly because of Shelley's vegetarianism but mostly because of the cost—and his pattern of life was as orderly and regular as was his practice of painting. Gabriel, of course, was as much as ever a stranger to order and regularity. He rose, ate, slept, and in general lived as the passing fancy took him. Without warning he might suddenly appear at the studio accompanied by several fellow students from the Maddox Street drawing school, perhaps strangers to Hunt, who would be invited by Gabriel to feel at home and to examine and evaluate his colleague's pictures and sketches. On one occasion, soon after he and his friends had entered the studio, Gabriel said, 'Now, Hunt, don't keep us waiting any longer. I've promised them all supper.' Hunt could only invite them all to sit down and make the most of his simple meal.

If as a person Rossetti was exasperating to Hunt, as a painting companion he eventually became almost insufferable. Gabriel had plodded away at his picture, and by the end of autumn he was ready to begin the figures. He now faced the problem which was constantly to trouble him and his Brothers: the need for models. Good models were scarce and expensive: their usual rate of pay was a shilling an hour, five shillings for a morning sitting and seven shillings and sixpence for a whole day. Even Collinson and Millais could not easily afford to employ professional models, and so the Pre-Raphaelites customarily used relatives, friends, and acquaintances, or posed for each other. For *The Girlhood of Mary Virgin*, Gabriel engaged a handyman, who occasionally did odd jobs for his family, to model St Joachim; and he asked his mother and younger sister to sit for St Anne and the Virgin. (His treatment of Christina's hair, incidentally, shows that the Pre-Raphaelites did not insist on the literal reproduction of a model; Christina's hair was dark brown, Mary's is golden.) Painting St Joachim and the heads of the women was not too difficult for Gabriel, but the Virgin's drapery proved intolerably troublesome and often provoked a violent eruption of the notorious Rossetti temper. His greatest rages, however, were caused by the child-angel. He would ask the small girl modelling the angel to stand perfectly still; then she would move, and he would explode in anger. Hunt recalled an especially turbulent scene after Rossetti had tried unsuccessfully to use five or six children: 'The unsteadiness of one mild little girl so overtried his temper that he revealed his irritation beyond bounds, storming wildly, overthrowing his tools and stamping about, until the poor child sobbed and screamed with fright, clinging to her conductress, much too alarmed to listen to any comfort he repentantly offered her.'

This outburst, Hunt added, 'raised clouds of dust and destroyed my tranquillity of mind, further work that day was out of the question'. At last brought to the end of his patience, he asked Gabriel to join him in a stroll in Regent's Park, and there he told Gabriel that his fits of rage were not only self-destructive but were also harmful to the sharer of the studio (Hunt was then apprehensive about having his own picture ready for The Exhibition). Unless Gabriel took hold of himself and controlled his passions, the two of them would have to part, immediately. William once said of his brother that 'he could be managed, but not driven'; on this occasion he was properly 'managed'. He accepted Hunt's rebuke, returned to the studio, and proceeded to paint the angel without further ado.

Although he was an irritant to his studio companion, Rossetti also proved to be serviceable: Hunt's subject was Italian, and so Gabriel became the model for the leading figure of *Rienzi*. Both William and Stephens noted that the Roman warrior's face is an excellent likeness of Gabriel's as he approached manhood. According to Stephens, this is 'much the truest portrait of Rossetti as he appeared at that time . . . the large, dark eyes, strongly marked dark eye-brows, bold dome-like forehead, abundant long and curling hair falling on each side of the face, and especially the full lips conspicuous in the picture, are Rossetti to the life'. Gabriel also sat as the Fool in *Cordelia Watching at the Bedside of Lear*, Brown's principal picture of the current artistic year—and here too, said William, is a faithful representation of his brother.

Cordelia Watching at the Bedside of Lear is important not because Rossetti was one of the painter's models but because this picture was Ford Madox Brown's first truly outstanding work of art. The scene, taken from Act IV, Scene 7, of Shakespeare's play, shows Lear just before he awakens. Brown wrote the following description of this picture, which he always regarded as one of his finest achievements:

Found wildly running about the beach at Dover, Lear is secured, put to sleep with opiates, and the physician, about to wake him by means of music, has predicted his reason will return with consciousness. Cordelia, at the foot of the bed, awaits anxiously the effect of her presence on him, and utters the touching soliloquy beginning—

> Had you not been their father, these
> Had challenged pity of them.

. . . the young men gaily riding with hawk and hound contrast pathetically with the stricken old man. The poor fool . . . looks on with watery eyes. The Duke of Kent . . . is seen next the fool, having a wig on the alter his appearance. The physician, with his conjuring book, was a magician also in those days.

Brown's judgment of his own work was shared by many others, for this pathetic, intensely dramatic, beautifully realized scene has been one of his most highly praised efforts. F. G. Stephens declared that 'as a powerful illustration of Pre-Raphaelitism, a glory of the English School, [it is] worthy to be compared with any masterpiece of Rossetti in his riper days.[1] The Victorian art critic Sidney Colvin wrote, 'As an imaginative realization of a given scene from poetry, in which strenuous thought and vivid insight concur with complete pictorial sanity, I think it has hardly been surpassed in modern painting.'[1] *The Athenaeum*, twenty-four years after it had been painted, called it 'one of the most nearly perfect pictures of the English School'.

During the months that he was preparing for the 1849 Exhibition, Rossetti's creative energies were directed almost entirely to painting. Even his three poems from this period—the sonnets 'St Luke the Painter', 'Not as These', and 'The Husbandmen', which are grouped together in *The House of Life* under the title 'Old and New Art'—deal with painting. And, as William said, they 'deserve to be considered by persons who would like to understand the Pre-Raphaelite movement, and the temper in which Rossetti viewed it'. 'St Luke the Painter' pays tribute to the legendary patron saint of painters, who according to tradition founded religious art with his portrait of the Virgin Mary; the poem voices the hope that contemporary painters

[1] *Dante Gabriel Rossetti*, p. 40.
[2] 'Ford Madox Brown', *Portfolio*, vol. I, June 1870, p. 851.

may rehabilitate their art by re-establishing the sincerity of its earliest days, before artists 'sought talismans, and turned in vain to soulless self-reflections of man's skill'. 'Not as These' counsels artists who think themselves better than their contemporaries to turn from the present 'into the lights of the great Past', and to aspire after the best qualities of their forefathers. The third sonnet, 'The Husbandmen', is based on the parable in which labourers hired late in the day are paid the same as those employed earlier, and applies the lesson to contemporary artists who, although they have arrived late, should 'stand not idle in the market-place', for

> Which of ye knoweth *he* is not that last
> Who may be first by faith and will?

During the autumn of 1848 the third member of the 'big three', Millais, was finishing his commissioned picture, and in November was ready to begin his first Pre-Raphaelite painting. His subject followed the decision to draw on Keats's 'Isabella', which, based on a story from Boccaccio's *Decameron*, recalls the time and place of the Italian Pre-Raphaelites. The poem tells of a pair of lovers, Lorenzo and Isabella, whose love is unfulfilled because Isabella's two older brothers match her with a wealthy suitor and then murder Lorenzo, an act which brings about the death of Isabella. In his picture, *Lorenzo and Isabella,* Millais represents an imagined dinner in Isabella's home, with twelve guests, at the moment when a glance exchanged by the young couple reveals their love to the brothers, one of whom releases his anger by kicking Isabella's dog.

The other P.R.B.'s were happy to see the commencement of *Lorenzo and Isabella,* for as the Pre-Raphaelite social leadership rested with Rossetti, its artistic supremacy belonged to Millais. Without him they would not have dared to fire the first gun of their assault. But when Hunt learned of his projected undertaking—a highly intricate, exactingly detailed design containing thirteen human figures, each of whose dress, facial expression, and gestures would be distinctive and particularized—he doubted that even Millais could complete this project in the less than five months that remained before the sending-in day of The Exhibition. Millais remained unworried. For one thing, he knew that, unlike Hunt, he would not be distracted by the time-consuming, sleep-stealing, Rossetti-inspired social proceedings of the Pre-Raphaelite Brotherhood. And he also knew that he was a rapid worker—and since, as always, he had meticulously worked out every detail of his picture, complex though it was, he could proceed immediately and unhesitatingly with a sure brush. Because of his thoroughgoing advance planning, the execution of his designs was usually relatively easy to accomplish. Once he amazed Hunt as he energetically painted while carrying on a lively conversation on a topic unrelated to his picture. 'Oh, that's all right,' said Millais, in response to his friend's astonishment. 'I've painted every touch in my head long ago, and have now only to transfer it to canvas.' So Hunt's anxiety about the completion of *Lorenzo and Isabella* rapidly evaporated when he saw Millais working surely and unfalteringly 'at a pace beyond all calculation'. Stephens also watched his facile colleague and wrote that 'such tenacity and technical powers were never since the German followers of Dürer adopted Italian principles of working, exercised on a single picture.'

Despite his extraordinary technical proficiency, Millais, as he later acknowledged, still sought advice from Hunt: 'I was always glad to hear what he had to say . . . and not infrequently to act on his suggestions. We were working together then, and constantly criticized each other's pictures.' But he pointedly denied that he had been influenced by his second principal colleague. He was especially annoyed seven years before his death by an article in which Harry Quilter wrote of *Lorenzo and Isabella*:

Was there another mind which conceived this supper at the house of Isabella, and worked upon Millais to paint it, not in the artist's own manner, but in that of the seer? This may have been so, and when we remember the earlier drawings of Rossetti, and the great influence his art and his personality exercised over the Pre-Raphaelite Brotherhood, it is not difficult to know whose was the influence. To those who are acquainted with Rossetti's work . . . in its earlier purity and almost ascetic spirit, there is, indeed, no doubt possible as to the fact of Millais having painted the picture in question under the inspiration of his half-Italian comrade.[1]

According to Quilter, Millais was 'jumping into another painter's intellectual and emotion skin' and thereby produced a picture 'which is in subtlety of imagination, in penetration of character, in nationality, and general spirit, entirely alien to his genius, his birth, and his intellectual capacity'. 'My pictures would have been the same if I had never seen or heard of Rossetti,' Millais insisted. His only picture, he

[1] Harry Quilter, 'The Isabella Supper', *Universal Review*, 1889, pp. 146–7.

said, which had been affected by Gabriel was *Lorenzo and Isabella*, 'in which some of the vestments were worked out in accordance with a book of mediaeval costumes which he lent me'. (The book was Bonnard's *Costumes*, whose plates were highly useful to all the active Pre-Raphaelites.) Further on Rossetti, Millais said 'I liked him very much when we first met, believing him to be (as perhaps he was) sincere in his desire to further our aims—Hunt's and mine—but I always liked William much better. Rossetti was a queer fellow, and impossible as a boon companion—so dogmatic and so irritable when opposed.'[1] Gabriel was not at all irritable about posing for one of the guests in *Lorenzo and Isabella*, the man in the rear draining his glass, of whose portrait Stephens said 'the pallor of the face is overdone, but the likeness is otherwise perfect'. The balding William sat for Lorenzo, to whom Millais gave a full head of golden brown hair. This alteration was the only liberty Millais took with his models, all of whom, friends and relatives, were so realistically depicted that Stephens commented, 'Van Eyck did not study the details of "the life" more unflinchingly than Millais here.'

As spring drew near, it became almost certain that the three leading Pre-Raphaelites would be prepared on 10 April to take their completed pictures to Trafalgar Square. The first to finish his painting, surprisingly, was Rossetti. By mid-winter he was able to work without Hunt's assistance, and early in March he visited a shop on Wigmore Street and bought for two shillings an artificial lily, from which he painted the last detail of the picture. Then, a full four weeks before the Academy's sending-in day, he stood and gazed at his first truly original oil-painting. With pride he printed in the lower left-hand corner 'DANTE GABRIELE ROSSETTI', beneath which he wrote 'P.R.B. 1849'. This was one of the first instances in which he signed his name in its soon-to-be familiar form (it is not clear why he added the second 'e' to his middle name), and it was the only time that he inscribed the fraternal initials on a picture.

Perhaps because he was an inextricable fusion of painter and poet, and perhaps because he anticipated uncomprehending viewers, Gabriel could not let his painting hang unattended. He composed two explanatory sonnets, to be printed on a slip of gilt paper and attached to the picture frame:

[1] *The Life and Letters of Sir John Everett Millais*, p. 52.

I

This is that blessed Mary, pre-elect
God's Virgin. Gone is a great while, and she
Dwelt young in Nazareth of Galilee.
Unto God's will she brought devout respect,
Profound simplicity of intellect,
And supreme patience. From her mother's knee
Faithful and hopeful; wise in charity;
Strong in grave peace; in pity circumspect.
So held she through her girlhood; as it were
An angel-watered lily, that near God
Grows and is quiet. Till, one dawn at home
She woke in her white bed, and had no fear
At all,—yet wept till sunshine, and felt awed:
Because the fulness of the time was come.

II

These are the symbols. On that cloth of red
I' the centre in the Tripoint: perfect each,
Except the second of its points, to teach
That Christ is not yet born. The books—whose head
Is golden Charity, as Paul hath said—
Those virtues are wherein the soul is rich:
Therefore on them the lily standeth, which
Is Innocence, being interpreted.
The seven-thorn'd briar and the palm seven-leaved
Are her great sorrow and her great reward.
Until the end be full, the Holy One
Abides without. She soon shall have achieved
Her perfect purity: yea, God the Lord
Shall soon vouchsafe His Son to be her Son.

The Girlhood of Mary Virgin was now ready to go on display. And soon the picture was indeed placed on an exhibition wall—but the wall was not located in Trafalgar Square. After he had completed the sonnets, Gabriel carried his painting to Hyde Park Corner, where, beginning on 26 March, it was to hang as No. 368 at the third annual Free Exhibition.

Rossetti's action shocked and amazed his companions, especially Hunt and Millais. Since they had resolved to launch a unified attack on the Academy, they were baffled by the desertion of their most outspoken soldier on the very eve of the battle. Especially bewildering was Gabriel's forsaking *The* Exhibition in favour of the least prestigious art show in London. Because Rossetti stayed away from Gower and Cleveland Streets at this time, Millais and Hunt could only speculate on what had caused him to take this divisive step.

In his memoirs, Hunt explained Rossetti's action by the saying that it 'gave him a few extra days for finishing his contribution, although the Gallery opened a week before the Academy'. Hunt clearly had confused the 1849 Free Exhibition with its predecessor the year before, which had opened one week before the Academy. In 1849, in order to avoid competition with the R.A., the directors of the Free Exhibition advanced their opening by a month, with pictures to be received ten days earlier. Since the exhibition in Trafalgar Square began on the first Monday in May, with entries due no later than 10 April, Rossetti had, instead of 'a few extra days', nearly four *fewer* weeks for finishing his painting.

Hunt may be forgiven for not remembering the exact date of an event that had occurred more than half a century before. Not so easily condoned, however, are the later writers who have approvingly quoted Hunt and who have suggested other reasons for Rossetti's appearance in the Free Exhibition—such reasons as his wishing to be the first Pre-Raphaelite to come before the public. It may not have have been out of character for him to try to be one jump ahead of his companions, but he could hardly have expected to do this by hanging his picture at Hyde Park Corner. Earlier Free Exhibitions had been only moderately attended and briefly reviewed; and, with five hundred works vying for the attention of critics, none of whom was likely to write more than one short notice of the show, Rossetti could not reasonably have hoped even to be mentioned in print.

Among the other theories to account for the presence of *The Girlhood of Mary Virgin* in the erstwhile Chinese Gallery are that Rossetti wanted to be sure his picture would have an advantageous position; that, in the words of a recent biographer, the usually dependable Oswald Doughty, he might have been driven by a 'fear of too close an association with his rebel Brethren, in case their work and the movement they represented prove unpopular'; and that, behaving in his usual impulsive way, as R. L. Mégroz said, he 'changed his mind at the last minute.' None of these notions stands up. First, any unestablished artist then would have preferred to see his painting near the ceiling of the Academy than at eye level in the Chinese Gallery. Secondly, it would not be in character for Rossetti suddenly to fear guilt by association—especially in light of the plainly lettered 'P.R.B.' on his picture. Thirdly, a man who for weeks had been labouring with unusual care and perseverance to complete a painting by mid-March would scarcely give in to an impulse regarding the choice of hanging place. No, Rossetti's decision to hang his picture in the Free Exhibition seems to have been carefully premeditated. And its true explanation probably involves two powerful influences on his artistic attitudes at this time: Ford Madox Brown and the Royal Academy itself.

Brown's personal power over Rossetti was and would always be greater than Hunt's. Brown constantly denounced the Academy, and was again in 1849 taking his painting to the Free Exhibition. His attitude and conduct alone might have been enough to induce his protégé to follow him to Hyde Park Corner.

But also, quite simply, Rossetti was afraid of sending his picture to the Academy and letting it face the judgment of the Council which acted as the Selection Committee. We have seen how, as a boy, he had needed four years to summon up courage to take the entrance examination for the R.A. Schools; he would always suffer from this deeply ingrained fear of failure. As William said of his brother, he 'was in some respects a singular compound of self-reliance and self-mistrust. He relied on himself so far as working-impulse and actual work were concerned. He mistrusted himself with regard to the effect of his work on other minds.' In the winter of 1848–49, then, he was confident of completing his picture but fearful of its reception. And, in fairness, there were grounds for his diffidence. After all, Brown had had only one picture accepted for hanging in Trafalgar Square, and in 1848 even Millais's contribution had been rejected. Moreover, Rossetti himself had had the temerity to quit the Academy school before completing its most elementary curriculum. So it is not surprising that Gabriel felt nervous about subjecting his first oil-painting to the scrutiny of the Academic Council.

Not only was Rossetti fearful that his picture would be rejected, but, paradoxically, he must also have been afraid of its being accepted. His sensitivity to criticism was as acute as his dread of failure. Even as a child he had been hypersensitive to others' evaluation of his drawings and poems as in the summer of 1848 when he sent 'My Sisters' Sleep' to Aunt Charlotte and wrote, 'I should not wish the verses to be seen by anyone but yourself.' If by chance his picture were placed in one of the galleries of the Academy, he would suffer the agony of seeing and hearing (and imagining) it undergoing an ordeal of fire unlike anything that might take place in the Chinese Gallery. Millais once said, 'The fact is, the R.A. is the only place for a man to find his real level. All the defects come out so clearly no private puffing is worth a farthing. You can't thrust pictures down people's throats.' Rossetti was not blind to his own defects, but was too proud to let them be exposed unnecessarily.

And so he carried the *Virgin* to the badly-lit building which *The Literary Gazette* called 'a splendid gallery' because its roominess permitted nearly every picture to be well positioned. He hung his painting on a space that had cost him fifteen shillings a horizontal foot, posted a price tag of eighty pounds, and, keeping clear of his Brothers, awaited the opening.

The third annual Free Exhibition was being to some extent taken a little more seriously by artists and critics—and its opening was well-timed. So it was more promptly and extensively reviewed than either of its forerunners. Since most of the pictures were the quintessence of mediocrity, a commendable work by contrast would be conspicuous (and perhaps this was another factor in Rossetti's decision to exhibit there). Thus one of the most frequently mentioned of the five hundred paintings was *The Girlhood of Mary Virgin*. By the end of the exhibition's first week Rossetti's picture had been favourably cited by a number of periodicals. The prestigious *Literary Gazette* called it 'a very uncommon work in emulation of the old missal style, highly finished, indeed though in oil'; *The Builder* said it was 'in the manner of the early school, finished with extraordinary minuteness and displaying a high tone of mind . . . one of the most noticeable pictures in the Gallery.' *The Morning Chronicle* said that 'the picture demands highest praise'; according to *The Observer*, 'the traits of the Virgin and mother are ineffably sweet; and the arrangement of the parts of the picture are of correspondent grace and beauty'. The reviewer for the important, newly-named *Art Journal* remarked, 'This picture is the most successful as a pure imitation of early Florentine Art that we have seen in this country. The artist has worked in austere cultivation of all the virtues of the ancient fathers. . . . The expression and character of the features are intense and vivacious, and these, together with the draperies and accessories, are elaborated into the highest degree of nicety.'

These commendations of a first painting would have delighted any young artist beyond expectation, but the best was yet to come. In 1848, the most important weekly journal of the arts, *The Athenaeum*, had waited until September to mention the Free Exhibition; but this year its unnamed reviewer (the noted painter-critic Frank Stone) visited the Chinese Gallery early, and his report appeared in the issue of 7 April. After summarily and contemptuously dismissing the bulk of the pictures, he wrote:

> It is pleasant to turn from the mass of commonplace . . . to a manifestation of true mental power, in which Art is made the exponent of some high aim. . . . Such work will be found . . . not from a long-practised hand, but from one young in experience, new to fame, Mr G. D. Rossetti.[1] He has painted . . . a work which, for its invention and for many parts of its design, would be creditable to any exhibition. . . . The picture, which is full of allegory, has much of that sacred mysticism inseparable from the works of the early masters, and much of the tone of the poets of the same time. While immature practice is visible in the executive department of the work, every allusion gives evidence of maturity of thought—every detail that might enrich or simplify the subject has found a place in it. The personification of the Virgin is an achievement worthy of an older hand. Its spiritualized attributes, and the great sensibility with which it is wrought, inspire the expectation that Mr Rossetti will continue to pursue the lofty career which he has here so successfully begun.
>
> The sincerity and the earnestness of the picture remind us forcibly of the feeling with which the early Florentine monastic painters wrought; and the form and face of the Virgin recall the words employed by Savonarola in one of his powerful sermons. . . . Mr Rossetti has, perhaps unknowingly, entered into the feelings of the renowned Dominican, who in his day wrought as much reform in Art as in morals. The coincidence is of high value to the picture.

Without any knowledge of the Pre-Raphaelite Brotherhood and its objectives, most of the reviewers emphasized the resemblances between Rossetti's picture and the works of early Italians—though none noticed, or heeded, the initials 'P.R.B.'

In 1864 Rossetti saw his *Girlhood of Mary Virgin* while it was being reframed, and he wrote that it was 'a long way better than I thought. . . . It quite surprised me to see what I did fifteen years ago.' Many later visitors to London's Tate Gallery also have marvelled at the excellence of his first original painting. To be sure, it has its imperfections: the inexpert composition, the unskilful execution of the Virgin's legs and the embroidery frame indicate his lack of training

[1] In the catalogue Gabriel's name appeared as G. D. Rossetti.

and experience; the colours are bright but without the depth and richness which later became characteristic of Rossetti's paintings; and perspective was obviously of little concern to the artist. The deficiencies, however, are easily over-balanced by the merits: the excellent drawing; the faithfully delineated details, such as the vine leaves and the dove; Mary's drapery and the rose-winged angel (the execution of which proved that Rossetti could persevere until he had surmounted his most difficult problems); and, above all, the two principal faces—the serene, courtly St Anne and the delicate, childlike Mary, who, as Lucien Pissarro said, is 'a quite unconventional madonna'. Even with Hunt's assistance, the picture bears the unmistakable imprint of the personality of Gabriel Rossetti—and, as plainly as 'The Blessed Damozel' and 'My Sister's Sleep' are poems of a painter, so *The Girlhood of Mary Virgin* is the painting of a poet.

It would be difficult to over-emphasize the significance of *The Girlhood of Mary Virgin*. Prior to its completion, Rossetti had been just another vocal but untested student painter, unsure of himself and his future. As soon as his picture had been completed, hung, seen, and reviewed, his self-doubts and uncertainties passed out of his mind. He knew that he was and always would be a painter.

During the last week in March and the first in April of 1849 Millais and Hunt, who were finishing their pictures while their colleague feasted on the praise of his *Virgin*, were not exactly overjoyed. Hunt often asserted his rightful claim to a generous share of credit for Rossetti's artistic maturation. In his book of memoirs he wrote, 'had he not been very closely, thoughtfully, and affectionately guided by me, hour by hour, in my studio for seven or eight months, I unhesitatingly maintain he could not have appeared as a painter in 1849, and not even in 1850, if ever'. It will be remembered, also, that he and Millais, many months before becoming intimate with Rossetti, had discussed and experimented with the principles of painting which came to be known as 'Pre-Raphaelite'. And so to hear of Rossetti being acclaimed a solitary reviver of an early style of art was, as Hunt understated it, 'somewhat trying'.

Nor was this the last or worst of Hunt's Rossettian trials. For several weeks after he had taken his painting to Hyde Park Corner, Gabriel did not go near his studio; then a porter suddenly appeared and told the astonished Hunt that he had come to collect the belongings of Mr Rossetti, who had terminated his studio partnership on the preceding Lady Day, 25 March, and no longer held himself responsible for his share of the rent. The burden of the full rent—and the additional bedroom which Hunt had taken only because of Rossetti—was a severe blow to his meagre funds. Knowing the futility of remonstrating with Gabriel, he reached a compromise with his landlord, but even so he had to return temporarily to his father's house.

The pictures of Hunt and Millais, each adorned with its creator's fraternal insignia, were accepted by the Academy and hung just above eye level in the well-lighted large room. They were favourably noticed in a number of journals, including *The Athenaeum*, and were praised by such men as Augustus Egg (soon to become a prominent R.A.), who personally visited and congratulated Hunt; Edward Bulwer-Lytton, author of the book which had inspired the painting, who lauded *Rienzi* as a work which, 'full of genius and high promise', was a splendid visual realization of the scene from his novel; Ford Madox Brown, who wrote in his diary, 'Went to see Millais' *Isabella*; wonderfully painted, full of expression, sentiment, and colour, and extreme good painting'; and the poet Coventry Patmore, who regarded Millais's picture as 'far better than anything Keats ever did'.

Hunt himself voiced the widespread opinion of *Lorenzo and Isabella* when he called it 'the most wonderful painting any youth under twenty years of age ever did'. Its faithfully observed and delineated details; its fresh, harmonious colours; its individualized gestures; its dramatic intensity; its masterly handling of light and shade (which in 1849 was strikingly novel); and its unity, which is exceptional for a picture with thirteen human and two non-human figures—all of these attributes have aroused high praise for Millais's painting.

Rienzi is more difficult to evaluate because it deteriorated and so required, many years later, some fairly extensive re-painting. Two of its enduring features, however, are the expressive face of Rienzi (that is, Rossetti), and its realistic 'Pre-Raphaelite' details—in the vegetation, the armour, the shields, the horses, the costumes, and even the bumble-bee in the right foreground, drifting in the air over the foliage.

So for Hunt, Millais, and especially Rossetti, the 1849 season was an artistic success. Hunt fared well with his first 'Pre-Raphaelite' picture, Millais re-established himself after his disappointment of 1848, and Rossetti launched his career. On opening day, *Lorenzo and Isabella* was sold to three Bond Street tailors who bought the picture as a speculative investment (they paid Millais 150 pounds and one new suit of clothes). In June, the Dowager Marchioness of Bath (undoubtedly urged on by her governess, who happened to be Gabriel's Aunt Charlotte Polidori) purchased *The Girlhood of Mary Virgin* for its asking price of eighty pounds.[1] He who needed money most waited longest for a sale. Hunt had hoped his picture would solve his money problems, but after six weeks on exhibition it was still unsold. However, a few days later, when the dejected artist was despairing of ever receiving an offer, a collector (sent by Augustus Egg) appeared at his home and paid the posted price of one hundred guineas for *Rienzi*.

Yet in spite of all these successes, in one respect the year was an abysmal failure for the Pre-Raphaelites. They had expected to raise a storm in the world of art, but they had produced not even a ripple in the sea of officialdom. No one was angered or alarmed. No one outside the Brotherhood was aware that an attempt had been made to revolutionalize British art. No one had even mentioned the initials which each of the three youths had painted with pride. So the Brothers were disappointed—though not disheartened. Already all of them, even the non-exhibitors, were eagerly looking forward to the next year. And, with the possible exception of Collinson,[2] each had resolved to do whatever he could to prevent another year of artistic tranquillity.

[1] When he heard of the purchase of *The Girlhood of Mary Virgin*, Millais wrote to Rossetti that he was 'stunning delighted' by the sale of the picture, 'and to such a nobby person—The success of the PRB is now *quite certain*.'

[2] Collinson had also exhibited a painting at the Academy, *Image—Boys at a Roadside Alehouse*. Although it did not command much attention, *The Art Journal* said of it: 'The scene is rendered with much spirit, and the characters individually with becoming truth.'

7

The Germ and the Launching of a Poet

The first taste of success led Gabriel Rossetti to start immediately looking forward to more. In May 1849, he wrote to Aunt Charlottte,

> As my picture this year has created some interest it is desirable that I should come before the public next year as prominently as possible, so as to succeed in establishing at once some degree of reputation. I am therefore about to commence immediately another work, hoping thus to get two done before the next exhibition.

But, for all his hopes and plans, Rossetti felt he deserved a brief interlude to enjoy some of the benefits of 1849. As soon as the doors of the Free Exhibition were permanently closed, early in the summer, he began to repaint the head of his troublesome angel (throughout his life he would forever be revising poems and retouching paintings). At the end of July he sent *The Girlhood of Mary Virgin* to the Marchioness of Bath, from whom without delay he received eighty pounds. For the first time Gabriel held in his hands money that he himself had earned, a sum that almost equalled his brother's yearly income. It is no wonder that he wanted to have two paintings completed for the next exhibition season. Whether any of Gabriel's earnings, like most of William's, went to help his family's finances is not clear; but it is certain that he did not hesitate to start spending money on himself.

In mid-July, after the sale of *Rienzi*, Rossetti had spoken with Hunt about visiting the Continent, and now, in August, he excitedly looked forward to the trip they would take—after Hunt had returned from the Lea marshes where, in the thick of the river and meadows, he was painting the background and foreground for his next picture. The journey would be pleasant and relaxing, but also edifying: Britain's inadequate public galleries and the crude methods of reproducing pictures made it essential for British artists to visit galleries, museums, and churches in Europe. Naturally they asked Millais to accompany them, and naturally Millais had no time for travel. Hoping to exhibit no fewer than three paintings in 1850, he was now in Oxford painting the first of these, and when he was working at full swing, nothing could divert John Everett Millais.

Early in the afternoon of 27 September, the two young men boarded a train at London Bridge Station to begin the five-hour ride to their embarkation port, Folkestone. They shared a compartment with four others, and in 'London to Folkestone', a poem written on the train, Gabriel briefly pictured his travelling companions. In these verses, and in all of the others written during the journey, William Rossetti observed, 'the writer was bent on the Pre-Raphaelite plan—that of sharply realizing an impression on the eye—and through the eye on the mind'. Hunt sat beside Gabriel, reading Dumas,

> hard-lipped, with heavy jowl
> And brows hung low, and the long ends of hair
> Standing out limp.

Seated on Rossetti's other side was a woman whose physical plainness suggested she was 'fair in soul, no doubt', carrying flowers which, the poet said, were 'half upon my knees'. Directly opposite him sat a 'poor young muff'

> pitiful in loose collar and black tie
> His latchet-button shaking as we go.

After crossing the Channel, they spent a night and morning in Boulogne, and at three o'clock began the eight-hour journey to Paris. Transportation in a French third-class rail carriage in the middle of the nineteenth century could hardly be called restful:

> This cursed pitching is too bad. My teeth
> Jingle together in it; and my legs
> (Which I got wet at Boulogne this good day
> Wading for star-fish) are so chilled that I
> Would don my coat, were not these seats too hard
> To spare it from beneath me, and were not
> The love of ease less than the love of sloth.

Apparently some of his fellow travellers in politically sensitive France were suspicious of Gabriel's writing tablet:

> Hunt has just stretched to tell me that he fears
> I and my note-book may be taken for
> The stuff that goes to make an 'émissaire
> De la perfide.' Let me abate my zeal:
> There is a stout gendarme within the coach.

Finally, as eleven o'clock approached, he saw the lights of Paris and said 'Dieu merci.'

During their sixteen days in Paris, where they lived in a room at 4 Rue Geoffroy Marie in Faubourg Montmartre, Hunt and Rossetti followed some of the usual tourist paths. They went to Notre Dame, which Rossetti said was 'inconceivably stunning' and contained 'most glorious things to put in pictures', and they climbed to the top, where Gabriel looked out over Paris and 'shouted in the spirit'. They also visited a cabaret to see a performance of the can-can, which inspired the following incomplete sonnet, whose 'numerical characteristics', Rossetti said, 'refer to the *danseuses*':

> The first, a mare; the second, 'twixt bow-wow
> And pussy-cat, a cross; the third, a beast
> To baffle Buffon; the fourth, not the least
> In hideousness, nor the last; the fifth, a cow;
> The sixth, Chimera; the seventh, Sphinx; . . . Come now,
> *One* woman, France, ere this frog-hop have ceased,
> And it shall be enough. A toothsome feast
> Of Blackguardism . . . and bald row,
> No doubt for such as love those same. For me,
> I confess, William, and avow to thee,
> (Soft in thine ear) that such sweet female whims
> . . .
> Are not a passion of mine naturally.
> . . .

Rossetti's reaction to the can-can girls was typical of the hyper-critical attitude of this thoroughgoing Englishman towards all things French. He complained about 'tiled floors in bedrooms', and narrow, winding streets 'which lead to the first place you came from', and the native 'who spit their oaths at you and grind their r's'. Here is a typical observation, written a week after his arrival: 'We have not seen six pretty faces since we have been in Paris, and those such as would not be in the least remarkable in London.'

The Parisian works of art did not escape Rossetti's disparagement. The paintings in the Louvre that he found praiseworthy could be contained in a few lines of a letter: 'There is a most wonderful copy of a fresco by Angelico, a tremendous Van Eyck, some mighty things by that real stunner Lionardo, some ineffably poetical Mantegnas, several wonderful Early Christians whom nobody ever heard of, some tremendous portraits by some Venetian whose name I forget, and a stunning *Francis I* by Titian. Gericault's *Medusa* is also very fine on the whole. . . . There is a wonderful head by Raphael; another wonderful head by I know not whom; and a pastoral by Giorgione [*Venetian Pastoral*], which is so intensely fine that I condescended to sit down before it and write a sonnet.' As for the rest of the pictures in the Louvre, Gabriel wrote, 'there is a monosyllable current amongst us which enables a P.R.B. to dispense almost entirely with details on the subject'. The monosyllable was the Brotherhood's term of derogation: 'slosh.'

The Luxembourg Palace was even more disappointing than the Louvre. Rossetti liked fewer than a dozen of its pictures: two by Delaroche, two by Robert-Fleury, one Ingres, one by Hesse, and several by Ary Scheffer and Granet. The remaining paintings, he reported, 'with a few mediocre exceptions, we considered trash'. For all but one of the works of Ingres, he said, 'I wouldn't give two sous—filthy slosh.' Delacroix, he remarked, 'except in two pictures which show a kind of savage genius, is a perfect beast'.

Rossetti, however, did find two pictures in Paris about which he could rave:

> Hunt and I solemnly decided that the most perfect works, taken *in toto*, that we have seen in our lives, are two pictures by Hippolyte Flandrin (representing Christ's entry into Jerusalem, and his departure to death) in the Church of S. Germain des Prés. Wonderful! wonderful! ! wonderful! ! !

Altogether he saw in all of Paris only about 'forty first-rate paintings, —or indeed fifty mayhap'.

So Rossetti was not unhappy on 15 October to leave Paris for Brussels, as is apparent from his three 'Last Sonnets at Paris', of which the following is the first:

> Chins that might serve the new Jerusalem;
> Streets footsore; minute whisking milliners,
> Dubbed graceful, but at whom one's eye demurs,
> Knowing of England; ladies, much the same;
> Bland smiling dogs with manes—a few of them
> At pains to look like sporting characters;

Vast humming tabbies smothered in their furs;
Groseille, orgeat, meringues à la creme—
Good things to study; ditto bad—the maps
Of sloshy colour in the Louvre; *cinq-francs*
The largest coin; and at the restaurants
Large Ibrahim Pachas in Turkish caps
To pocket them. *Un million d'habitants:*
Cast up, they'll make an Englishman—perhaps.

Rossetti's distaste for the Continent did not abate in Brussels. He wrote to William, 'There is a most servile aping of the French here, notwithstanding that they seem to be held in hatred. The English are victimized to a beastly extent everywhere. One of the great nuisances at this place, as also at Waterloo, is the plague of guides, from which there is no escape.' In one day, he said, he and Hunt took in everything in the city 'except a lot of scientific and industrial silliness'. The Brussels Museum contained 'a few very fine early German pictures, among them a wonderful Van Eyck', but when they entered one room and found it 'full of Rubenses', they 'held aloof'. As a matter of course they visited the site of England's greatest continental triumph, but, Gabriel reported, 'between you and me, William, Waterloo is simply a bore.'

From Brussels they travelled to Antwerp, where Rossetti enjoyed the paintings of Memling and the Van Eyck brothers but was repelled by the omnipresent Rubens. After Antwerp came Ghent, where a visit to the celebrated convent, the Béguinage, was described by Gabriel in a letter to Collinson:

Each nun has a house to herself, over which is written not her name, but that of some saint under whose protection she has been pleased to put it. In some cases where the name was more than usually quaint, we felt disposed to knock at the door and ask if he was in; but refrained, as it was rather late, and we feared he might be gone to bed. We witnessed the vesper service, which rather surprised us, as we thought that among the tunes played we could recognize 'Jim Crow' and 'Nix my dolly'. At the end, each nun finds a kind of towel somewhere, which she folds up and puts on the top of her head; during the service, a rather sloshy one goes about with a policeman's bull eye, collecting coppers. At our entrance and departure, Hunt dipped his fingers in the holy-water stoup and commenced some violent gesticulations, which I was obliged to bring to an abrupt conclusion.

Ghent was followed by the artistic highlight of the journey, Bruges, which, Rossetti wrote, was 'a most stunning place, immeasurably the best we have come to', with 'a quantity of first-rate architecture, and very little or no Rubens'. He was captivated most of all by 'the miraculous works of Memling and Van Eyck'. Memling was Rossetti's principal continental discovery; of the large triptych in the Hospital of St John he declared that 'the perfection of character and even drawing, the astounding finish, the glory of colour, and above all the pure religious sentiment and ecstatic poetry . . . is not to be conceived or described'.

After they had seen Bruges, Rossetti and Hunt were ready to return home. Interestingly, neither showed any desire to go to the birthplace of Pre-Raphaelitism, Italy. Hunt was eager to resume his work, and Gabriel felt that he had seen enough Italians in Charlotte Street to last a lifetime.

From their month's travelling—the longest journey Rossetti would ever make—they brought back souvenirs including, in Gabriel's words, 'an extraordinary self-concocting coffee-pot for state occasions of the P.R.B.' and a book 'containing a receipt for raising the devil'. More importantly, they returned with renewed faith in the idea of Pre-Raphaelitism. As Hunt said, 'We came back with richer minds, but without any change of purpose.'

Refreshed and eager to go back to work, they were soon busily studio-hunting. At first they went to Cheyne Walk, a quiet tree-lined street, greatly favoured by artists and writers, running alongside the river in Chelsea, where they looked at a large house which they thought was suitable for the entire Brotherhood. The dwelling commanded an excellent view of the Thames and could provide accommodation for four—a studio, a bedroom, and a small reading room each. All of the Pre-Raphaelites except Millais, who would have nothing to do with this scheme, met in Woolner's studio and excitedly discussed the proposal. They decided, among other things, that they would paint on the front door 'P.R.B.' which they would tell non-members meant 'Please Ring Bell'. Three days later their enthusiasm had subsided, and they abandoned the project.

Rossetti then suggested to Hunt that they share a studio again; and when Rossetti discovered a satisfactory house, also in Cheyne Walk, Hunt amazingly almost agreed—because, he remarked, on their recent trip Gabriel had been 'a perfect travelling companion, ever in the best of temper'. But his better judgment prevailed: as he wrote, 'remembering my experience in Cleveland Street, and that my resources and chances would not warrant an uncertain expenditure, I relinquished the idea'.

On 10 November, Rossetti found and agreed to rent a studio at 72 Newman Street, just above Oxford Street, two blocks from Soho Square. An extension of Cleveland Street, two blocks in length, Newman Street once had been inhabited by many artists—including Benjamin West, the second president of the Royal Academy, and, in 1826, five of the forty R.As. By 1849 the street had deteriorated, but was still well equipped with studios. Gabriel's was on the second floor of a house whose ground floor was used by the proprietor of a dancing academy; a short time earlier, its rent had been forty pounds, but the landlord agreed (presumably after some blandishments) to lease it for twenty-eight pounds. Rossetti would use his Newman Street accommodation only for painting and entertaining, and would continue to sleep at his family home.[1] A few days later Hunt moved into temporary quarters in Bayswater, where he remained until 5 January, when he took an attractive house at 5 Prospect Place, a few steps from Cheyne Walk.

In the middle of November, when Hunt and Rossetti returned to their easels, the third member of their triumvirate had completed one painting and was preparing to put the finishing touches on a second. Millais painted the first in Oxford during the summer; it was a portrait of his host, one James Wyatt, a merchant of pictures, prints and frames, together with his young granddaughter. Its highly meticulous details, ranging from wall portraits and gilt frames to mahogany tables and antimacassars led one writer late in the century to observe that Millais had worked on this picture 'with the eye of a conscientious insect'.[2] While in Oxford, Millais had also begun *Ferdinand Lured by Ariel*. Inspired by Act I, Scene 2 of Shakespeare's *Tempest*, it shows Ferdinand standing perplexed as he listens to the invisible Ariel, accompanied in the air by several attending spirits, who, according to Millais, are 'half human and half like birds'. Because of all the assorted herbiage and foliage surrounding Ferdinand, the picture has often been called the first Pre-Raphaelite landscape. The manner in which the vegetation was painted is indicated by a sentence

[1] The character of Charlotte Street, incidentally, seems to have improved since the days of Rossetti's early boyhood. The 1850 Post Office Directory listed among its inhabitants six artists, including Copley Fielding, two architects, one solicitor, one professor of music, one district clerk, and one Sir William Pym.

[2] *Saturday Review*, 15 January 1898, p. 74.

from the 23 July 1849 entry of the *P.R.B. Journal*: 'Millais said he had thoughts of painting a hedge (as a subject) to the closest point of imitation—with a bird's nest—a thing which has never been attempted.' Soon after returning to London, Millais painted Ferdinand's head, modelled from Stephens, in one uninterrupted sitting which began at ten and ended just before five o'clock, when the artist laid down his brush and said, 'There, old fellow, it's done!' Stephens told of how he had felt after standing motionless for nearly seven hours: 'For me, still leaning on a stick and in the required posture, I had become quite unable to move, rise upright, or stir a limb, till, much as if I were a stiffened lay-figure, Millais lifted me up and carried me bodily to the dining-room, where some dinner and wine put me on my feet again.'

Now in mid-November, Millais was sketching Ariel and the other spirits, Hunt was returning to the picture he had begun in the Lea marshes, and Rossetti was ready to go to work in his new studio. Gabriel had several ideas in mind, including an enormous canvas containing at least thirty figures, based on a song from Browning's *Paracelsus*, 'Hist, said Kate the Queen'. But at last he decided to undertake a more modest venture, at least in his first painting (for he still intended to exhibit two pictures in 1850). The following is the 25 November 1849 entry in the *P.R.B. Journal*: 'Gabriel began making a sketch for *The Annunciation*. The Virgin is to be in bed, but without any bedclothes on, an arragement which may be justified in consideration of the hot climate; and the angel Gabriel is to be presenting a lily to her. The picture, and its companion of the Virgin's Death, will be almost entirely white.'[1] This painting, which at first would bear a Latin title, *Ecce Ancilla Domini* (Behold the Handmaid of the Lord), was an obvious companion piece to *The Girlhood of Mary Virgin*.

The incident was a familiar one in art, but—naturally—Rossetti's conception of it was highly unconventional, as Stephens observed when he contrasted it with traditional representations of the Annunciation:

The Virgins Annunciate of Angelico, Memmi, Taddeo Bartoli, Fra Bartolommeo, and others, were generally handsomely clad, if not crowned and jewelled, and most are enthroned under arched canopies, adorned with sculptures. The Flemings and Germans went beyond this and expended all

[1] Rossetti never painted the picture of the Virgin's death.

the resources of their skill on Mary's brocade, precious stones, goldsmithery, and even illuminations of the sumptuous breviary they bestowed on her. Rossetti gave her no ornaments, except a gilded nimbus, which, as in other pictures, glows round her hair, and was kindled as the angel spoke. She is covered from head to foot-heel by a simple robe of lawn, leaving her arms bare, and her dark auburn tresses fall on her shoulders . . .

Ruskin also remarked on the differences between Rossetti's Virgin (again modelled after Christina) and earlier Madonnas:

Rossetti's 'Annunciation' differs from every previous conception of the scene known to me, in representing the angel as waking the Virgin from sleep to give her his message. . . .

. . . consider . . . how the pious persons who had always been accustomed to see their Madonnas dressed in scrupulously folded and exquisitely falling robes of blue, with edges embroidered in gold,—to find them, also, sitting under arcades of exquisite architecture by Bernini,—and reverently to observe them receive the angel's message with their hands folded on their breasts in the most graceful positions, and the missals they had been previously studying laid open on their knees,—consider, I repeat, the shock to the feelings of all these delicately minded persons, on being asked to conceive a Virgin waking from her sleep on a pallet bed, in a plain room, startled by sudden words and ghostly presence which she does not comprehend, and casting in her mind what manner of Salutation this should be.[1]

Rossetti's second figure, his angelic namesake (whose face was drawn principally from William and whose hair was taken from Woolner) is equally unorthodox. Stephens described the conventional delineation of the angel Gabriel:

Nearly all the more ancient pictures of Italian, German, and Low Country Schools, not less than cognate sculptured representations of this subject, give magnificent if not royal habiliments—sometimes even (as if gentle Gabriel were the warlike Michael) archangelic coronets, armour, and weapons to the harbinger of Heaven when appearing to Mary. He is usually winged, and his vast pinions, glittering in gold, azure, and vermillion, and *semée* with stars, reach from his superb tiara to the floor.

Rossetti's angel, devoid of supernatural features and dressed simply in white, holds out a lily—but, again in the words of Stephens, 'unlike the Gabriels of Angelico, Memmi, Durer, Del Sarto, Raphael, Giovanni Santi, Tintoretto, and Rembrandt—makes no obeisance to Mary, not yet crowned Queen of Heaven'.

[1] 'The Three Colours of Pre-Raphaelitism', *Nineteenth Century*, November 1878, pp. 926, 928–9.

Although the picture was small—28 by 17½ inches—and relatively simple, nothing he had yet attempted had been nearly as troublesome to Rossetti as *Ecce Ancilla Domini.* The necessity of painting alone in a studio generated and aggravated many of the difficulties; frequently he exclaimed angrily that he had abandoned his picture. But he always came back to it, with the help and encouragement of Brown, Stephens (who helped him with the ever-irksome perspective), and, most of all, his former studio companion, Holman Hunt.

Rossetti habitually visited Hunt's living quarters, and often came with his drawing folio seeking professional advice. Hunt himself was busy with what was then his largest and most elaborate endeavour—a painting with nine principal figures, more than two dozen minor persons, and an abundantly varied foreground and background, entitled *A Converted British Family Sheltering a Christian Missionary from the Persecution of the Druids.* Reflecting his interest in the conflict between the Druids and Christians of ancient Britain, Hunt's picture would disclose a hut containing nine Christians—a family of eight converts and a missionary—hiding from their enemies, shown in the background with a group of victims.[1]

Now more than ever it seemed clear that the Pre-Raphaelite objectives in art would be carried forward only by the three successful exhibitors of 1849. Their only colleague who might join them in 1850 was Collinson, who was painting a picture and, according to the 8 October 1849 entry of the *P.R.B. Journal,* was 'finishing up the trees outside to a pitch of the extreme minuteness'. Woolner was turning out commissioned works (including a portrait medallion of Tennyson) which were good but irrelevant to Pre-Raphaelitism; and although Stephens made several designs for a picture, he and William were soon to decide that they could best convey their artistic ideas by means of the written word.

These two non-exhibiting Brothers soon had an opportunity to put their opinions in writing: in the autumn of 1849 literature became as important a mode of Pre-Raphaelite expression as painting. Once again the way was led by Gabriel Rossetti. On 18 September 1849, he wrote to William, who was holidaying with Collinson in the Isle of Wight:

[1] In a letter of 31 March 1855 to his Oxford friend and patron Thomas Combe, Hunt said of his picture of the Druids, 'I would as soon rely on that to express my idea of Pre-Raphaelitism as any picture I ever painted.'

I have wasted several days at the Museum, where I have been reading up all manner of old romaunts, to pitch upon stunning words for poetry. I have found several and also derived much enjoyment from the things themselves, some of which are tremendously fine.

Rossetti wanted to write poems: his first love had always been poetry. Painting was laborious and tedious, so he did not derive much pleasure from the act itself; but he enjoyed writing verse, which came easily to him, and he knew he was a better poet than painter. Also, he was publicly a recognized visual artist but a mute and inglorious poet. Thus, naturally, after his success with his painting, he wanted to display his other (and greater) talent. But there was no literary equivalent of the Free Exhibition. So Rossetti suggested that the Pre-Raphaelites produce their own journal.

He put forward this proposal in July, and it received the speedy approval of four of his fellows—Hunt, Woolner, Stephens and William—along with one important outsider. This was Coventry Patmore, who through Woolner had become acquainted with the other Pre-Raphaelites—a twenty-six-year-old poet who was then still unknown but whose book of verse, published five years earlier, had been warmly applauded by Rossetti (who later placed Patmore's name on the List of Immortals).

Gabriel's powers of persuasion had little difficulty in infecting most of the Brothers with his enthusiasm for the new venture. He won over Hunt by appealing to his desire to propagate Pre-Raphaelitism. He excited Woolner, who was modestly proud of his poetry (which had received hearty approbation from Patmore), by offering him a chance denied him as a sculptor—to become a 'Pre-Raphaelite' artist. He enlisted William and Stephens by showing them a way to become art critics and productive members of the Brotherhood. Even Collinson was sufficiently stirred to contemplate writing a religious poem; and Millais, who could not then spare time from his painting, promised a contribution if the magazine's life extended past the opening of the Exhibition.

Since the undertaking was too large to be confined to the seven Pre-Raphaelites, they were aided in various ways by about a dozen other like-minded persons: Patmore, of course; Christina Rossetti, Brown, William Bell Scott; two young sculptors named John Hancock and John Lucas; a pair of youthful painters, Walter Deverell and Cave Thomas; and the Tupper brothers—John, a would-be writer of prose and verse, and George, who was a partner in the printing firm that agreed to produce the journal.

Before Rossetti's departure for France, he and the others had decided that they would put out a monthly magazine of about forty pages which would sell for one shilling; that each issue would contain two etchings and several literary works; that the editor would be William Rossetti; and that each Brother would subscribe one guinea, thereby becoming a joint proprietor of the journal. (Hancock and Deverell also contributed a guinea each and became co-proprietors with the seven Brothers.) They had even settled the contents of the first number, and by 25 September had agreed on terms with the publishers, who were to be ready to bring out the first issue in December. They apparently agreed on everything except the title. Their first selection was *Monthly Thoughts in Literature, Poetry and Art*; later, at Gabriel's suggestion, this cumbersome combination of words was replaced by another name, not much more memorable, *Thoughts Towards Nature*.

Soon after Hunt and Rossetti had returned from the Continent the proprietors decided that the first number would come before the public in January. They also agreed that because of their precarious finances, they would not advertise the journal; that they would not be concerned with religion or politics; and that they would not sign their contributions—because, William wrote, they 'entertained a general feeling that to appear publicly as writers, and especially as writers opposing the ordinary current of opinions of fine art, would damage their professional position, which already involved uphill work more than enough'.

The magazine's name continued to pose a problem, for they were not satisfied with the lacklustre *Thoughts Towards Nature*. But the issue was not resolved until two or three days before the cover was to be printed, when on the night of 19 December the Pre-Raphaelites and a few others gathered in Gabriel's studio to consider a list of about sixty-five possible titles which had been drawn up by Cave Thomas. Among those discussed and discarded were *The Acorn*, *The Advent*, *The Alert*, *The Chariot*, *The Die*, *The Goad*, *The Harbinger*, *The Illuminator*, *The Precursor*, *The Seed*, *The Sower*, *The Spur*, and *The Truth-Seeker*. Ultimately all were eliminated but *The Germ* and *The Scroll*, and when *The Scroll* was defeated by a vote of six to four, the journal of the Pre-Raphaelite Brotherhood was named *The Germ*, sub-titled *Thoughts Towards Nature in Poetry, Literature and Art.* (The ten participants have not been identified, nor is it known how anyone voted.) The word *germ*, of course, did not have the modern connotation of a microbe; it was used in its original, hopeful sense of an embryo, a seed, the beginning of something.

On the day after the title had been chosen Gabriel stayed up all night to write most of his prose tale 'Hand and Soul', which on the morning of 21 December became the last piece of writing for the first issue to be delivered to the printing shop of G. F. Tupper and Sons. On 31 December, the publishers, Aylott and Jones, known principally for books on evangelical religion, received fifty copies of *The Germ*, most of which were sent to the principal periodicals and to twenty-one leading clubs; and by the middle of January the full printing of seven hundred copies was complete.

England's newest literary magazine measured eight by five inches, and its fifty pages included nine poems, one prose tale, one essay, one book review, and one double etching. Of all the contributors only the creator of the etching was identified; at the top of the white cover just below 'No. 1 (Price One Shilling) JANUARY 1850' appeared the words 'With an Etching by W. Holman Hunt'. The cover also bore a sonnet by William Rossetti which, he said, was meant to 'express the spirit in which the publication was undertaken':

When whoso merely hath a little thought
  Will plainly think the thought which is in him,—
  Not imagining another's bright or dim,
Not mangling with new words what others taught;
When whoso speaks, from having either sought
  Or only found,—will speak, not just to skim
  A shallow surface with words made and trim,
But in that very speech the matter brought:
Be not too keen to cry—'So this is all!—
  A thing I might myself have thought as well,
But would not say it, for it was not worth!'
  Ask: 'Is this truth?' For is it still to tell
That, be the theme a point or the whole earth,
Truth is a circle, perfect, great or small?

The sonnet makes clear why William Rossetti's literary reputation does not rest on his verse. It is remarkable that a man who consistently wrote straightforward, lucid prose could also compose this incomprehensible poem, which Oswald Doughty accurately calls 'one of the worst sonnets in the English language'.[1]

Hunt's double-etching immediately followed the table of contents and illustrated two passages from the opening pair of poems, 'My Beautiful Lady' and 'Of My Lady in Death', which marked the Pre-Raphaelite debut of Thomas Woolner. Few modern readers would agree with Patmore's praise of these poems,[2] the first of which begins:

> I love my lady; she is very fair;
> Her brow is white, and bound by simple hair;
> Her spirit sits aloof, and high
> Altho' it looks thro' her soft eye
> Sweetly and tenderly.
>
> As a young forest, when the wind drive thro'
> My life is stirred when she breaks on my view.
> Altho' her beauty has such power,
> Her soul is like the simple flower
> Trembling beneath a shower.

Hunt's upper, and principal, etching, depicting the arboreal and floral scene where the 'lady' kneels and picks a weed while her lover holds her other hand and shoulder, cannot be compared with his paintings, but still is a satisfactory piece of work—and easily the best etching to appear in *The Germ*. (In the lower picture the lover is prostrate on a grave in front of a procession of mourners.)

Woolner's second poem was followed by Brown's tolerable sonnet 'The Love of Beauty', followed in turn by an eight-page essay by John Tupper entitled 'The Subject in Art (No. 1)', which supposedly sets forth some of the principles favoured by the Pre-Raphaelites. Two main ideas are laid down by Tupper. In the first place, he says that a work of art should affect us just as its subject might affect us if we encountered it in nature. Thus anything in nature that stimulates us is a proper subject for a work of art. Secondly, Tupper maintains that a contemporary subject need not be any less valuable than a

[1] Disturbed by the frequent charges of unintelligibility, William wrote a prose explanation of his sonnet: 'A writer ought to think out his subject honestly and personally, not imitatively, and ought to express it with directness and precision; if he does this, we should respect his performance as truthful, even though it may not be important. This indicated, for writers, much the same principle which the P.R.B. professed for painters—individual genuineness in the thought, reproductive genuineness in the presentment.'

[2] Gabriel wrote that 'the only defect he [Patmore] found [was] that they were a trifle too much in earnest in the passionate parts, and too sculpturesque generally. He means by this that each stanza stands too much alone, and has its own ideas too much to itself'. In 1863 a revised version of the poem was republished in the volume, *My Beautiful Lady*.

subject taken from the past. Whatever value the essay might have had, however, is diminished by its preposterous style: one of its sentences contains 378 words and eighty-one marks of punctuation.

Tupper's verbiage is followed by three poems which, taken together, are the *pièce de resistance* of the inaugural issue of *The Germ*: Patmore's fine twelve-line lyric 'The Seasons'; one of Christina Rossetti's best known and best loved poems, 'Dream Land'; and Dante Gabriel Rossetti's 'My Sister's Sleep'.

Immediately succeeding 'My Sister's Sleep' is Gabriel's prose tale 'Hand and Soul', which purports to be the biography of a thirteenth-century Italian artist named Chiaro dell' Erma. Because of certain self-revelations 'Hand and Soul' has fascinated some commentators, such as Rossetti's friend, the minor poet William Sharp, who in his 1882 book on Gabriel wrote a fifteen-page summary of the eleven-page story. We need not linger over the narrative, because its 'directly personal utterances' (so Sharp justified his lengthy discussion) add nothing to our picture of its creator—and because as an imaginative work of art it is one of Rossetti's worst efforts. Its tedium suggests that Gabriel's talent for writing prose fiction was on a par with William's for composing poetry.

'Hand and Soul' was followed by four selections which completed the first issue of the journal: William's commendable twelve-page review of Arthur Hugh Clough's narrative poem *The Bothie of Toper-no-fuosich*; some worthless poems by William and by John Tupper; and Christina's tender lyric 'An End'.

The penultimate page contained a declaration of editorial policy, which stated that the 'endeavour held in view throughout the writings on Art will be to encourage an entire adherence to the simplicity of nature', and that the 'chief object of the etched designs will be to illustrate this aim practically, as far as the method of execution will permit'. The first number ended with a full-page advertisement by the Provident Life Insurance Company.

It is unlikely that Provident Life would have issued a long term policy on the magazine. Of the seven hundred printed copies, fewer than two hundred were sold, and the proprietors were left with a deficit of twenty pounds. The journalistic response to this new journal, moreover, was less than enthusiastic. The only two major periodicals that took note of *The Germ* each allotted it one derogatory paragraph. *The Spectator* [12 January 1850, p. 43] observed that the magazine was dominated by 'poetry of the school of Tennyson, pushed to an exaggeration of the master's exaggerations'. *The Literary Gazette* [19 January 1850, p. 47] commented that *The Germ* 'belongs to a school which, in aiming at nature and simplicity, often shows how hard the strain is to hit, or it may be to miss, the mark, and which thinks nothing of incongruities or anomalies, so that it can occasionally pump out a new sort of phraseology or the semblance of a new idea. Its standard is hoisted in the clouds, and out of ken of reason and the rational world. Indeed where there is the greatest obscurity, there seems to be the claim for the most admirable poetry.' (One brief favourable notice appeared in January, in *The Builder* [19 January, p. 34], which said that the new publication was 'edited by some young artists who, if their powers be equal to their enthusiasm and desire, will one day be in the first rank'. In February *The Critic* devoted a complimentary page to this first number of *The Germ*, especially singling out for praise 'My Sister's Sleep', commenting, after quoting the entire poem, 'What *a picture* it is. A *poet's tongue* has told what an *artist's eye* has seen'.)

The Germ would have died a speedy death had not Rossetti persuaded his colleagues to bring out a second number, which appeared in February.

The new issue began with William's same cover sonnet and ended with the same insurance advertisement. The intervening pages contained an etching by Collinson, a book review by William, essays by Stephens and Brown, and poems by Woolner, Scott, Collinson, Patmore, Calder Campbell, Deverell, and the three Rossettis. The strict policy of anonymity was abandoned and seven of the authors, including the Rossetti brothers, signed their contributions. Christina would not consent to the use of her name, and so her three fine lyrics —'A Pause of Thought' (later published as Part I of 'Three Stages'), 'Song: Oh roses for the flush of youth', and 'A Testimony'—bore a pseudonym devised by Gabriel, 'Ellen Alleyn'. Gabriel's own contribution included the crowning achievement of *The Germ*: the first published version of 'The Blessed Damozel'.

The February sales report was even more disheartening than its predecessor. The printing had been reduced to five hundred copies, but no more than forty were sold. The magazine seemed unquestionably dead; even Gabriel saw the futility of trying to keep it alive. After the publisher had given him the bad news, William wrote in the

P.R.B. Journal, 'This is the last knockdown blow. We certainly cannot attempt a third Number.' Then suddenly the magazine received a reprieve: the printers offered to bring out another number or two at their own risk. This action might be seen as a rare instance of mercantile magnanimity; but remember that John Tupper was one of the printer's sons. The author of the long-winded article 'The Subject in Art (Part I)' had some unused material which he surely knew could have been published nowhere else, and so John Tupper, anxious to prolong his literary career, probably persuaded his father and brothers to extend the journal's life.

The end of March brought forth the third number of the periodical, renamed (at the suggestion of John Tupper's brother Alexander) *Art and Poetry*, subtitled *Being Thoughts towards Nature*. It contained Brown's mediocre etching of a scene from *King Lear*, done six years earlier in Paris; a body of prose and poetry that was trivial or execrable; and four praiseworthy pieces—Patmore's 'Essay on Macbeth', Christina's reflective lyric 'Sweet Death', and two poems Gabriel Rossetti had written during his Continental journey, 'The Carillon, Antwerp and Bruges', and 'From the Cliffs, Noon' (which later was revised and renamed 'The Sea-limits').

The public response to the third issue was no more encouraging, but the Tuppers bore the cost of yet another number, which appeared on the last day of April, one week before the opening of the Royal Academy Exhibition. Since Christina and Patmore had contributed nothing this time, its only creditable selections were seven of Gabriel's Continental poems: 'Pax Vobis' (later republished as 'World's Worth') and six 'Sonnets for Pictures', each of which deals with a painting Rossetti had seen on his journey—*A Virgin and Child*, by Hans Memling, in the Academy in Bruges; *The Marriage of St Katherine*, also by Memling, in the Hospital of St John in Bruges; *A Dance of Nymphs*, by Andrea Mantegna, in the Louvre; *A Venetian Pastoral*, by Giorgione, in the Louvre; and, the subject of two sonnets, *Angelica Rescued from the Sea*, by Ingres, in the Luxembourg.

Several of those who were closely associated with the magazine personally advertised its fourth issue by carrying posters in front of the Academy during the first week of The Exhibition; but, as William wrote, 'All efforts proved useless. People would not buy *The Germ*, and would scarcely consent to know of its existence.' And so 'the magazine breathed its last, and its obsequies were conducted in the strictest privacy'. The proprietors of *The Germ* were left with a debt of more than £30, most of which was probably never liquidated. As late as 9 September 1852, John Tupper wrote to Stephens that his father, the P.R.B.'s principal creditor, was still impatiently waiting to be paid the balance due him. In his letter Tupper said, '. . . let it be determined who *will* and who *will not pay at once* . . . I know and greatly feel that it will fall very heavy upon Wm. Rossetti who has paid so *much more* than any one else, and *so much more promptly*.'

Can we assign any significance to the episode of *The Germ*? Its circulation hardly made it a conversation piece—the total number of copies sold was under four hundred. Its propagation of Pre-Raphaelite doctrines proved to be of little consequence; and its art and literature gave it no great distinction, since only Hunt created an etching surpassing bare tolerability and only Patmore and the two most gifted Rossettis produced writings above mediocrity. But in the end *The Germ* did serve one worthwhile purpose: it unified and strengthened the Pre-Raphaelite Brotherhood by giving the minor members a chance to become creatively active participants. During the initial Pre-Raphaelite year, as we have seen, only Rossetti, Hunt and Millais were productive within the framework of the Brotherhood. It is doubtful if the society could have endured much longer had this state of affairs not been changed by *The Germ*. Woolner, who never carved a Pre-Raphaelite statue, wrote Pre-Raphaelite verse; Collinson wrote and etched; and, most important, William Rossetti and Stephens became practising critics. For these last two Brothers, *The Germ* marked a turning point in their lives. As an immediate result of the magazine, in February 1850, William was hired (without pay) by one of *The Germ*'s very few friendly reviewers, *The Critic*, to comment on literary and artistic topics, and not long after Stephens too was employed as a practising critic. For the remainder of the century both wrote prolifically, and became invaluable fountainheads for devotees of the Rossettis and the Brotherhood.

The Germ also gains importance through providing the formal public inauguration of the poetic career of Dante Gabriel Rossetti. (Although two of her short poems had appeared in *The Athenaeum*, the Pre-Raphaelite journal performed a similar service for Christina.) Gabriel now was a published poet. That *The Germ* had been his own creation and reached few readers moderated only slightly, if at all, his excitement at seeing his poems in print, and his pleasure greatly increased when his works, especially 'The Blessed Damozel', were praised by a handful of discriminating readers. For Rossetti, the insignificant Pre-Raphaelite journal served as a counterpart of the insignificant Free Exhibition, by providing him with public exposure and approbation, and by strengthening his self-confidence. Again, as after he had received the letter from Leigh Hunt, his belief in his poetic gifts was sustained.

But during these months of *The Germ* Gabriel had not stopped being a painter. Now and then his thoughts turned to 'Hist, said Kate the Queen' and to imagined representations of Francesca da Rimini and of Giotto painting a portrait of Dante; but eventually he dropped the idea of exhibiting two pictures and concentrated on *Ecce Ancilla Domini*. Naturally, the time he gave to his painting was less than that expended on theirs by his two principal colleagues, who were not diverted by *The Germ*. Hunt proceeded in his usual methodical way with his large picture, and Millais, after finishing *Ferdinand Lured by Ariel* in December, immediately began the design for his third, and major, work of the current artistic year. This was to be an untitled work depicting an imaginary incident from the life of Jesus, to which would be attached a verse from the Book of Zechariah (xiii, 6): 'And one shall say unto him, What are these wounds in thine hands? Then he shall answer, Those with which I was wounded in the house of my friends.' The picture would show Jesus as a child standing in Joseph's carpenter shop, holding up a hand slightly cut by a nail. Kneeling comfortingly beside him would be his mother, while grouped solicitously around a work bench, from left to right, would be a carpenter's helper, St Anne, Joseph, and young John the Baptist. In the background, crowding behind an open door, would be a flock of sheep. Because, as he told Hunt, he was 'determined to choose a real carpenter, whose frame and muscles had been formed by the very exercise that had been the toil of the Virgin's husband', Millais took a cot and his painting equipment to a carpenter's shop in Oxford Street, where he stayed until he had faithfully delineated the workman and everything in his shop, including the shavings on the floor. Since live animals were not readily available in London, he painted his flock from two unsheared heads of sheep bought from a neighbouring butcher.

One evening while his picture was unfinished, Millais said to Hunt, 'I declare to you, when painting the body of little St John, as I finished it and turned my eyes from the boy who stood for me, and back to the painting, so thoroughly in relief did it appear that on looking again to the model I could not at the moment tell which was which.' Indeed, none of the paintings he had then done gratified him as much as this one. Hunt, too, was pleased with the progress of his own work, and both eagerly looked forward to the opening of The Exhibition, feeling confident that their pictures would attract attention, and hoping that the year might be memorable for the Pre-Raphaelite Brotherhood. For Rossetti, 1850 already had been noteworthy: he had become a published poet, and was completing the first painting he had executed while working alone.

But none of the Pre-Raphaelite brothers had any idea just how unforgettable the year 1850 was to be.

8

The Battle of 1850

1850 was to be a momentous year for Rossetti in a way other than artistic—it was the year he met Elizabeth Siddal. She was introduced to him by another artist, Walker Deverell, a close friend of his. The son of the Secretary of the Government School of Design, Deverell was a promising painter who twice, in 1847 and 1848, had exhibited a painting in the Royal Academy Exhibition, and a cheerful, convivial person; he was well liked by the Brothers, had been a schoolmate of theirs at the Academy, and was one of the proprietors of *The Germ*, to which he had contributed an etching and two poems. Only Hunt's insistence on limiting the membership to seven had prevented Deverell from becoming the eighth P.R.B.

In March 1850, while accompanying his mother to one of the millinery shops in Cranbourne Street, Deverell was struck by the beauty of one of the shop assistants. But he looked at the young lady with the eyes of an artist, not a potential lover; he was painting a scene from *Twelfth Night*, and there before him was what he urgently needed, an ideal model for Viola. His mother inquired on his behalf about the possibility of the girl's sitting for him; the shop owner agreed to reduce her employee's working hours (perhaps because Mrs Deverell was a steady patron); and the girl herself, Elizabeth Siddal, agreed to pose for the handsome young artist.

Miss Siddal's first sitting took place on the next day, after which Deverell called on Hunt, where he also found Rossetti. In recollecting that evening, Hunt wrote

Deverell had not been seated many minutes, talking in a somewhat absent manner, when he bounded up, marching, or rather dancing to and fro about

Ashmolean Museum, Oxford.

Early Britons sheltering a Missionary from the Druids (*A Converted British Family*) by Holman Hunt.

Reproduced by courtesy of the Trustees of the Tate Gallery, London.

Christ in the House of His Parents (*The Carpenter Shop*) by Millais.

Reproduced by permission of Lord Sherfield.

Mariana by Millais.

By courtesy of the Guildhall Art Gallery, London.

The Woodman's Daughter by Millais.

By permission of the Museum and Art Gallery, Birmingham.

Valentine Rescuing Sylvia from Proteus by Holman Hunt.

Ashmolean Museum, Oxfor

Convent Thoughts by Charles Collins.

By permission of the Bradford Art Gallery and Museums Committee.

Wickliffe Reading his Translation of the Bible by Ford Madox Brown.

Reproduced by courtesy of the Trustees of the Tate Gallery, London.

The Death of Ophelia by Millais.

the room, and, stopping emphatically, he whispered, 'You fellows can't tell what a stupendously beautiful creature I have found. By Jove! she's like a queen, magnificently tall, with a lovely figure, a stately neck, and a face of most delicate and finished modelling; the flow of surface from the temples over the cheek is exactly like the carving of a Pheidean goddess. Wait a minute! I haven't done; she has grey eyes, and her hair is like dazzling copper, and shimmers with lustre as she waves it down. And now, where do you think I lighted on this paragon of beauty? Why, in a milliner's back workroom. . .'

Since she was to return to his studio the next afternoon, Deverell invited his friends to come and meet this 'miraculous creature'. With the Academy's sending-in day a month away, Hunt could spare no time from his work; but Rossetti felt no such compunction, and he was in Deverell's studio long before Elizabeth arrived.

When she entered the room, Gabriel saw that Deverell had not exaggerated. Apparently about nineteen years old (though actually younger), she was tall and slim, with a well-formed, finely chiselled head, which Gabriel himself said (quoting Spenser) rested on a 'neck like a tower'. To these attributes were added her fresh complexion, her full, sensuous lips, and, especially for Rossetti, her red-gold hair. (If Deverell had mentioned only her hair, Gabriel would have been eager to meet her, for throughout his life no physical feature attracted him more than a fine head of hair.)

Rossetti was captivated—not only by Elizabeth's appearance, but by a quality she possessed which a friend called 'an unworldly simplicity and spirituality'. He was also enchanted by her movements and speech. Deverell had said that his model was 'really a wonder; for while her friends of course are quite humble, she behaves like a real lady, by clear common sense, and without any affectation, knowing perfectly, too, how to keep people at a respectable distance'. During the sitting, as Rossetti watched, she remained poised and graceful, carrying herself with an almost regal dignity and an aloofness that sometimes approached disdain. She had a clear, low-pitched, slightly sibilant voice, which she used sparingly; when she did speak, it was in a dryly humorous, lighthearted manner, as if she were being careful not to disclose her thoughts. William Rossetti wrote:

I hardly think I ever heard her say a single thing indicative of her own character, or of her serious underlying thought. All her talk was of a 'chaffy' kind—its tone sarcastic, its substance lightsome. It was like the speech of a person who wanted to turn off the conversation, and leave matters substantially where they stood before. Now and again she said some pointed thing, which might cast a dry light, but ushered one no further. She was not ill-natured in talk, still less was she scandal-mongering, or chargeable with volatility or levity personal to herself; but she seemed to say—'My mind and my feelings are my own, and no outsider is expected to pry into them.'

Miss Siddal's conduct and diction were surprising in the light of her family and environment. Her father was a poorly educated, unprosperous cutler from Sheffield; the family (the parents, Elizabeth, a younger sister, and two brothers, one of whom was feeble-minded) lived across the river in the near-slum of Southwark, so it is something of a mystery how Elizabeth overcame the giveaway manners and speech of Southwark and managed almost to pass for a resident of the West End.[1] But then Elizabeth Siddal was in many ways a woman of mystery. Not even her closest friends knew her age—although we now know that when she met Rossetti she was not yet seventeen. Those who knew her intimately even disagreed on her appearance—for instance, the colour of her eyes, was variously described as greenish-blue, grey-green, and golden brown.

The mystery was undoubtedly part of her fascination for Gabriel—to which he had completely succumbed by the time he left his friend's studio. As the second sentence of his self-revelatory story 'Hand and Soul' says: 'The extreme longing after a visible embodiment of his thoughts strengthened as his years increased, more even than his sinews or the blood of his life . . .' The longing was Rossetti's, not Chiaro dell' Erma's—and now it was ended. In his diary, Brown wrote, 'Rossetti once told me that, when he first saw her, he felt his destiny was defined.' Gabriel was in love—though probably not at first sight. William wrote that Gabriel 'saw her, admired her enormously, and was soon in love with her—*how* soon I can't exactly say'. One another occasion, William said, 'In 1850 he fell seriously in love.' Gabriel's conduct suggests that perhaps as early as March, but certainly before the end of the summer, he had been caught up in what would be his most enduring passion. As for Elizabeth, she was quickly charmed by this courteous, eloquent, Latinesque young

[1] The Siddal family home was in Kent Place, which in 1850 was occupied by fifteen other residents, all but one of whom maintained a business on his premises: two grocers, two fruiterers, two butchers, two beer retailers, one shoemaker, one cheesemonger, one silversmith, one ham and beef dealer, one leather dresser, one hardwareman, and a certain Miss Akin.

man, and before long, William said, 'she was sincerely in love with him'.

At their first meeting, she consented to sit for Gabriel, but he had no immediate need of a model. Instead, he watched her pose for Deverell and Hunt; and in less than two months her likeness was exhibited twice and her hair three times. Her debut in paint occurred on 8 April, when Deverell's scene from *Twelfth Night* went on display. On the last day of April, the final number of *The Germ* contained an etching by Deverell showing another scene from *Twelfth Night*, with Elizabeth as Viola. Finally, on 7 May, Hunt's picture was placed on exhibition, and because he wanted the young woman ministering to the priest to be 'a fair Celt with red hair', he had copied the hair from Elizabeth.

Since posing for artists was more enjoyable than working for a milliner, Elizabeth Siddal became a part-time employee in Cranbourne Street and the favourite model of the Pre-Raphaelites, to whom she was known as 'Lizzy'. She remained friendly with them all, but it was tacitly understood that for only one of them was she anything more than a model. When he met Lizzy, Rossetti was finishing *Ecce Ancilla Domini*. Again he had changed his mind about submitting his picture to the Academy, and was once more getting ready for the opening of the Free Exhibition—which was holding its show in the Portland Gallery in Regent Street, and had gained a higher-sounding name, The National Institution of Fine Arts. The exhibition opened on 8 April, and late in March Rossetti and Deverell took their pictures to the Portland Gallery, whose four large rooms *The Literary Gazette* called 'exceedingly good both for light and form,' where *Ecce Ancilla Domini* was listed as No. 225 and priced at fifty pounds. It was signed 'D G R March 1850'—without the fraternal initials.

Ecce Ancilla Domini has some of the faults of *The Girlhood of Mary Virgin*—including its weak perspective and rigid forms—but it also has the strong points of the 1849 painting; and taken as a whole it shows Rossetti's progress. The handling of colours anticipates Rossetti's later pictures: the white is skilfully used in the drapery, couch and floor, and is adroitly relieved by the crimson embroidery frame, the bright blue curtain, and the blue sky behind the open window. As for the Virgin, nothing Gabriel had yet done in the visual arts equals his delineation of this delicate, tremulous, awe-stricken girl—of whom

Stephens said, 'Fra Angelico never produced a maiden more passionless than this.'[1]

While acknowledging its 'naïve charm', Holman Hunt insisted that *Ecce Ancilla Domini* is not 'fundamentally Pre-Raphaelite in character', because it 'still reflected Brown's early Christian phase'. But this was a minority opinion (perhaps due to Hunt's continuing coolness towards Brown). Rossetti's second painting has usually been cited as one of the most striking embodiments of Pre-Raphaelitism. Lucien Pissarro, for example, said that it is 'rightly considered most typical of Rossetti's "Pre-Raphaelite" period', and Stephens called it 'the one perfect outcome of the original motive of the Pre-Raphaelite Brotherhood by its representative and typical member'. This picture is Rossetti's only truly Pre-Raphaelite painting because for once he worked in complete fidelity to nature (although he was forced to use a cloth model of a lily, a real lily not being available in winter), and because he made his greatest effort to portray an event exactly as it might have occurred. *Ecca Ancilla Domini* eventually became the "world's choice" among paintings treating of that subject'[2] but, as Robert De La Sizeranne wrote, 'if it is borne in mind that it was painted in 1850, it will be evident that it was a revolution in the way of simplicity, humility, and up to a certain point, realism in religious painting.

Hunt did agree that the painting 'attracted considerable admiration from thoughtful artists'. Since it was an improved specimen of the same genre as his well received painting of 1849, Rossetti expected that reviewers, thoughtful or otherwise, also would admire *Ecce Ancilla Domini*. And it did receive a few favourable (though qualified) notices. *The Observer* commended its 'singularly artistic' execution 'not withstanding its curious style'; and *The Builder* called attention to Rossetti's genius, 'misdirected though it be', and complimented his picture even though it was 'a performance full of affectation'. He also received some faint praise from *The Times*—surprisingly, since this mightiest of England's newspapers had ignored the 1849 Free Ex-

[1] Stephens and William did not entirely agree on how closely the Virgin's head resembled Christina's. According to Stephens, 'the face of Mary was a just and true likeness of Christina, and was painted with hardly any alteration of her features or expression'. William, while acknowledging that the 'head resembles Christina sufficiently to be accounted a likeness', contended 'it is less like her than the head in *The Girlhood of Mary Virgin*'.

[2] Ernest Radford, *Dante Gabriel Rossetti*, p. 15.

hibition and seldom noticed unestablished artists. *The Times'* critic wrote:

Mr Rosetti, a young artist evidently of talent and originality, carries his predilection for the mediaeval so far that his *Salutation of the Virgin* might be a leaf torn out of a missal. The figures are tall and lank, the expression of the girlish virgin is intense to the highest degree, but there is nothing human in this intensity. . . . Mr Rosetti's picture is the work of a poet, and the frozen character of the style is counterbalanced by the visible fervour of the artist.

This brief notice, which misspelled his name and misnamed his picture, provided Rossetti with his only journalistic success of 1850. He was disappointed that some of the best known periodicals had ignored his work. But Frank Stone of *The Athenaeum*, whose praise of *The Girlhood of Mary Virgin* had so delighted Rossetti in 1849, did not neglect him. In the 20 April issue of *The Athenaeum*, Stone anonymously commented:

What shall we say of a work . . . which we notice less for its merits than as an example of the perversion of talent which has recently been making so much way in our school of art, and wasting the energies of some of our most promising aspirants? We allude to the *Ecce Ancilla Domini* of Mr D. G. Rossetti. Here a certain amount of talent is distorted from its legitimate course by a prominent crotchet. Ignoring all that has made the art great in the works of the greatest masters, the school to which Mr Rossetti belongs would begin the work anew, and accompany the faltering steps of its earliest explorers. This is archaeology turned from its legitimate uses, and made into a mere pedant. Setting at nought all the advanced principles of light and shade, colour, and composition, these men, professing to look only to Nature in its truth and simplicity, are the slavish imitators of artistic inefficiency. Granted that in these early masters there is occasionally to be seen all that is claimed for them of divine expression and sentiment, accompanied by an earnestness and devotion of purpose which preserved their productions from oblivion—are such qualities inconsistent with all subsequent progress in historical excellence, or do these crotchet-mongers propose that the art should begin and end there? The world will not be led to that deduction by such puerilities as the one before us; which, with the affectation of having done such a great thing, is weakness itself. An untintelligent imitation of the mere technicalities of old art—golden glories, fanciful scribblings on the frames, and other infantile absurdities—constitutes all its claim. A certain expression in the eyes of the ill-drawn face of the Virgin affords a gleam of something high in intention, but it is still not the true inspiration. The face of the Angel is insipidity itself. One arm of the Virgin is well drawn, and there is careful though timid workmanship in the inferior and accessorial part of the work, but this is, in many places, where it would have been better left out. Yet with this we have exhausted all the praise due, in our opinion, to a work evidently thrust by the artist into the eye of the spectator more with the presumption of a teacher than in the modesty of a hopeful and true aspiration after excellence.

These remarks threw Rossetti into a state of shock. Characteristically, he first vowed never again to exhibit a picture in public. Next he sent *The Athenaeum* a scathing letter which the editor refused to publish because of its virulence. (Unfortunately, no copy was preserved.) And that fury was apparently the only immediate effect of *The Athenaeum* review. Neither he nor Hunt nor Millais stopped to ask themselves why this reviewer, who a year earlier had praised to the skies a lesser picture in the same style as the object of his present denunciation, should have changed his mind. They saw no significance in the allusions to 'the school to which Mr Rossetti belongs', and to 'these men' who profess 'to look only to Nature in its truth and simplicity', and are 'slavish imitators' of 'early masters'. It simply did not occur to them that these remarks indicated that *The Athenaeum*'s art critic was privy to the secret of the P.R.B.

The Pre-Raphaelites should again have been a little shaken on the following Saturday, when *The Spectator*, though ignoring Rossetti in its review of the National Institution's exhibition, referred to Walter Deverell as an 'absurd . . . nonsensical . . . practical joker, a self-burlesquer . . . aping the imperfections of art on its revival after the middle ages'. It might have seemed ominous that the brief notice in *The Spectator*, which mentioned only two other exhibitors, should have singled out for particular abuse the closest friend and associate of the Pre-Raphaelites. But if Hunt or Millais, or any others, reacted in any way at all to the *Athenaeum* and *Spectator* reviews, no documentary record of their response has survived.

It was clear—in fact, blatantly obvious—that the P.R.B.'s veil of secrecy had been penetrated. And one week later, the Saturday before the opening of the eighty-second Exhibition of the Royal Academy, all remaining doubts must have been discarded. The weekly *Illustrated London News* contained a regular column of chitchat, 'Town Talk and Table Talk', written by a Scotsman named Angus B. Reach. In the 4 May number, Reach reminisced on Wordsworth, who had died on 23 April; he noted signs of approaching spring, such as parties of picnickers and sail boats on the Thames; and he repeated rumours concerning the Government. Then he ended his column with the following paragraph:

Has any casual reader of art-criticisms ever been puzzled by the occurrence of three mysterious letters as denoting a new fashioned-school or style in painting lately come into vogue? The hieroglyphics in question are 'P.R.B.', and they are the initials of the words 'Pre-Raffaelite Brotherhood'. To this league belong the ingenious gentlemen who profess themselves practitioners of 'Early Christian Art', and who—setting aside the Mediaeval schools of Italy, the Raffaelles, Guidos, and Titians, and all such small-beer daubers—devote their energies to the reproduction of saints squeezed out perfectly flat—as though the poor gentlemen had been martyed by being passed under a Baker's Patent—their appearance being further improved by their limbs being stuck akimbo, so as to produce a most interesting series of angles and finely-developed elbows. A glance at some of the minor exhibitions now open will prove what really clever men have been bitten by this extraordinary art-whim, of utterly banishing and disclaiming perspective and everything like rotundity of form. It has been suggested that the globe-shape of the world must be very afflicting to the ingenious gentlemen in question. Sydney Smith said that the Quakers would, if they could, have clothed all creation in grey. The 'P.R.B.' would be bolder still, for they would beat it out flat, and make men and women like artfully-shaped and coloured pancakes.

Hunt recounted how the worried Brothers gathered together to discover who 'had played traitor' and 'insisted upon a searching investigation being made'. Then Rossetti admitted that his friend the Scottish sculptor Alexander Munro 'had persisted for long in beseeching him to tell the riddle, till, under pledge of secrecy, the mysterious monogram had been explained'. Munro, they concluded, must have carried the tidings to his fellow Scot Angus Reach. Thus nearly all biographers of Rossetti and commentators on the Pre-Raphaelite Brotherhood have charged Gabriel with being the betrayer of his Brothers. Unquestionably, Hunt's account is true, and Rossetti did speak imprudently to Munro, who may have given the information to Reach. But Hunt's story does not contain the whole truth. It implies that the Pre-Raphaelite secret would have remained inviolate, at least for the time being, if it had not been for that single paragraph in the 4 May issue of *The Illustrated London News*. Oddly, no one seems to have considered, in this context, *The Athenaeum*'s 20 April condemnation of Rossetti, which surely implies the knowledge of a society of rebellious young artists. More oddly, no one seems to have noticed the appearance on 4 May of similarly knowing articles in two other well-known periodicals: *The Spectator* and *The Literary Gazette*.

The *Gazette* printed two notices of the Free Exhibition: that of 27 April did not mention Deverell or Rossetti, but a week later its second notice contained the following:

No. 143, W. Deverell. This very clever scene belongs to a somewhat novel phase in our fine arts, which has been designated the *Pre-Raphael School*. . . .

No. 225. *Ecce Ancilla Domini*. D. G. Rossetti. If one class be Pre-Raphael, this is *Pre-Pre*, or ancient Byzantine. . . .

In 1850 the Academy held its first preview for the press, which took place on Friday, 3 May. The next day *The Spectator* published a brief report of The Exhibition. The writer cursorily viewed the galleries and only once stopped in his tracks, in the West Room:

In this room the two most singular pictures are, a design of the young Jesus, by Millais, and 'A Converted British Family sheltering a Christian missionary from the persecution of the Druids' by William Holman Hunt—leading types of the pre-Raphael school: both are full of ability, especially that by Millais; both monstrously perverse, Millais still being the greater culprit. If one can penetrate through the nonsense of the manner to what is really in the artist, he may be conjectured to possess more power than any man in the place: but a painter who can spontaneously go back, not to the perfect schools, but through and beyond them to the days of puerile crudity, seems likely to be conscious of some fatal constitutional disease in his genius; or he would hardly, in malice prepense, make a deliberate choice of impotency.

Therefore, all in all, and unless Alexander Munro had been exceedingly garrulous, it would seem that by the beginning of May 1850, the existence of the Pre-Raphaelite Brotherhood had become common knowledge in the London art world. Indeed it would have been surprising if the news had not come to light by then. During the period of *The Germ*, the Pre-Raphaelites had worked closely with non-members who certainly knew about the organization. William's *P.R.B. Journal* relates that when the members talked of renting a communal house, they decided to ask Deverell to join them; that later they discussed the question of whether or not to call their magazine *The P.R.B. Journal*; that after rejecting this proposal, they deliberated on whether or not to print their monogram on the cover; and that at a meeting on 10 December, which non-members attended, they 'debated the propriety of having an article explanatory of the principles in Art of the P.R.B.' All of this shows that the Brothers did not conceal from their friends the fact of their society; and as the privileged circle widened, inevitably more and more people would be in on their secret. So, although Rossetti was perhaps more indiscreet than any of his fellows, it is unfair to give him the entire blame for the disclosure. In fact, all the Pre-Raphaelite painters seem to have been apprehensive before the beginning of May, for none of their current pictures bore the initials of their society.[1]

When Hunt and Millais entered the Academy on touching-up morning, they were pleased to discover that of the five Pre-Raphaelite pictures only Collinson's,[2] suspended just below the ceiling, and Millais's *Ferdinand Lured by Ariel*, hanging near the floor, had been given unsatisfactory positions. Hunt's painting—the highly realistic picture of the Christian family and the Druids, in which the figures, the lighting, the draughtsmanship, and the over-all unity raised it above the artistic level of *Rienzi*—and Millais's scene in the carpenter shop were favourably placed in a room that contained pictures by such highly regarded artists as Turner, Landseer, Watts, Ward, and Armitage. But the morning was marred by an incident that may have seemed ominous. Hunt and Millais were standing in front of the latter's principal work when two students stopped and, after looking at the picture, turned towards Millais and laughed. Millais furiously advanced on them and almost shouted, 'Do you know what you are doing? Don't you see that if you were to live to the age of Methuselah both of you, and you were to improve every day of your life more than you will in the whole course of it, you would never be able to achieve any work fit to compare with that picture.' When one of the students pleaded that they had not said anything, Millais replied, 'No, but you did this, you laughed at my painting, and you did so defiantly in my face, so that you should not be surprised at my telling you that you were egregious fools.' This unusual touchiness on the part of the usually self-controlled Millais reveals the state of his nerves as he awaited the verdict of the experts.

The first important pronouncement appeared on 9 May in *The*

[1] Even the usually accurate William Fredeman follows his predecessors in his recently published *Pre-Raphaelitism* by stating that Angus Reach's column in *The Illustrated London News* was the first public notice of the Brotherhood. Mr Fredeman shows no knowledge of the 4 May notices in *The Literary Gazette* and *The Spectator*, and although he cites *The Athenaeum's* 20 April review of the Free Exhibition, he seems unaware of its significance.

[2] *Answering the Emigrant's Letter*, a rather good picture of a young boy reading the newspaper *Australian News* to the other six expressively individualized members of his family.

Times, where Millais's painting (which came to be known as *The Carpenter Shop*) was the object of more than passing curiosity:

His picture is plainly revolting. The attempt to associate the Holy Family with the meanest details of a carpenter's shop, with no conceivable omission of misery, of dirt, of even disease, all furnished with a surpassing power of imitation, this picture serves to show how far mere imitation may fall short by dryness and conceit all dignity and truth.

These remarks were neutralized two days later when *The Illustrated London News*, in its first notice of the Exhibition, included an engraving of *The Carpenter Shop* and allotted more space to this picture than to any of the other 1,455 works on display:

. . . a picture painted, it is said, on a wrong principle, but with a thousand merits, and many intentional defects. . . . What is called, somewhat slightingly, the *pre-Raphaelism* of this picture, is its leading excellence. We may look in vain throughout the whole of the Exhibition for another picture (Mr Dyce's alone excepted) in which we shall find a sincerity of look in the heads of the principal figures at all comparable to this. The intentional deformities, such as the frost-bitten toes of Joseph, the sore heel of the Virgin, etc., are not at all to our taste; but the picture has so many merits, that all its eccentricities may be very well excused, though they cannot be overlooked.

Thus, contrary to popular belief, the critical response to the Pre-Raphaelites in 1850 was not unanimously hostile. Other friendly critiques appeared in May; though they were outnumbered by adverse reviews, for a fortnight none of the latter had the prestige to distress Hunt and Millais. Then, on 25 May, the influential *Literary Gazette* finally commented on the most talented Brother:

No. 429, Portraits, J. E. Millais. No. 504, Ferdinand Lured by Ariel, with nothing alluring, by the same, and No. 518, a nameless atrocity, supposed to represent a verse of Zechariah. A miserable carpenter's shop, with two children embracing in front of the bench, and a naked distorted boy on the right side, are presented to us as high art: in which there is neither taste, drawing, expression, or genius. And yet this style pertains to an imitative School; the sooner which is sent back to the dryness and wretched matter-of-fact of old times will be the better. Such things are simply disagreeable, if not worse. . . .

This brief paragraph opened the floodgates of enmity. A week later Frank Stone, who had earlier lacerated Rossetti, now turned his attention to the entire Brotherhood—'a school of artists whose younger members unconsciously write its condemnation in the very title which they adopt'. Here is part of his long diatribe in *The Athenaeum*:

This school of English youths has, it may be granted, ambition, but not of that well-regulated order which, measuring the object to be attained by the resources possessed, qualifies itself for achievement. Their ambition is an unhealthy thirst which seeks notoriety by means of mere conceit. Abruptness, singularity, uncouthness are the counters by which they play for game. Their trick is to defy the principles of beauty and the recognized axioms of taste. . . . Let us conjure these young gentlemen to believe that Raphael may be received as no mean authority for soundness of view and excellence in practice. They stand convicted of insincerity by the very cleverness of some of their pictures. What a wilful misapplication of powers is that which affects to treat the human form in the primitive and artless manner of the Middle Ages, while minor accessories are elaborated to a refinement of imitation which belongs to the latest days of executive art! By the side of their affected simplicity and rudeness they write in the condemnation of the same, saying, 'You see by the skill with which we can produce a shaving that we could joint and round these limbs if we would. We show you that which some of us could, if we chose, do as well as they who use the enlarged means and appliances of art; we can also do and choose to do as ill as they who wanted our knowledge. We desire you to understand that it is not for want of knowing what nature is that we fly to affectation.' In point of religious sentiment Mr Rossetti stands the chief of this little band. Mr Hunt stands next in his picture of 'A Converted British Family' . . . Mr Millais, in his picture without a name . . . has been most successful in giving the least dignified features of his presentment, and in giving to the higher forms of characters and meanings, a circumstantial Art Language from which we recoil with loathing and disgust. There are many to whom his work will seem a pictorial blasphemy. Great imitative talents have here been perverted to the use of an eccentricity both lamentable and revolting. 'Ferdinand Lured by Ariel', . . . though better in the painting, is yet more senseless in the conception, a scene built on the contrivances of the stage manager, but with very bad success.

These statements alone would have put the Pre-Raphaelites' names on everyone's lips—but they were followed by many other assaults. On 15 June came the worst of all, from an unexpected source: the most famous and most popular man of letters in the English-speaking world, Charles Dickens. On 30 March 1850, Dickens had begun his own twopenny weekly family magazine, *Household Words*. In its eleventh issue, the leading article, 'Old Lamps for New Ones', is a rare piece of Dickensiana:

In the fifteenth century, a certain feeble lamp of art arose in the Italian town of Urbino. This poor light, Raphael Sanzio by name . . . was fed with a preposterous idea of beauty—with a ridiculous power of etherealizing, and exalting to the very Heaven of Heavens, what was most sublime and lovely in the expression of the human face divine on Earth—with the truly contemptible conceit of finding in poor humanity the fallen likeness of the angels of God, and raising it up again to their pure spiritual condition. This very fantastic whim effected a low revolution in art, in this wise, that Beauty came to be regarded as one of its indispensable elements. In this very poor delusion, artists have continued until this present nineteenth century, when it was reserved for some bold aspirants to 'put it down'.

The Pre-Raphaelite Brotherhood, Ladies and Gentlemen, is the dread Tribunal which is to set this matter right. Walk up, walk up; and here, conspicuous on the wall of the Royal Academy of Art in England, in the eighty-second year of their annual exhibition, you shall see what this new Holy Brotherhood, this terrible Police that is to disperse all Post-Raphael offenders, has been 'and done!'

You come—in this Royal Acadmy Exhibition . . . to the contemplation of a Holy Family. You will have the goodness to discharge from your minds all Post-Raphael ideas, all religious aspirations, all elevating thoughts; all tender, awful, sorrowful, ennobling, sacred, graceful, or beautiful associations; and to prepare yourselves, as befits such a subject—Pre-Raphaelly considered—for the lowest depths of what is mean, odious, repulsive, and revolting.

You behold the interior of a carpenter's shop. In the foreground of that carpenter's shop is a hideous, wry-necked, blubbering, red-haired boy in a nightgown, who appears to have received a poke playing in an adjacent gutter, and to be holding it up for the contemplation of a kneeling woman, so horrible in her ugliness that (supposing it were possible for any human creature to exist for a moment with that dislocated throat) she would stand out from the rest of her company as a monster in the vilest cabaret in France or the lowest gin-shop in England. Two almost naked carpenters, master and journeyman, worthy companions of this agreeable female, are working at their trade; a boy, with some small flavour of humanity in him, is entering with a vessel of water; and nobody is paying any attention to a snuffy old woman who seems to have mistaken that shop for the tobacconist's next door, and to be hopelessly waiting at the counter to be served with half an ounce of her favourite mixture. Wherever it is possible to express ugliness of feature, limb, or attitude, you have it expressed. Such men as the carpenters might be undressed in any hospital where dirty drunkards, in a high state of varicose veins, are received. Their very toes have walked out of Saint Giles's.

This, in the nineteenth century, and in the eighty-second year of the annual exhibition of the National Academy of Art, is the Pre-Raphael representation to us, Ladies and Gentlemen, of the most solemn passage which our minds can ever approach. This, in the nineteenth century, and in the eighty-second year of the annual exhibition of the National Academy of Art, is what Pre-Raphael Art can do to render reverence and homage to the faith in which we live and die!

Dickens's vehemence may seem startling if we remember that part of his fame was due to the stark and sordid realism of such books as *Oliver Twist*, *Nicholas Nickleby*, and the novel then being serialized, *David Copperfield*. He did, however, congratulate Millais for his admirably painted 'shavings which are strewn on the carpenter's floor'; but then he went on to remind the Academy that 'Art includes something more than the faithful portraiture of shavings, or the skilful colouring of drapery', and that 'mere handicraft' is rather less important than 'considerations of common reverence or decency'. And he concluded by prophesying that if the Royal Academy persisted in its hospitatlity to the Pre-Raphaelites, it 'might place Her Gracious Majesty in a very painful position, one of these fine Private View days'.

The last major blow in the unilateral battle was struck by one of the most celebrated British monthly periodicals, *Blackwood's Magazine*. In 'Pictures of the Season', its discussion of the current exhibitions, *Blackwood's* declared:

> *A propos* of aberrations, we have a word to say. . . . Affectation, however, is a more suitable word for the mountebank proceedings of a small number of artists, who stimulated by their own conceit, and by the applause of a few foolish persons, are endeavouring to set up a school of their own. We allude to the Pre-Raphaelites. . . . It appears that they have got into their wise heads certain notions that the ideal of expression is to be found in the works of the artists who flourished previously to Raphael. And they have accordingly set to work to imitate those early masters, in their errors, crudities, and imperfections—renouncing, in fact, the progress that since then has been made; rejecting the experience of centuries, reverting for models, not to art in its prime, but to art in its uncultivated infancy. And a nice business they make of it. Regardless of anatomy and drawing, they delight in ugliness and revel in diseased aspects. Mr Dante Rossetti, one of the high-priests of this retrograde school, exhibits at the Portland Gallery. Messrs Millais and Hunt favour the saloons of the Academy. Ricketty children, emaciation and deformity constitute their chief stock in trade. They apparently seek bad models, and then exaggerate their badness till it is out of all nature. . . . We can hardly imagine anything more ugly, graceless, and unpleasant than Mr Millais's picture. Such a collection of splay feet, puffed joints and misshapen limbs was assuredly never before made within so small a compass! . . . Another specimen from the same brush inspires rather laughter than disgust.

The recently published first volume of the *Wellesley Index to Victorian Periodicals*, edited by Walter E. Houghton, identifies the author of 'Pictures of the Season' as Frederick Hardman, who, like

Dickens, was a prolific writer of fiction and non-fiction, and, again like Dickens, was not notably qualified to discuss the visual arts of Hardman's 177 other essays listed in the *Wellesley Index*, only two are in any way concerned with painting. It seems reasonable to surmise that Dickens and Hardman, well-known, facile, but not artistically knowledgeable writers, had been persuaded by influential R.A.'s to join the assault upon the P.R.B. in periodicals that normally did not contain reviews of art exhibitions.

Thus discussed and ridiculed all over London, the Pre-Raphaelites were, as William wrote on 21 July, 'unquestionably . . . one of the topics of the season'. William further observed that 'The "notoriety" of Millais's picture may be evidenced by the fact, received from an undoubted authority, of the Queen's having sent to have it brought to her from the walls of the R.A., which her recent accouchement had prevented her from visiting.'

One of the factors at the root of this concerted attack, which was virtually unprecedented in the history of British art, was the name the youths had chosen for their society. Since Raphael was acclaimed the king of painters and idol of art students, it seemed the height of impudence for a group of youngsters to call themselves Pre-Raphaelites. The name seemed to imply, the critics believed, that they arrogantly regarded themselves as greater than Raphael himself, and that they looked on all post-Raphael art as valueless. The reviewers further inferred from the name that the young men intended slavishly to copy everything, including blemishes and crudities, in early Italian paintings. Here, the critics felt, was a group of insurgent fledglings trying to uproot the foundation of contemporary British painting. The Pre-Raphaelite Brotherhood, then, could be no less than an organized conspiracy to overthrow the conventions and traditions to which the officialdom of English art swore allegiance. Furthermore, if these rebels would subvert their country's art, might not they try to tear down the proprieties in other areas of national life, such as morality and religion.

The challenge of the Pre-Raphaelites could not be ignored, since several of their abominations hung on hallowed walls next to works by venerated R.A.'s—and, above all, since one of the rebels was John Everett Millais. We have stressed that Millais was particularly valuable to the Pre-Raphaelite movement because he was the best known young painter in the country. For the same reason, Millais bore the brunt of the attack—though, of course, in the middle of the nineteenth century his picture, treating sacred personages as if they were ordinary flesh and blood creatures, was a genuine shocker.[1] But Millais was the most talented, the most celebrated, and therefore the most feared member of this band of artistic revolutionists. (Collinson, the least gifted of the four currently exhibiting Pre-Raphaelites, was almost ignored by the critics.) Without Millais the Brotherhood might have drawn a few supercilious comments; but with him they became a *cause célèbre*.

Soon it became fashionable to deride the Pre-Raphaelites, or at best to regard them, in the words of *Punch*, as 'dear silly boys'. Hunt described the typical reaction to their works: 'Sometimes I went stealthily to the Exhibition, hoping to hear some favourable opinion expressed, but as soon as the public arrived at my picture they invariably said, "Oh, this is one of those preposterous Pre-Raphaelite works", and went on to the next without looking again.' And their pocketbooks were hurt as well as their pride. By the end of the season neither Rossetti nor Hunt nor Collinson had received an offer, and Millais, who had sold his pictures before sending-in day, had to lower the price of his *Carpenter Shop* because its buyer had become unnerved by its notoriety.

When this never-to-be forgotten season finally came to an end, the Pre-Raphaelites breathed a collective sigh of relief. But, creditably, they were not prepared to surrender or to agree with those who prophesied doom for the Brotherhood. They were confident that they would survive the disaster, and would bounce back stronger than ever in 1851. Millais went to Oxford to paint his next background, and Hunt was executing a new preliminary design, both determined to make their critics eat their words. As Hunt declared, they regarded the condemnation of their work 'to be none other than the inspiration of personal jealousy and party interest. This conviction, forced upon both of us, brought no thought of surrender in either, but rather the disposition to be the more unflinching.'

[1] When the painting was submitted to the Academy, before the Pre-Raphaelites had become notorious, it was viewed unfavourably by most of the Council. F. B. Barwell wrote: 'I well remember Mulready, R.A., alluding to the picture some two years after its exhibition. He said that it had few admirers inside the Royal Academy Council, and that he himself and Maclise alone supported its claims to a favourable consideration.'

9

Ruskin Intervenes

Rossetti was not rushing ahead with new artistic plans: he was intending to abstain from exhibitions in 1851, and, besides, he was too caught up with Lizzy to concern himself with future plans. But he was not by any means giving up. There had, however, been one casualty from the attacks on the P.R.B. in 1850. On 21 May Rossetti had received a letter from Collinson, whose exhibited work had been largely neglected by the critics declaring that, although he reverenced the Italian Pre-Raphaelites, 'as a sincere Catholic' he no longer could allow himself 'to be called a P.R.B. in the brotherhood sense of the term'. His main reason for withdrawing, he said, was that 'I love and reverence God's faith, and I love His holy Saints; and I cannot bear any longer the self-accusation that, to gratify a little vanity, I am helping to dishonour them, and lower their merits, if not absolutely to bring their sanctity into ridicule.' The letter ended with a postscript: 'Please do not attempt to change my mind.' Collinson's reconversion was probably as genuine as any action of his could be; but its timing, and the vague allusions to the supposed incompatibility of Catholicism and Pre-Raphaelitism hint that he might have been more troubled by the thought of ridicule being heaped on James Collinson than on the 'holy Saints'. In any event, one of his fears was groundless: no one tried to change his mind.

Millais was spending the summer and early autumn in Oxford working on two pictures inspired by recent poems—Tennyson's 'Mariana' and Coventry Patmore's 'The Woodman's Daughter'. Because of his faith in himself, and because of his comfortable financial status, Millais was not unduly disturbed by the furore; but a passage from a letter he wrote in December, 1850, shows that his thoughts were not wholly tranquil:

I shall endeavour to forget . . . present and future miseries that keep me from sleep. You will perhaps wonder what these ailments can be. I will enumerate them. First, a certainty of passing an unusually turbulent life (which I do not like); secondly, the inevitable enemies I shall create if fully successful; thirdly, the knowledge of the immense application required to complete my works for the coming exhibition, which I feel inadequate to perform.

Hunt, as always, was short of money, and so, with Stephens, was forced to accept a commission to clean and restore a mediocre painting on the ceiling of Trinity House. It was unsatisfying drudgery, but between them the youths earned fifty-four pounds. Meanwhile Hunt was designing two pictures, both to be based on scenes from Shakespeare: the prison interview between Isabel and Claudio, from *Measure for Measure*, and Valentine's rescue of Sylvia, from *Two Gentlemen of Verona*.

While Millais and Hunt were getting on with their work, their principal associate, in the words of William Bell Scott, was 'floundering about'. Rossetti suffered considerably more than they from the hostile reviews; and additionally he was distressed by his failure to sell *Ecce Ancilla Domini*, even after he had re-worked the picture and reduced the price to forty guineas. He eventually realized that, however he felt, he would have to exhibit pictures until his name and reputation had a monetary value. His greatest problem then became the choice of a subject for his next painting. Because of the reception of *Ecce Ancilla Domini*, he decided to abandon religious subjects. By then, although his two major works were religious pictures, he had also completed a dozen minor unexhibited pieces, chiefly pen-and-ink drawings, which were related not to religion but to poetry—Dante, Goethe, Coleridge, Poe, and Browning. Of these the most notable was his first completed water-colour (painted in 1849 shortly after his return from the Continent), a small, vividly pigmented, imaginative interpretation of Browning's study of impassioned jealousy, 'The Laboratory'. This picture of an inflamed court beauty waiting to take from the chemist the potion with which she will poison her rival at the ball is, as Stephens said, 'the prototype of that larger class of works of his which are studies in human passion and sentiment dramatically expressed and delineated with success of the most precious kind'.

Now in the summer of 1850, Rossetti reconsidered Browning and his abandoned project, *Hist! Said Kate the Queen*; but soon seeing the impossibility of his carrying out this enormous undertaking, he discarded it in favour of a scene from *Much Ado About Nothing*, which in turn gave way to Dante's *Vita Nuova*, which yielded in rapid order to numerous other designs, each of which was begun and cast aside. By summer's end his artistic efforts had produced almost nothing.

While he was 'floundering', Rossetti remained on good terms with the other Pre-Raphaelites, none of whom blamed him for the disaster. But apparently Millais's parents did—as Hunt found when he visited them shortly after Dickens's onslaught. After quoting from the essay, Mrs Millais asserted, 'Is that not wicked? I declare the article has the essence of malice, and is expressed so rankly that the abuse reaches the sacred personages represented, and cannot be designated as other than blasphemous.' While she was speaking, Hunt reported, Mr Millais 'was walking about with a cane in his hand, . . . clenching his fist and swearing that if he knew where to find the anonymous brood of abusers he would drag them out into the street and thrash them within an inch of their lives'. His wife observed that it was a pity their son had changed his style, for this had brought on the assaults, and then added an emphatic *non sequitur*: 'I wish that you had never had anything to do with that Rossetti!' When Hunt pointed out that he and Millais had agreed to change their style long before they had become friendly with Rossetti, she replied, 'Ah, I don't like the look of him; he's a sly Italian.' Mr Millais sustained her opinion and added, 'I don't admire his behaviour; he loudly indulges in insulting denunciation of persons who have the right to be treated with respect, and asserts himself generally so as to offend people quite unnecessarily.'

During the summer, Rossetti did not see Millais (who was in Oxford) but he often visited Hunt, and once they talked about travelling together to Palestine, where Hunt could paint a realistic scene from the life of Ruth. Then, early in autumn, Hunt unexpectedly sold his maligned painting for £150 (to an Oxonian who had been directed to it by Millais) and was willing to take a trip with Rossetti, who had 'borrowed' money from Aunt Margaret. On 23 October they began their journey, not to Palestine but to Sevenoaks. There, in the great deer park of the fifteenth-century baronial mansion Knole, Hunt planned to paint a woodland background for *Valentine Rescuing Sylvia*.

Gabriel was not attracted to the magnificent scenery of Knole Park;

for him, as A. C. Benson said, 'the smallest touch of human beauty had more significance than the noblest natural prospect'. Even if he had been a nature lover, he would probably not have enjoyed the cold and wind and rain which marked their three weeks' stay in Sevenoaks. At first he made an effort to paint in the rain, as he related in a letter to John Tupper: 'I myself had to sketch under the canopy of heaven, without a hat, and with my umbrella tied over my head to my button-hole . . . (N.B. Trousers turned up.)' But his good humour declined in the bad weather, and Hunt told of a typical episode in Knole Park: 'He set himself to paint, near my place of work, a boscage for a background. I went sometimes to see him at work, but I found him nearly as if engaged in a mortal quarrel with some leaf which had perversely shaken itself off its branch just as he had begun to paint it, until he would have no more of such conduct and would go back to his lodgings.' Still, he did manage to do some work: Woolner, who with Stephens had joined his friends in Sevenoaks, wrote (early in November) that 'he gets up at seven o'clock, is painting his background with mystic feeling'. (The tolerably good background was completed before he returned to London, but was not incorporated into a picture until 1872.)

While he was at Sevenoaks, Rossetti turned again to poetry. Woolner reported that he 'translates canzoni at a great rate of evenings', and eight days later William recorded in the *P.R.B. Journal* that Gabriel had returned to London 'with a great quantity of translations from the old Italian, and one or two short original poems'. The original poems were the brief lyric 'A Young Fir-Wood' and 'Autumn Idleness', which became Sonnet LXIX of *The House of Life*. In early adulthood, Rossetti wrote verse to ease his mind and release his tensions but felt, as he explained in a letter to Aunt Charlotte, that poetry was only a 'minor employment', that his 'real career' was painting. Yet because he could not sell *Ecce Ancilla Domini* (which eventually he called 'the blessed white eyesore') and could not decide on a subject for his next picture, he occupied himself more and more with his 'minor employment'. In November he sent his translation of *Vita Nuova* to the new poet laureate himself, Alfred Tennyson, who, according to the *P.R.B. Journal*, called it 'very strong and earnest'; two months later Coventry Patmore, with his usual hyperbole, declared that some of Rossetti's translations were the only true love poems he had seen.

After returning from Sevenoaks, instead of beginning a new work, he spent many days repainting portions of *Ecce Ancilla Domini*. He then started several designs, including at least two that would form bases for later paintings—*Borgia* and *Beatrice at a Marriage Feast Denying Her Salutation to Dante*—but he could settle on nothing. Early in 1851, Brown wrote in his diary, 'Rossetti has just thrown up a *third* picture, and will have nothing [to exhibit] . . . he has made some fine designs which are perfectly divine. I mean by that, finer than anything I have ever seen, but paint he *will not*. He is too idle.' Long before the earliest of the sending-in days, it seemed that Rossetti would in fact, as he had often vowed, never exhibit again.

But then, at this time, he had other troubles. In the summer of 1850 the dancing master beneath his studio had absconded; and in accordance with the law, the property of the sub-tenant, Rossetti, was seized by the landlord as compensation for loss of rent. Gabriel and William, however, sneaked out some personal effects, mostly books, which they left at Brown's. Gabriel then seems to have gone into hiding, for Christina, briefly resting in Brighton, wrote to William, 'If his whereabouts is to be kept secret, pray do not let me have his address.' His departure for Sevenoaks was probably speeded by a desire to escape the landlord: in a letter of 25 October to John Tupper he wrote, 'I have not seen you for an age, though I marked you among the four or five to be routed out before I left town—after which I was forced at last to bolt o' sudden, with my tail between my legs, whereby hang particulars of acute anguish.'

Upon returning to London, Gabriel must have negotiated a peace with the landlord, for he moved into a studio at 74 Newman Street, only two doors from his former workshop, paid for with more money from Aunt Charlotte.

His home address was still 50 Charlotte Street, where the family's finances were more precarious than ever, and might have been calamitous had not William had a piece of good fortune. In the autumn of 1850 a libellous critique brought on the resignation of *The Spectator*'s art critic, who before quitting his post happened to speak to Brown, who recommended William as a successor. The editor of *The Spectator* interviewed William, looked at some of his articles for *The Critic* and hired him in November at an annual salary of fifty pounds. William was amazed that one of Britain's leading weekly journals should select as its art critic a twenty-one-year-old youth, who was unknown except for his connection with a notorious artistic coterie. The editor, showing commendable fairness and objectivity, probably hired William simply because he considered him to be a highly promising, talented young writer who certainly would not demand exorbitant wages. Although *The Spectator* had been one of the most vehement disparagers of the Pre-Raphaelites, William happily learned that he would be free to express his own opinions: in the *P.R.B. Journal* he recorded that 'considerable latitude is allowed to the writer', and he would 'be but little hampered with any antécédens'. Then another minor Pre-Raphaelite had good luck, for when William left *The Critic*, his place was taken by Stephens. As Holman Hunt wryly said, to its originators the Pre-Raphaelite Brotherhood brought trouble and adversity, but 'to its nominal members it has been a lifelong source of fortune'. William wrote, 'With this moderate sum supplementing my salary in the Inland Revenue (which may now have been something like £110) I figured almost as a capitalist among the P.R.B. Millais perhaps alone made more than this in the course of a year; most of the others, much less or hardly anything.'

Most of William's earnings continued to support his family, but even so at the end of 1850 they had to leave Charlotte Street and move to a smaller, less expensive house at 38 Arlington Street, in Camden Town. There the enfeebled Gabriele Rossetti had a garden to sit in, when the weather permitted. Also, Camden Town, being a relatively new district, gave Mrs Rossetti and Christina an opportunity to open a day school, as a possible source of extra income.

Mrs Rossetti's pupils were only a few daughters of local tradesmen whose tuition never appreciably helped the household finances, but the school did act as a kind of therapy for Christina. When Collinson had returned to the Catholic Church, she had immediately broken off their engagement, and although she kept a stoical silence on the topic, William said that she took this decisive step 'with deep sorrow and reluctance', and for a long time 'a blight was on her heart and spirits'. A few months after the end of the betrothal, she encountered Collinson near Regent's Park, whereupon she fainted on the spot. At home Gabriel's once vivacious younger sister became unusually reserved and taciturn, and for a while she wrote no poems. So she welcomed the chance to devote herself to an impersonal occupation.

Since Maria earned little from her work as a governess or from the few Italian lessons she gave, the Rossettis were almost entirely dependent on William. Gabriel continued to live at home after the move to Arlington Street, and continued to contribute nothing in support of the household. As always he asked and got money from relatives, not only from Aunt Charlotte but also from his hard-pressed mother and brother. In the spring of 1851 Brown noticed that William seemed to be avoiding Gabriel, and in his diary he wrote, 'I had thought for some time there had been some estrangement between Rossetti and his brother, and I asked Deverell who was sitting next to me this morning. He said no. That he believed they were as good friends as ever, but that he supposed his brother did not call on him oftener than he could help because he was ordered peremptorily to hand over all the cash he had about him.'

Because of his financial irresponsibility and his irregular living habits, Gabriel's relations with his father became more strained than ever, and they often exchanged angry words. Perhaps it was after one of these scenes that Gabriel surprised everyone early in 1851 by actually inquiring into the possibility of getting a job. There were a number of positions for which he might have applied—in the British Museum, or in Mudie's thriving circulating library in Oxford Street, or in one of W. H. Smith's newly opened railway station bookstalls. But he sought none of these. Instead, he went to a railway terminal—not the nearby London and North-Western Railway's Camden Town depot, only a few blocks from his home, but rather one of the most inconveniently located stations in London, the South-Western Railway's terminal at Nine Elms, south of the Thames above Vauxhall Bridge. There Rossetti, who had never shown the slightest interest in or aptitude for mechanics of any sort, said that he was interested in becoming a railway telegrapher. He wanted to see the recently installed telegraph machinery; Hunt gives an account of the episode:

> Without waste of time he asked to be shown the work that would be expected of him. He was assured it would be the simplest in the world, and this was demonstrated by the sight of the instrument at work. There were two dials like clock faces, and to each there was an index. The operator took hold of a handle. Rossetti laughed to hear the thing going 'clock, click, click' and to see the needle going about in fits. 'There, you see,' said the gentleman, 'that's all.' 'Nothing else?' commented Gabriel. 'I am extremely obliged to you. It is really amusing. I won't tax your kindness more. It would be absolutely useless for me to undertake the work. I could not do it.'

Of course he could not do it; but now no one could say he had not looked for work. The trip to Nine Elms perhaps appeased Gabriele;

in any case Gabriel resumed his usual way of life with no further thought to employment.

At this time, Rossetti was no longer using the studio in Newman Street; it was dark, gloomy, and, when rain struck its slanting skylight, distinctly noisy. Late in December 1850, Deverell rented the second floor of a house at 17 Red Lion Square, in Holborn, one of whose three rooms, facing the square, would make an ideal studio. In January, Gabriel accepted Deverell's invitation to share his studio, under the landlord's condition (as recorded in the *P.R.B. Journal*) that their models had to be 'kept under some gentlemanly restraint, "as some artists sacrifice the dignity of art to the baseness of passion"'. The two young painters assured him they were gentlemen, and Gabriel set up his easel in Deverell's room.

No one was surprised that the principal founder of the Pre-Raphaelite Brotherhood was sharing a studio with a non-member. The society, which had not met since the opening of the R.A. Exhibition, was no longer functioning actively. William Rossetti and Stephens, who missed the Pre-Raphaelite camaraderie, called a meeting in January at Hunt's lodgings, where those present included themselves, their host, and Millais; and in February another meeting was held, attended by all six members. At these gatherings, the Brothers tried to regenerate their society by adopting a code of principles and regulations, including a statement that 'no engagement with any other person can supersede the obligation of a P.R.B. meeting', and a provision whereby any member who absented himself from a meeting would be fined five shillings. They also considered electing new members, likely choices being Deverell and the talented young painter, Charles Collins, son of the late distinguished Royal Academician William Collins, and younger brother of the soon-to be-famous 'sensation' novelist Wilkie Collins. A youth who had enrolled in the Academy schools when he was only fifteen, Charles Collins had already exhibited six pictures at the past four R.A. Exhibitions, and his work was so strongly influenced by the Brothers that *The British Quarterly Review* called him 'in fact more obstinately Pre-Raphaelitesque than any of the others'. But the rules were not enforced, and no new members were elected. Subsequent meetings were infrequent and irregular; social activities became almost extinct; and from then on the P.R.B. existed only nominally.

The society's decline was inevitable. Only William, Stephens and

Hunt showed any desire to revitalize it, and Hunt lost some of his zeal when he realized that Pre-Raphaelitism could be carried forth by only three of the Brothers, one of whom was mostly devoid of fraternal loyalty. Woolner was kept busy with non-Pre-Raphaelite work, and during the early months of 1851 was preoccupied with his entry in a public competition for a statue to adorn Wordsworth's burial place in Grasmere Churchyard. Millais, who had never been enthusiastic about the society, now saw it as a possible obstacle to his own success: he suggested, in view of the public hostility toward them, that they should cease to call themselves Pre Raphaelites. But it was Rossetti who was most to blame for the decline of the P.R.B., as it was he who had been most responsible for its birth and its active life of nearly two years.

Rossetti's restless temperament, which had caused him to leave the Royal Academy Schools and Brown's studio, probably in any case would have made him tire of the group—especially since, unlike Hunt or Millais, who fervently went out into nature with paint boxes and easels, he never had been at heart a genuine Pre-Raphaelite. The recent notoriety, moreover, had greatly dampened his ardour for the association. But, primarily, his loss of interest was due to his increased passions elsewhere.

On 7 December 1850, William noted in the *P.R.B. Journal* that he had encountered Millais, Hunt and Collins 'parading Tottenham Court Road . . . on the search for models'. Since good models, especially females, were not readily obtainable, the Pre-Raphaelites sometimes combed the streets for likely subjects, and prior to the summer of 1850 no one had enjoyed 'model hunting' more than Rossetti. But for many months prior to 7 December, he had had no need or wish to go out for this purpose; he was held spellbound by his one and only model, Elizabeth Siddal. As Gabriel's love for Lizzy kept him off Tottenham Court Road, it also kept his mind away from the thoughts of the Brotherhood.

Lizzy continued to work a shortened schedule in the milliner's, but her off-duty daytime hours were regularly spent with Gabriel. His preoccupation with her prevented him from having anything ready for an exhibition—and yet she was also his artistic inspiration. He made innumerable sketches and drawings of her, including a nine by seven water-colour drawing, *Rossovestita* (Red-clad), his first extant portrait of his first love. Although *Rossovestita* apparently was not an especially good likeness, Rossetti did capture Lizzy's characteristic posture of proud, enigmatic aloofness—a protective covering for a working-class girl who had been thrust among a group of artists.

Lizzy continued to sit for others in the Pre-Raphaelite circle—her principal role this year was Hunt's heroine in *Valentine Rescuing Sylvia*—but everyone knew she belonged to Rossetti. He made no attempt to conceal his love from his intimates; and, while Lizzy was not demonstrative, there can be little doubt of her love for Rossetti. Neither in 1850 nor in 1851 did Gabriel meet any member of Lizzy's family, and the only other Rossetti whom she saw was William. Gabriel had no need to be ashamed of this beautiful, well-spoken young lady who was usually, as Brown once put it, 'beautifully dressed for about three pounds, altogether looking like a queen'. To present her to his family at this time, however, would have been unthinkable unless they were formally betrothed. No engagement announcement was made during 1850–1, but it seems as if, before the end of 1850, it was tacitly understood by themselves, and probably by his friends, that they were pledged to each other. It also seems likely that when they were alone together, their behaviour was only what might have been expected of a passionate, uninhibited young couple who were devoted to one another and who took it for granted that one day they would be man and wife. Several of Rossetti's biographers have maintained that their pre-marital relations were strictly platonic; but this opinion seems improbable in the light of Rossetti's personality—and in terms of *The House of Life* sonnets, which celebrate the pleasures of physical love or, in Rossetti's own words, 'all the passionate and just delights of the body'.[1] In *The House of Life*, he repeatedly declares that true love is an indivisible union of the physical and spiritual, of body and soul. In a typical passage, in Sonnet V, he says:

> Lady, I fain would tell how evermore
> Thy soul I know not from thy body . . .

In the sonnets, moreover, the lady is also shown to enjoy both aspects of love; in Sonnet IX she clearly enunciates her desire for both 'Passion' and 'Worship'. For Rossetti, a platonic relationship with someone he loved would have been as purposeless as a physical relationship with a Haymarket streetwalker. During the spring of 1851, Lizzy sat as Gabriel's principal figure in his water-colour

[1] Dante Gabriel Rossetti, 'The Stealthy School of Criticism'.

Beatrice at a Marriage Feast Denies Dante her Salutation; but in real life she now was somewhat less ethereal than Dante's Beatrice, and probably was denying her lover nothing.

Rossetti's portrait of Beatrice is an excellent likeness of Lizzy, and the picture itself would beautify the wall of any gallery; but it was not finished in time for the 1851 season. Since his only completed picture, *Rossovestita*, was a minor performance which he did not seriously think of exhibiting, it was clear that this year Gabriel would not have to undergo the pain of reading reviews of his work. But his closest associates, Hunt, Millais, Brown, Deverell, Collins, and even Collinson, had worked hard during the year, and each would exhibit at least one picture. All of them were apprehensive, but watched hopefully for signs of a modified public and critical attitude towards Pre-Raphaelitism. There had been few favourable straws in the wind since the preceding cataclysmic summer: the Pre-Raphaelites had remained notorious, and had been frequently degraded or lampooned—as in the 'Fine-Art Gossip' column of the 7 December issue of *The Athenaeum*:

> The soi-disant Pre-Raphaelite ignores the principles of Art, and affects to despise all the approaches hitherto made towards the establishment of fixed ideas on the subject of beauty and taste . . . he sits down before some model in the selection of which he has taken no further account than as it may answer his desire to imitate the ugliness of some early master, and searching out its—perhaps disgusting—details with microscopic eye, things that he has achieved all by a successful imitation, and hopes by this process to work out a patent way to the true and the beautiful.

Occasionally, however, one might have inferred that the Pre-Raphaelites had exerted a small positive influence on their contemporaries—or at least that some of their principles had been adopted independently by others. Thus in February a correspondent to *The Athenaeum* wrote the following answer to an article defending the contemporary practice of painting with dull colours:

> If we consult ancient manuscripts, we find our forefathers dressed in all sorts of gay colours. Again, every old collection of portraits of British worthies give us many examples of bright colours in dress. Coming down still later, who has not mourned with Pepys the rent in his gay doublet? or exulted with him on his first Sunday exhibition of some exquisite velvet coat with gold buttons and embroidery? Who can forget poor Goldsmith's trying to hide with three-cornered hat the patch of unfaded colour in his second-hand scarlet coat, exposed by the removal of its first owner's star? Hogarth's heroes, too, are somewhat gay. The old-fashioned blue-coat boy has bright yellow legs,

a blue body and a red girth round it. What tropical bird can beat him? I grieve to say that the bright red cloaks of village crones are nearly extinct. Again, if we scrape off the modern whitewash in our churches, we frequently find the remains of very gay colours underneath, in addition to the gorgeous splendour of the old painted glass . . . I do not believe that colour is wicked in England, or even in Scotland; and I hail the advent of cheerful colours, and an escape from universal sad colour, ashes and mud, with the utmost delight. I am not sure that in this dullness we modern English are right, and that all our forefathers are wrong . . . Why are we to aggravate the dullness of our sunless climate by denying ourselves gay colours in obedience to very doubtful inferences? . . . Let us emancipate ourselves, and be natural. Colour is the inheritance of all the earth, and will prevail in spite of philosophy.

The Pre-Raphaelites clung to the hope that comments like these, rare though they were, might herald a more tolerant attitude towards them.

For the fifth consecutive year the season was ushered in by the Free Exhibition, which again held its show in the Portland Gallery and called itself the National Institute of Fine Arts. Opening on 14 April, the exhibition included works submitted by two weaker associates of the Pre-Raphaelite group, Deverell and Collinson. Deverell's contribution, *The Banishment of Hamlet*, was a large picture of Claudius informing Hamlet of his impending departure for England; Collinson's entry, an even larger painting, forty-eight by seventy-one inches, based on an episode in Charles Kingsley's poem *The Saint's Tragedy*, was entitled *An Incident in the Life of St Elizabeth of Hungary*. The depicted 'incident' supposedly took place at the high mass on the feast of the Assumption, when Elizabeth was said to have removed her coronet and knelt before the crucifix to be reprimanded by the Landgravine of Thuringia. Unquestionably Collinson's finest effort, even *The Athenaeum* acknowledged it as 'one of the most carefully treated works in the Exhibition', the picture, containing more than three dozen well arranged figures, was his only work whose details, such as the mosaic floor were executed with Pre-Raphaelite exactitude; clearly he had suffered no artistic ill-effects by withdrawing from the Brotherhood.

The journalistic response to the Portland Gallery exhibition presaged another year of notoriety for the Pre-Raphaelites. Even though one of these two exhibitors had resigned from the Brotherhood, and the other had never been an actual member, Collinson and Deverell were treated almost as if they had originated the movement. In nearly every review, they received more attention than any of the other exhibitors, and often more space was given to their paintings than to all of the remaining 447 entries; but the only favourable critique was published in *The Spectator* and was written by William Rossetti. The notice in *The Illustrated London News* was typical, beginning thus:

The 'P.R.B.' school figure in the paintings of two of their disciples. . . . The perversion of taste which drives clever young men into a wild-goose chase of imitation of the early and semi-barbarous stages of art, is one of the strangest manias of the day, involving, as it does, the repudiation of all natural and flowing lines of beauty; the substitution for them of the most utterly ungraceful and stiffly rigid attitudes and postures; while the general effect is an uncomfortable persuasion that the artist must have taken his models from an unfortunate set of ladies and gentlemen who had all their limbs broken early in life, and never enjoyed the advantages of a competent surgeon to set them to rights again.

The almost universal denunciation of 'two of their disciples', whom *The Athenaeum* called representatives of a 'crotchetty school of would-be-antique moderns', must have caused Hunt and Millais some worry about the reception awaiting them. But they and their colleagues were not the only persons who were troubled by the general savagery of contemporary art criticism. In 1851 members of the press for the first time were admitted to the annual Royal Academy dinner, held as always on the Saturday preceding the opening; and on this occasion His Royal Highness Prince Albert, who delivered the main speech, aimed several remarks especially at the newly-invited guests:

The production of all works in art or poetry requires, in their conception or execution, not only an exercise of the intellect, skill and patience, but particularly a concurrent warmth of feeling, and a free flow of imagination. This renders them most tender plants, which will thrive only in an atmosphere calculated to maintain that warmth, and that atmosphere is one of kindness—kindness towards the artist personally, as well as towards his production. An unkind word of criticism passes like a cold blast over their tender shoots, and shrinks them up, checking the flow of the sap which was rising to produce, perhaps, multitudes of flowers and fruit. But still criticism is absolutely necessary to the development of art, and the injudicious praise of an inferior work becomes an insult to superior genius. In this respect our times are peculiarly unfavourable when compared with those when Madonnas were painted in the seclusion of convents; for we have now, on the one hand, the eager competition of a vast array of artists of every degree of talent and skill, and, on the other, as judge, a great public, for the greater part wholly uneducated in art; and this led by professional writers, who often strive to impress the public with a great idea of their own artistic knowledge, by the merciless manner in which they treat works which cost those who produced them the highest efforts of mind and feeling.

The Royal Academy faced some unprecedented competition this year, for on 1 May the first world's fair—the so-called Great Industrial Exhibition—was inaugurated in Hyde Park in the presence of Queen Victoria. The annual Exhibition, which opened four days later in Trafalgar Square, nevertheless stimulated as much excitement as ever in the art world; and among its works none seemed likelier to stir public interest than the six paintings contributed by the Pre-Raphaelite circle. Three of the six came from Millais, who had never worked harder than during the preceding year. He had laboured from dawn to dusk until 10 February, when he wrote to a friend, 'Tonight I commence for the first time this year evening work which lasts till twelve and which will continue for the next few months.' His entries were the pictures he had begun during the preceding summer—*Mariana* and *The Woodman's Daughter*—and a painting commenced in February, *The Return of the Dove to the Ark*.

Millais regarded *Mariana* as his major work of the year, and the painting has been highly praised by many others, including John Ruskin, who called it 'on the whole the perfectest of [Millais's] works, and the representative picture of that generation'.[1] It was intended to portray the heroine of Tennyson's early poem 'Mariana', four lines of which were quoted in the Exhibition catalogue:

> She only said 'my life is dreary,
> He cometh not!' she said;
> She said 'I am aweary, aweary,
> I would that I were dead.'

The picture, however, rather more successfully illustrated Pre-Raphaelitism than Tennyson. The splendidly luxurious accessories—such as Mariana's rich blue dress, her jewelled girdle, the embroidery on the table, the ornate lamp and the colourful flower garden—are all faithful to the tenets of the Brotherhood, but they hardly seem appropriate to Tennyson's 'moated grange', where

> With blackest moss the flower-plots
> Were thickly crusted, one and all:
> The rusted nails fell from the knots

[1] 'The Three Colours of Pre-Raphaelitism', *Nineteenth Century*, December 1878.

> That held the pear to the gable-wall.
> The broken sheds look'd sad and strange:
> Unlifted now was the clinking latch:
> Weeded and worn the ancient thatch. . . .

One of Millais's biographers, J. Ernest Phythian, has defended *Mariana*'s elegance: 'The whole point of the picture is that the lady's surroundings are extremely beautiful, and yet she is unutterably sad. The picture . . . opens up to us one of the tragedies of life, that no luxury, no beauty, can fill the place of un-requited or ill-requited love.' If this is true, the painting then has only a tenuous relationship to its poetic model. Even more typically Pre-Raphaelite than *Mariana* is the excellent landscape *The Woodman's Daughter*, whose every shadow, branch, leaf, and blade of grass was skilfully delineated with absolute fidelity to nature. The picture shows a lord's son offering four strawberries to a woodman's daughter; Millais painted the berries in March, and since he would not be satisfied with imitation fruit, he paid five shillings and sixpence for four berries, which, after painting them, he and Collins ate.

Since *Claudio and Isabella* was not yet finished, Hunt's only work to be exhibited was *Valentine Rescuing Sylvia from Proteus*, whose models included Rossetti (Valentine) and Elizabeth Siddal (Sylvia). With its realistic foreground and background (painted in Sevenoaks), its splendid colours, and its four vividly portrayed main figures, this work clearly excelled any of Hunt's earlier productions. This painting and those of Millais moved Brown to write magnanimously in his diary that they 'kill everything in the exhibition for brilliancy . . . I think Millais's pictures as small pictures, more wonderful than any I have yet seen, and Hunt's picture is a truly noble one.'

Despite the Pre-Raphaelite notoriety, none of Millais's or Hunt's entries was turned down by the Council, and only *Valentine Rescuing Sylvia* was unfavourably hung. The Council's action should have answered those critics who repeatedly charged that prejudice and bias lay behind the selection and hanging of R.A. pictures. The Academy also accepted works from two men who were close associates of the Pre-Raphaelites: *Convent Thoughts*, by Collins, which shows a young nun standing in a variegated garden contemplating a passion flower, and *Geoffrey Chaucer Reading the 'Legend of Custance' to Edward the Third and His Court on the Anniversary of the Black Prince's Forty-Fifth Birthday*, by Brown, who after an absence of ten years was appearing for the second time in a Royal Academy Exhibition. Brown had begun the design for this enormous painting, one of his finest, in 1845; six years later he had had to work almost continuously for three days and nights in order to have it ready for sending-in day. Its size, its vivid colours, its lively group of well-drawn personalities, and its dramatic intensity make *Chaucer* a striking, spectacular picture and one of Brown's best.[1] Apart from its artistic qualities, the picture is of interest because Deverell had sat for the page talking to the lady in the foreground, William Rossetti posed for the minstrel looking up at Chaucer, Elizabeth Siddal represented the lady whose hands are clasped, and Gabriel was the model for Chaucer, whose likeness, William said, was 'recognizably like Chaucer and also a very fair portrait of Rossetti'. Brown's luck, incidentally, seems at last to have turned: in 1850 his painting of *Cordelia at the Bedside of King Lear* had been exhibited and well received in Dublin, and shortly after the Exhibition opened, his *Chaucer* had a 'sold' sign posted beside it.

Because of his recent sale, Brown was uncharacteristically cheerful on opening day; and Millais and Hunt also had a few happy moments when they were congratulated by several non-Pre-Raphaelite artists. Their pleasure was short-lived, however, for two days later *The Times* published its first notice of the exhibition—a notice which showed that this bulwark of the Establishment had ignored the admonitions of Prince Albert:

We cannot censure at present as amply or as strongly as we desire to do, that strange disorder of the mind or the eyes which continues to rage with unabated absurdity among a class of juvenile artists who style themselves P.R.B., which, being interpreted, means *Pre-Raphael-brethren.* Their faith seems to consist in an absolute contempt for perspective and the known laws of light and shade, an aversion to beauty in every shape, and a singular devotion to the minute accidents of their subjects, including, or rather seeking out, every excess of sharpness and deformity. Mr Millais, Mr Hunt, Mr Collins—and in some degree—Mr Brown . . . have undertaken to reform the art on these principles. The Council of the Academy, acting in a spirit of toleration and indulgence to young artists, have now allowed these extravagances to disgrace their walls for the last three years, and though we cannot prevent men who are capable of better things from wasting their talents on ugliness and conceit, the public may fairly require that such offensive jests should not continue to be exposed as specimens of the waywardness of these

[1] The reader perhaps should be reminded of Brown's comment on his experimentation with lighting in his picture, *Chaucer*, quoted on page 39.

artists who have relapsed into the infancy of their profession. . . . These young artists have unfortunately become notorious by addicting themselves to an antiquated style and an affected simplicity in Painting, which is to genuine art what the mediaeval ballads and designs in *Punch* are to Chaucer and Giotto. With the utmost readiness to humour even the caprices of Art when they bear the stamp of originality and genius, we can extend no toleration to a mere servile imitation of the cramped style, false perspective, and crude colour of remote antiquity. We do not want to see what Fuseli termed drapery 'snapped instead of folded', faces bloated into apoplexy or extenuated to skeletons, colour borrowed from the jars in a druggist's shop, and expression forced into caricature. It is said that the gentlemen have the power to do better things, and we are referred in proof of their handicraft to the mistaken skill with which they have transferred to canvas the hay which lined the lofts in Noah's Ark, the brown leaves of the coppice where Sylvia strayed, and the prim vegetables of a monastic garden. But we must doubt a capacity of which we have seen so little proof, and if any such capacity did ever exist in them, we fear that it has already been overlaid by mannerism and conceit . . . the authors of these offensive and absurd productions have continued to combine the puerility or infancy of their art with the uppishness and self-sufficiency of a different period of life. That morbid infatuation which sacrifices truth, beauty, and genuine feeling to mere eccentricity deserves no quarter at the hands of the public, and though the patronage of art is sometimes lavished on oddity as profusely as on higher qualities, these monkish follies have no more real claim to figure in any decent collection of English paintings than the aberrations of intellect which are exhibited under the name of Mr Ward.

For Hunt this diatribe signified a 'studied determination to destroy us altogether', and Millais agreed that *The Times* had sold 'itself to destroy us'. Their alarm was not unwarranted, for as always lesser papers and periodicals would follow the lead of Britain's journalistic monarch. Since they could hardly survive two consecutive years of damnation, if *The Times'* critique should set the pattern for this season's critical reaction to them, the Pre-Raphaelites and their associates could consider themselves artistically dead. Indeed, not long after the appearance of *The Times* article, Sir Charles Eastlake, the new President of the Royal Academy, was reported to have said that never again would the walls of his institution be sullied by paintings of the Pre-Raphaelites.

The level-headed Millais realized they would have to act immediately if they were to stave off the final blow. So as soon as he had read *The Times'* invective, he hurried off to suburban Highgate to see the poetic companion and admirer of the Pre-Raphaelites, Coventry Patmore—who, as Millais knew, was a close friend of John Ruskin. As we saw in an earlier chapter, in 1843 Volume I of *Modern Painters* had created a sensation in the world of art, and Ruskin's critical reputation had soared with the publication of each of three additional volumes—*Modern Painters*, Volume II (1846), *The Seven Lamps of Architecture* (1849), and *The Stones of Venice*, Volume I (March 1851). Now, although only thirty-two, he was Britain's most important and most influential art critic, who, in the words of Millais's son, John Guille Millais, 'was all but universally accepted as the final authority in matters of art'. Millais had not read any of Ruskin's books, but he hoped that because of his strong influence on Hunt, he might be partial to the Pre-Raphaelites, and might be willing to rescue them from disaster. Patmore promised that without delay he would ask Ruskin to rebut *The Times*' art critic in a letter to the editor.

Ruskin himself was then a man of means who was living with his young wife in their town house at 31 Park Street, Mayfair. Although the Pre-Raphaelites may have thought he was a partisan of theirs, in fact Ruskin had taken little note of their works. His interest was aroused, however, when Patmore visited him the day after Millais had sought his help; Patmore must have pointed out that the philosophical impulse of Pre-Raphaelitism lay in the two volumes of *Modern Painters*. At the moment Ruskin was preparing for publication a revised edition of Volume I, and he may suddenly have recognized in the Pre-Raphaelites ardent practitioners of his own preachings.[1] In any event, after he had examined the controversial paintings, he returned home and composed a letter to *The Times*.

When it was done, Ruskin showed it to his father, whose advice he frequently sought, who warned him against mailing it because of its caustic tone—whereupon he destroyed it and wrote a milder version which he posted on the afternoon of 9 May. Four days later *The Times* published the letter which Hunt said appeared like 'thunder out of a clear sky'. It is important enough to be reproduced here almost in its entirety:

[1] We can only speculate on what the two men said to each other, for there is no known documentary account of their meeting. According to Ruskin's best biographer, Derrick Leon, 'Patmore . . . approached Ruskin, who, his natural belligerence, no less than his natural generosity, immediately aroused, ordered the carriage and drove to the Academy in order to re-examine with punctilious care the egregious paintings which were arousing so much censure.' (*Ruskin: the Great Victorian*, p. 143.)

Sir:

Your usual liberality will, I trust, give a place in your columns to this expression of my regret that the tone of the critique which appeared in *The Times* of Wednesday last on the works of Mr Millais and Mr Hunt, now in the Royal Academy, should have been scornful as well as severe.

I regret it, first, because the mere labour bestowed on those works, and their fidelity to a certain order of truth (labour and fidelity which are altogether indisputable), ought at once to have placed them above the level of mere contempt; and, secondly, because I believe these young artists to be at a most critical period of their career—at a turning-point, from which they may either sink into nothingness or rise to very real greatness; and I believe also, that whether they choose the upward or the downward path, may in no small degree depend upon the character of the criticism which their works have to sustain. I do not wish in any way to dispute or invalidate the general truth of your critique on the Royal Academy; nor am I surprised at the estimate which the writer formed of the pictures in question when rapidly compared with works of totally different style and aim; nay, when I first saw the chief picture by Millais in the Exhibition of last year, I had nearly come to the same conclusion myself. But I ask your permission, in justice to artists who have at least given much time and toil to their pictures, to institute some more serious inquiry into their merits and faults than your general notice of the Academy could possibly have admitted.

Let me state, in the first place, that I have no acquaintance with any of these artists, and very imperfect sympathy with them. No one who has met with any of my writings will suspect me of desiring to encourage them in their Romanist and Tractarian tendencies.[1] I am glad to see that Mr Millais's lady in blue [Mariana] is heartily tired of her painted window and idolatrous toilet table; and I have no particular respect for Mr Collins's lady in white, because her sympathies are limited by a dead wall, or divided between some gold fish and a tadpole. . . . But I happen to have a special acquaintance with the water plant, *Alisma Platago*, among which the said gold fish are swimming; and as I never saw it so thoroughly or so well drawn, I must take leave to remonstrate with you, when you say sweepingly that these men 'sacrifice *truth* as well as feeling to eccentricity.' For as a mere botanical study of the water-lily and *Alisma*, as well as of the common lily and several other garden flowers, this picture would be invaluable to me, and I heartily wish it were mine.

But, before entering into such particulars, let me correct an impression

[1] Herein lay the only present major point of disagreement between Ruskin and the Pre-Raphaelites. In *The P.R.B. Journal*, William wrote, 'Ruskin says something of P.R.B. "Romanist and tractarian tendencies," in reference to the *Mariana* and to Collins' picture. Such tendencies, as utterly non-existent in fact, it might not be amiss to repudiate. . . . But perhaps it will be preferable to wait for Ruskin's sequel.' Later William pointed out that Ruskin 'was at that time a very earnest Protestant Christian', and that his 'vague idea that the Pre-Raphaelites were leagued in some Puseyite or Roman-catholic propaganda' had been 'fostered by public rumour.'

which your article is likely to induce in most minds, and which is altogether false. These pre-Raphaelites (I cannot compliment them on common-sense in choice of a *nom de guerre*) do not desire nor pretend in any way to imitate antique painting as such. They know very little of ancient paintings who suppose the works of these young artists to resemble them. As far as I can judge of their air—for, as I said, I do not know the men themselves—the pre-Raphaelites intend to surrender no advantage which the knowledge or inventions of the present time can afford to their art. They intend to return to early days in this one point only—that, as far as in them lies, they will draw either what they see, or what they suppose might have been the actual facts of the scene they desire to represent, irrespective of any conventional rules of picture-making; and they have chosen their unfortunate though not inaccurate name because all artists did this before Raphael's time, and after Raphael's time did *not* this, but sought to paint fair pictures, rather than represent stern facts; of which consequence has been that, from Raphael's time to this day, historical art has been in acknowledged decadence.

Now, sir, presupposing that the intention of these men was to return to archaic *art* instead of to archaic *honesty*, your critic borrows Fuseli's expression respecting ancient draperies 'snapped instead of folded', and asserts that in these pictures there is a '*servile* imitation of *false* perspective'. To which I have just this to answer:

That there is not one single error in perspective in four out of the five pictures in question;[1] and that in Millais's 'Mariana' there is but this one—that the top of the green curtain in the distant window has too low a vanishing point; and that I will undertake, if need be, to point out and prove a dozen worse errors in perspective in any twelve pictures, containing architecture, taken at random from among the works of the popular painters of the day.

Secondly: that, putting aside the small Mulready, and the works of Thorburn and Sir W. Ross, and perhaps some others of those in the miniature room which I have not examined, there is not a single study of drapery in the whole Academy, be it in large works or small, which for perfect truth, power, and finish could be compared for an instant with the black sleeve of the Julia or with the velvet on the breast and the chain mail of the Valentine, of Mr Hunt's picture; or with the white draperies on the table of Mr Millais' 'Mariana,' and of the right-hand figure in the same painter's 'Dove returning to the Ark'.

And further: that as studies both of drapery and of every minor detail, there has been nothing in art so earnest or so complete as these pictures since the days of Albert Dürer. This I assert generally and fearlessly. On the other hand, I am perfectly ready to admit that Mr Hunt's 'Silvia' is not a person whom Proteus or any one else would have been likely to fall in love with at first sight; and that one cannot feel very sincere delight that Mr Millais's 'Wives of the Sons of Noah' should have escaped the deluge; with

[1] Ruskin was alluding to the works of Millais, Hunt, and Collins; he ignored Brown's painting.

many other faults besides, on which I will not enlarge at present, because I have already occupied too much of your valuable space, and I hope to enter into more special criticism in a future letter.

None of the condemned painters could have dreamed of a more eloquent defence. But would even Ruskin be able to forestall disaster? The Pre-Raphaelites could only sit back and wait for the answer which would probably determine the fate of all of them, including the Brother standing, or perhaps lying, in Red Lion Square, aloof from the battlefield.

10

The Turn of the Tide

Two days after the publication of Ruskin's letter, Hunt, Millais, the Rossetti brothers, Brown and Collins assembled in Millais's studio to discuss Patmore's suggestion that they send a note of thanks to their benefactor. Although boundlessly grateful, they decided against writing to Ruskin because, Hunt explained, 'as there is a promise of a second letter, it would be better not to thank Mr Ruskin until that has appeared, so that he would, if necessary, be able to say that he is not in communication with us, which fact, it is evident, gave his first letter so much more importance than if it could have been said to result from friendly motives'. Hunt also thanked Patmore himself, not only for asking Ruskin to write his letter but also for briefing him—as he clearly must have done—on the objectives of the Pre-Raphaelite Brotherhood.

On 15 May, the date of this informal meeting, William wrote in the *P.R.B. Journal*, 'As to abuse, it seems to be in the air, so much does the infection spread among critics in word and print.' During the next fortnight, the Brothers detected little perceptible effect on their detractors from Ruskin's declaration of 13 May. They received various written and verbal insults: a note was sent to Millais by an acquaintance warning him that he would be snubbed when next they met in public; a lecture was delivered by a professor in the R.A. Schools ridiculing their efforts; and a newspaper article demanded that the walls of the Academy be immediately stripped of their paintings.

The month of May, however, was not unrelievedly bleak. Thomas Carlyle, according to Woolner (who was doing his portrait medallion), said, 'These Pre-Raphaelites they talk of are said to copy the thing as it is, or invent it as they believe it must have been: now there is some sense and hearty sincerity in this. It is the only way of doing anything fit to be seen.' Brown's painting was treated kindly by *The Athenaeum* and was warmly praised by *The Illustrated London News*, which called it 'the leading picture of the Middle Room'. On 24 May, the latter journal included in its third notice of The Exhibition a large engraving of *The Return of the Dove to the Ark* and some faintly complimentary remarks on Millais, who, it said, 'is young enough to mend, and has talent to do better things'. *The Illustrated London News* also observed that Collins had painted the landscape of *Convent Thoughts* 'with a microscopic minuteness perfectly wonderful'—but added that it was comparable to writing the Lord's Prayer 'on a silver penny of Maunday money'.

Valentine Rescuing Sylvia was the only Pre-Raphaelite painting to go unmentioned in *The Illustrated London News*. This neglect was probably what Hunt had expected, for among his circle at this time he was the most dejected. Brown and Millais had sold their pictures, and Collins was living in comparative comfort; but Hunt's painting was unsold, and his financial prospects looked hopeless. A publisher who had asked him to illustrate an edition of Longfellow's poems refused to accept his drawings; no one would commission him to paint a portrait; and his father complained of being ridiculed by friends, one of whom was willing to bet that *Valentine Rescuing Sylvia* would be taken down before the close of The Exhibition. At one point Hunt even contemplated abandoning art and emigrating to Australia or Canada; but Millais rescued him from these depths by saying that he had saved and put aside five hundred pounds which were as available to Hunt as to himself.

Hunt was encouraged more by his friend's confidence in him than by the generous offer itself. But even without Millais's encouragment, he would have forgotten the colonies after the publication on 30 May of Ruskin's second letter to *The Times*. After devoting five paragraphs to a detailed analysis of Millais's and Hunt's currently exhibited pictures, Ruskin declared:

> I wish them all heartily good-speed, believing in sincerity that if they temper the courage and energy which they have shown in the adoption of their systems with patience and discretion in framing it, and if they do not suffer themselves to be driven by harsh or careless criticism into rejection of the ordinary means of obtaining influence over the minds of others, they may,

as they gain experience, lay in our England the foundation of a school of art nobler than the world has seen for three hundred years.

The Times had published Ruskin's first letter without comment, but in its 30 May issue it editorially answered him with a defence of its position. Part of the editorial accused Ruskin of inconsistency for claiming to be a devotee both of Turner and the Pre-Raphaelites:

Mr Ruskin's own works might prove the best antidote to [Pre-Raphaelitism] . . . for, if we remember rightly, he has laid it down, in his defense of Mr Turner's landscapes, that truth in painting is not the mere imitative reproduction or image of the general effect given by an assemblage of the objects as they *appear* to the sight. The Pre-Raphaelites have taken refuge in the opposite extreme of exaggeration from Mr Turner . . . They combine a repulsive precision of ugly shapes . . . with monotony of tone . . . or distorted expression.

On the following day *The Spectator* added its voice to Ruskin's defence of the Pre-Raphaelites—not surprisingly since William Rossetti was still *The Spectator*'s art critic. Even so, an extended commendation in a prestigious journal could not but be helpful to their cause, especially following on the heels of Ruskin's letter. Above all, it contained a clear explanation of the basic Pre-Raphaelite principle:

This principle may be broadly laid down as 'the truth, and nothing but the truth': we should add, 'the whole truth', were it possible to *reproduce* the facts of nature, instead of merely *representing* them proximately. But, it is to be asked, the truth of what? for surely every object in nature is not *per se* a subject for a picture. The objection is well founded, but ill addressed: let the still-life painters answer it—the flower, the animal painters—any, in short, before those who deal with the highest themes of human life and emotion. But, as certainly as painting is an imitative art—and that it is so who will dispute?—so certainly is the correct and faithful preferable to the careless imitation of the accessory portions of a picture. Thus stated, our assertion seems an impertinent truism: but it will not become so until the conscientious labour bestowed on such asccesories, as on the more important parts, shall have ceased to be matter for ridicule.

All through the month of May, *The Athenaeum* and *The Literary Gazette* had ignored Millais, Hunt, and Collins. But on 7 June, after a week in which to digest Ruskin's second letter and *The Spectator*'s observations, both journals' reviewers took note of the Pre-Raphaelites. In 1850, *The Athenaeum* had given an entire notice to its denunciation of Millais and Hunt and the Brotherhood, and in April of 1851 it had used three-fourths of its commentary on the Portland

Gallery show to condemn Collinson and Deverell; but now it could spare only one brief paragraph for the season's leading Pre-Raphaelite exhibitors:

Of the pre-Raphaelite brethren little need now be said,—since what has been already said was said in vain. Mr Charles Collins is this year the most prominent among the band, in *Convent Thoughts*. There is an earnestness in this work worth a thousand artistic hypocrisies which insist on the true rendering of a buckle or a belt, while they allow the beauties of the human form divine to be lost sight of. Mr Millais exhibits his old perversity in a scene from Tennyson, *Mariana*, and in the *Return of the Dove to the Ark*. The last is a good thought marred by its art-language. *The Woodman's Daughter* is of the same bad school:—and Mr Hunt brings up the rearward move by a scene from 'The Two Gentlemen of Verona'—*Valentine rescuing Sylvia from Proteus*.

The Literary Gazette's entire 7 June critique dealt with the Pre-Raphaelites. They were more or less mildly censured—but most important, for the first time in a major periodical other than *The Spectator* they were treated as artists whose works deserved serious examination and discussion. The tone of the review was established in the first paragraph:

If these pictures were badly painted, if the drawing were false, if they showed no study, or a coarse and clumsy carelessness, with neither meaning nor expression, we should be disposed to join with the Jupiter tonans of the daily press in considering them a disgrace to the walls of the Academy. But none of these faults can be brought against them. . . . We believe the 'brethren' are in earnest, and that they mean well, and their intentions are pure and devoted to art, however injudiciously directed.

Although the Pre-Raphaelites were guilty of 'heresy in art', it had

arisen from a desire to avoid conventionalism and theoretical style, and rely entirely upon nature. It is certainly better to see men following nature's teaching than painting eternally out of their own heads, repeating again the same forms, colours, and expressions.

Probably the point of greatest significance in this article was the acknowledgement that minuteness of detail ought not be a basis for derision:

With enthusiasm and a most devoted study of nature, evinced in the marvellous perfection with which every leaf and flower is painted in the *Convent Thoughts*, or in the drawing of the young shoots of the ash and the oak trees; in the bark of the trunks, and other minutiae of detail, in Mr Millais's picture of the *Woodman's Daughter*; and no less in the surprising labour bestowed upon the dead leaves, and the draperies in Mr Hunt's *Valentine rescuing Sylvia from Proteus,* the pre-Raffaelites employ all the modern appliances of painting in giving an exact resemblance of the objects. . . . It is for this devoted and faithful study that we have hopes of the pre-Raffaelites; that they will become *naturalistic* in the way the Caracci Guido, and Correggio did.

Finally the reviewer sounded almost like a convert to Pre-Raphaelitism (or perhaps to Ruskin) when he wrote, 'Nature is like the conscience to a painter, a faithful monitor who, if he follow truly, will not mislead him.'

If a single day can stand as the turning-point in the war waged by the Pre-Raphaelites that day was 7 June 1851, when one of their most vehement foes held out a large olive branch and another confined its hostility within the limits of a perfunctory, face-saving paragraph.

Now that they could properly express their gratitude to Ruskin, Hunt and Millais wrote a joint letter of thanks, attaching to it Millais's address (perhaps because, as Derrick Leon suggested, Gower Street would provide a 'more imposing heading' than Prospect Place). Ruskin must have been highly pleased with the letter, for on the afternoon of its arrival he and his beautiful twenty-two-year-old wife drove to 83 Gower Street and became acquainted with Millais, whose charm and affability moved them to invite him to spend a week at the Fuskin family estate on Denmark Hill, in the southern suburb of Camberwell. Millais naturally seized on the opportunity to be a guest of the nation's most influential art critic, and his 'exuberant interest in human experience', Hunt related, 'as well as his childlike impulsiveness in conversation made him in a few days like an intimate of many years' duration'. The Ruskins even invited him to join them on a vacation in Switzerland.

Millais had to decline this last invitation. Now that the critical tide had begun to turn, he and his friends were eager to plunge into their pictures for 1852, which they sanguinely thought would be a year of triumph and vindication for Pre-Raphaelitism. Early in July, he and Hunt and Collins went down into neighbouring Surrey, where they took lodgings for the rest of the summer and set up their easels. Millais began the foreground and background for two pictures—the drowning of Ophelia and a rendezvous of two bygone lovers—while Hunt was beginning the first Pre-Raphaelite picture to have a contemporary subject, a scene which would show a young shepherd courting his mistress and neglecting his flock.

Meanwhile on Denmark Hill it became clear that John Ruskin had not written his last word of the year on the Pre-Raphaelites. If he had not been censured by *The Times*, and had not struck up a friendship with Millais, Ruskin might have gone off on the Continental holiday and left it at that. Certainly nothing would suggest that he had originally intended to extend his published support of the Pre-Raphaelites beyond his second letter. But after being angered by *The Times* and charmed by Millais, he decided that these talented young men deserved further encouragement. So he added a new closing paragraph to the new edition of Volume I of *Modern Painters* before it went to press:

> I would further insist on all that is advanced in these paragraphs, with special reference to the admirable, though strange, pictures of Mr Millais and Mr Holman Hunt; and to the principles exemplified in the efforts of other members of a society which unfortunately, or rather unwisely, has given itself the name of Pre-Raphaelite; unfortunately, because the principles on which its members are working are neither pre- nor post-Raphaelite, but everlasting. They are endeavouring to paint, with the highest possible degree of completion, what they see in nature, without reference to conventional or established rules, but by no means to imitate the style of any past epoch. Their works are, in finish of drawing, and in splendour of colour, the best in the Royal Academy; and I have great hope that they may become the foundation of a more earnest and able school of art than we have seen for centuries.

One paragraph obviously could not do justice to the Brethren, and so Ruskin immediately began a lengthy essay, which was completed late in July and published in August as a sixty-eight page pamphlet entitled *Pre-Raphaelitism*. In the preface, he told of how his earlier exhortation to artists to seek their inspiration, 'in all singleness of heart', directly from nature was now being 'carried out, to the very letter, by a group of men who, for their reward, have been assailed with the most scurrilous abuse which I ever recollect seeing from the public press.'[1] He 'therefore thought it due to them to contradict the directly false statements which have been made respecting their works; and to point out the kind of merit which, however, deficient in some respects, those works possess beyond the possibility of dispute'.

Ruskin spelled out the objectives of the Pre-Raphaelites, praised

[1] This scurrilous abuse, Ruskin revealed, even extended to their public defender: 'The very day after I had written my second letter to *The Times* . . . I received an anonymous letter . . . from some person apparently hardly capable of spelling, and about as vile a specimen of petty malignity as ever blotted paper.'

their works, and refuted their critics' principal charges. The Pre-Raphaelites, Ruskin said, were only fulfilling the 'true duty' of all painters: 'the faithful representation of all objects of historical interest, or of natural beauty existent at the period'. In living up to their 'true duty', the Pre-Raphaelites, necessarily and deliberately, were going against all conventional art instruction, which began 'by telling the youth of fifteen or sixteen, that Nature is full of faults, and that he is to improve her; but that Raphael is perfection, and that the more he copies Raphael the better, and that . . . he is to try to do something very clever, all out of his own head, but yet this clever something is to be properly subjected to Raphaelesque rules'. Ruskin then enumerated some of these rules, 'which through various channels, Royal Academy lecturings, press criticisms, public enthusiasms, and not least by solid weight of gold, we give to our young men. And we wonder we have no painters!' The Pre-Raphaelites, 'exceedingly young men, of stubborn instincts and positive self-trust', refused to bow down before these rules and produce 'works enriched by plagiarism, polished by convention, invested with all the attractiveness of artificial grace, and recommended to our respect by established authority'. Instead, these independent youths 'have produced works in many parts not inferior to the best of Albert Dürer'. For their praiseworthy originality, they deserved to be lauded, not vilified. The accusations, furthermore, hurled at the Pre-Raphaelites, Ruskin said, were baseless. They did not imitate the early Italian Masters, they did not paint without a system of light and shade, and they did not neglect proper perspective. Ruskin concluded by asking the public 'to give their pictures careful examination, and look at them once with the indulgence and the respect which I have endeavoured to show they deserved'.

The foregoing paragraph summarizes the main points of Ruskin's pamphlet insofar as it deals with the Pre-Raphaelites. Less space, however, was devoted to the P.R.B. than to Turner. E. T. Cook observed that 'it may indeed apart from the title be called the first of Ruskin's many pamphlets on Turner', and *The Athenaeum*'s review of the booklet stated, 'If Turner be not a Pre-Raphaelite, more than half the pamphlet has nothing to do with "Pre-Raphaelitism".' Ruskin might have retorted that precisely what he was trying to establish was that Turner *was* a Pre-Raphaelite. Disturbed by *The Times*' contention that it was inconsistent to extol both Turner and the Pre-Raphaelites, he set forth the essential similarities between the elderly landscapist and the young rebels, both of whom were 'equally impressed with a humble desire to render some part of what they saw in nature faithfully,' and were 'among the few men who have defied all false teaching, and have, therefore, in great measure, done justice to the gifts with which they were entrusted'. The principal Brothers, Ruskin wrote, 'had the same desire for truth in natural facts, for realism in presentation, and for pure colour, as were to be found in Turner, in the painters praised in *Modern Painters*, and in the early Italian painters.'

Some commentators have suggested that Ruskin did not really understand Pre-Raphaelitism and that his explanation of its principles was inaccurate and too greatly coloured by his own ideas. One might, it is true, take exception to certain aspects of his booklet. His generalizations, especially those dealing with Pre-Raphaelite theory, sometimes apply to only one of the Brothers, Holman Hunt. He seems to have thought that these seven youths shared his own enthusiasm for medievalism. He read too much significance into their almost casually selected name: '. . . they have opposed themselves . . . to the entire feeling of the Renaissance schools; a feeling compounded of indolence, infidelity, sensuality, and shallow pride.' Finally, despite his bias towards medievalism, nowhere does he allude to the only medievalist among the seven, Dante Gabriel Rossetti. Even with these limitations, however, the essay taken as a whole does show that Ruskin understood what the Pre-Raphaelites were trying to do, and that he fairly and correctly expounded the doctrines that had been worked out by Hunt.

Pre-Raphaelitism generated considerable interest, and the detractors were quick to respond and deride. *The Athenaeum*, which for years had carried on a running battle with Ruskin, declared that he had

> betaken himself, in all the pomp of his infallibility, to induce us to put trust in two opposite faiths at once,—to satisfy that hot and cold are one,—that licence and pedantic formality are alike to be reverenced,—and that with Turner-*olatry* as strongly professed by him as ever, the canonization of *St* Millais, and other Pre-Raphaelites is entirely compatible and on every ground to be defended.

The lampooners and disparagers nevertheless were forced to acknowledge the importance and influence of the booklet and its author. In its unfavourable review, *The Art Journal* recognized that

> Pre-Raphaelitism, left to its own merits would have passed away like any other similar specimen of conceit or craft. . . . The author of *Modern*

Painters has, however, conferred a factitious importance on the 'school' as he calls it, by taking it under his protection, and by giving it the benefit of his public advocacy. . . . The hopeful school of P.R.B. . . . are abetted in their folly by the Oxford graduate.

That the Pre-Raphaelites had been 'abetted' by Ruskin was undeniable; even those who wished they had 'passed away' now had to take them seriously. Furthermore, if England's most eminent art critic approved of these young men, less valiant and knowledgeable souls became able to summon up courage to discuss candidly and even admit a liking for a P.R.B. picture.

The most convincing demonstration of the respectability conferred by Ruskin on the Brotherhood came in November 1851. Early in August, Hunt and Millais had travelled from Surrey to London to collect their paintings from The Exhibition, which closed on August Bank Holiday. Since Millais's pictures had been sold, he merely arranged to distribute them to their owners, but Hunt decided to exhibit his unsold *Valentine Rescuing Sylvia* in Liverpool. Founded in 1810, the Liverpool Academy had held its first exhibition in 1814, and seventeen years later gave its first annual price of £50 to the work which was judged to be the best in the show. (Since its exhibition began late in August, it welcomed entries that had hung in Trafalgar Square.) Hunt received by mail, shortly after the opening, a few insulting letters and abusive newspaper clippings; but after this emotional eruption subsided he gave little thought to his picture until one morning early in November he received a letter from Liverpool announcing, to his astonishment, that he had won the £50 prize with *Valentine Rescuing Sylvia from Proteus.* William Rossetti excitedly declared in *The Spectator* that 'one of the most advanced signs of the times shoots meteorlike from the provinces across the London fog which encrusts Trafalgar Square'.[1] He might have added that, however open-minded the directors of the Liverpool Academy were, even they almost certainly would not have honoured a Pre-Raphaelite painter if the trail had not been blazed by John Ruskin.

[1] *The Art Journal,* on the other hand, expressing the prevailing journalistic point of view, declared that the Liverpool Academy 'has procured itself a somewhat unenviable notoriety . . . this act . . . has already thrown dissension among its members . . . there cannot be a doubt that many of its friends will be alienated from the institution by the perpetration of such a folly of a few of the Liverpool academicians'. He who should receive most credit (or blame) for giving the award to Hunt was William L. Windus, a talented painter who had seen and admired the Pre-Raphaelite works in London and then spoken persuasively to his colleagues in Liverpool. Soon thereafter Windus himself became a convert to Pre-Raphaelitism.

Hunt's good fortune did not end there. Soon he received a letter from a Belfast shipping agent, one Francis MacCracken, offering to buy *Valentine Rescuing Sylvia* (without seeing it) for Hunt's posted price, £150.

But one Brother was not sharing the newly-won limelight and prosperity. Rossetti's name had never been publicly mentioned by Ruskin, who was hardly aware of his existence—clear indication of why it was essential for an unestablished artist to exhibit his work. Gabriel's attitude towards exhibitions, however, had not greatly changed. In August he wrote to his Aunt Charlotte concerning Lady Bath's advice that he exhibit *Ecce Ancilla Domini* in Liverpool:

> As regards Lady Bath's idea about sending my little picture to Liverpool, I should certainly have done so (or else to Manchester or Birmingham) last year, had the thing been of a more popular character. Even were it only a *little* less peculiar, I would have done so for the sake of the chance; but, as it is, I know by experience that you might as well expect a Liverpool merchant to communicate with his Chinese correspondent without the intervention of someone who knows the language as imagine that he could look at the picture in question with the remotest glimmering of its purpose. This is the reason which has prevented me from sending it anywhere; particularly as it would be sure to come back with the frame knocked to pieces, and as it is a very bad thing for any artist, without some definite chance of sale, to exhibit any picture a second time, and to let everyone know that he has not sold it.

When he wrote this piece of rationalization, Rossetti was no longer working with Deverell; late in May he had left Red Lion Square and gone to 17 Newman Street, where he again shared a studio with Ford Madox Brown. We cannot be certain why Gabriel left his congenial friend—but his jealousy and sensitivity concerning Elizabeth Siddal (on one occasion he had excoriated Stephens because of a harmless remark he regarded as a slur on his beloved) might well have led him to withdraw her from the constant company of one of the most remarkably handsome young men in London. This postscript to a letter dated 2 January 1851, to Stephens from John Tupper, who had expected Deverell to replace Collinson in the Brotherhood, might suggest why Rossetti may have been apprehensive about his handsome friend: 'Happy New Year to you! and P. R. B. to Deverell. I suppose tonight eh? You may interpret P.R.B. "Penis rather better" —which to him is important.' Moreover, Deverell lived as well as worked in the Red Lion Square studio, and so Rossetti could never have had much time alone with Lizzy. But in Newman Street Brown no longer maintained his residence—for he had apparently married again and was the father of an infant daughter.

In 1849, while he had been in Stratford-on-Avon painting a portrait of Shakespeare, twenty-eight-year-old Brown and Emma Hill, the fifteen-year-old daughter of a farmer's widow, met, fell in love, and contemplated marriage. Mrs Hill objected to Brown's suit, more because of what she fancied to be the disreputability of his profession than their disparate ages or his financial status; and so the couple eloped. Because young Emma was uneducated and uncultured, so it has been said, Brown concealed his marriage until the birth of his daughter early in 1851, after which he spent most of his time in their simple family cottage in Hampstead. Everyone who has written on the subject, including Brown's grandson, has been extremely vague concerning the time and place of the wedding. The cause of this vagueness might perhaps lie in the General Registry Office, in Somerset House, whose official, well-kept records make no mention of any union between Ford Madox Brown and Emma Hill. In any event, married or not Brown was frequently absent from London and 17 Newman Street was a most convenient place for Rossetti to paint and to entertain Lizzy.

Partly because of his unceasing obsession with 'Guggums', as he called Lizzy, Rossetti painted and wrote little at this time. From the day that he moved into Red Lion Square, in January 1851, until midsummer in 1852, he completed only two original poems—'Dante at Verona', begun several years earlier, and the sonnet 'On the "Vita Nuova" of Dante'—and only two pictures worthy of mention, the small water-colours *Beatrice at a Marriage Feast Denies Dante her Salutation* and *Borgia*.

On 11 November 1848, Gabriel had written to his father's friend and benefactor Charles Lyell, 'Ever since I have read the *Vita Nuova*, I have always borne it in mind as a work offering admirable opportunities for pictorial illustration: a task which I am now resolved to attempt.'

His three current compositions inspired by Dante, more particularly Dante's love of Beatrice, reveal the Italian poet's continuing influence on Rossetti—and also show his romantic readiness to relate his own passion to that of his Florentine namesake. The poems were prompted by his recently completed translation of the *Vita Nuova*, and pay tribute to Dante's adoration of Beatrice. The Dantesque water-colour drawing (fourteen by seventeen inches) shows the Florentine poet encountering a bridal procession, from which a child and three female attendants have stepped aside to pause before him. While the child hands him a flower, two of the women look interestedly at the solemn, black-garbed stranger, but the tall central figure, Beatrice, with her excellently formed head held high on her long neck, stands regally aloof, as unconcerned as if she were waiting on a customer in a Cranbourne Street bonnet shop.

Yet although Gabriel was not producing much, the quality of his output was high: both *Beatrice at a Wedding Feast* and *Borgia* were superior to more than a few works hanging on important gallery walls. The latter picture, only nine by ten inches, is a striking group centred round Lucrezia, who sits and plays a lute. While two children dance in the foreground, her father, the lecherous Pope Alexander VI, leans over her left shoulder, and immediately to her right, beating time with a knife against a wine glass and blowing rose petals from her hair, stands her cruel-faced brother Cesare. Perhaps because she was not modelled on Lizzy, Lucrezia's head is not outstanding; but her elaborately embroidered gown was excellently painted and the delineation of the two men showed that Rossetti could create superior male portraits. Taken as a whole, *Borgia* is a well-proportioned, dramatic composition, of which *The Quarterly Review* said, some years after his death, 'no drawing of Rossetti has finer qualities than this, regarded apart from its technical merits, and purely as a study of humanity'.[1]

In addition to the four completed works, during 1851 and the first half of 1852 Rossetti began one of his most celebrated poems, 'Sister Helen', and made the first designs for three important pictures—*How They Met Themselves*, *Found*, and *Giotto Painting the Portrait of Dante*, only the last of which was completed before the end of 1852. *How They Met Themselves* was not finished until 1860, and *Found* was never completed; but since they were conceived in 1851, it is worthwhile looking at them briefly here.

While Hunt was in Surrey painting his contemporary scene, Rossetti also turned to a modern subject in *Found*. This painting depicts a wealthy city dweller's discarded mistress, formerly a country girl, who is crouching against a wall and trying to hide her face from her childhood sweetheart, a drover, who has recognized her while on

[1] 'Dante Gabriel Rossetti,' July 1896, p. 1906.

his way to market. William Bell Scott always asserted that the impulse for *Found* came from his own poem 'Rosabell', which refers to a more or less similar incident. Rossetti may have been influenced by 'Rosabell', but the question is not important. Scott did not discover the 'fallen woman' theme; the idea had appealed to other Victorian artists, such as George F. Watts in *Found Drowned*, painted in 1850, and R. S. Stanhope, in *Thoughts of the Past*, a picture of 1852, and Rossetti himself had begun two poems—'Jenny' and 'A Last Confession'—which deal with variations of the theme. More important than connections between *Found* and 'Rosabell' is the fact that this painting was Rossetti's only endeavour conceived and begun, as Hunt said, wholly 'in accordance with our [Pre-Raphaelite] aims'. In painting *Found*, Rossetti intended to be as faithful to nature as Hunt or Millais or Collins might have been with the same subject matter. *Found* is not at all typical of Rossetti's work, for as *The Academy* observed less than a year after his death, this painting 'like the Jenny in his poems, is almost the only sign that this self-absorbed man ever looked beyond his own life and garden, and the sanctum of his fancy, into the street and palpitating world with which he lived surrounded'.[1]

How They Met Themselves is very different: a pen-and-ink design representing a young couple in a woodland at twilight, suddenly coming face to face with their own doubles. The lady faints, and her lover reaches for his sword. This curious creation bears some resemblance to the poem Rossetti began at this time, 'Sister Helen', which tells of a young woman who brings about the torturous death of her unfaithful lover by slowly melting his wax image. Neither the picture nor the poem can be called Pre-Raphaelite: both are unearthly, macabre products of a vividly active imagination which had been stimulated by reading.

Also at this time Rossetti was earning some money by executing a few fanciful Dantesque water-colours, which, according to Hunt, 'he sold for small sums to artists having independent means'. Producing these potboilers gave Rossetti some practice with water-colours, but not much else: certainly they were unrelated to Pre-Raphaelitism,

[1] 6 January 1883, p. 14. Rossetti's momentary preoccupation with realism is revealed by a postscript to an 1852 letter to John Tupper, who in a minor way was associated with one of London's hospitals: 'Are there any opportunities at the Hospital of seeing such a thing as a dying boy? Consequent emotions in bystanders face desirable—mother especially so—If you have any youth in such a position, and he is accessible, I wish you would let me know before the looks are entirely vacant.' *Letters of Dante Gabriel Rossetti*, ed. by Doughty and Wahl, vol. I, p. 106.

since, as Hunt remarked, they 'gave little opportunity of drawing from the life'. It was simply because he would not, or could not, 'draw from life' that Rossetti was not, and would never be, a Pre-Raphaelite painter. As a movement, Pre-Raphaelitism was both negative and positive: it rebelled against contemporary conventions of painting, but at the same time it insisted upon uncompromising fidelity to nature. Rossetti could be called a Pre-Raphaelite only in the negative sense of the term, for although he repudiated the traditions attached to the name of Sir Joshua Reynolds, he did not share his principal colleagues' devotion to nature. As we have seen, whereas Hunt had been stimulated by Ruskin, Rossetti had received his greatest artistic influence from Blake, who, like Ruskin, rejected Reynolds but, unlike Ruskin, turned not to nature but to himself. For Blake an artist should not appeal to any outside force, neither other artists nor nature, to supply the source of his creativity. This creativity was to be found only within his own individual, unique imagination. Rossetti followed in the footsteps of Blake partly because his own self-willed temperament was in tune with that of the earlier poet-artist and partly because his indolence made it difficult, if not impossible, for him to adhere for long to the stringent, demanding doctrines of Holman Hunt. His two Pre-Raphaelite paintings had each taken from him many months of arduous work, but now he was turning out acceptable water-colours in a few hours. Rossetti was not renouncing the principles of Pre-Raphaelitism, for he had never really accepted them. Working under the direct supervision of Hunt, he had painted two genuinely Pre-Raphaelite pictures, but now, possessed of a measure of self-confidence, Rossetti the painter would do as Rossetti the poet had always done. He would find his inspiration within himself, and he was never again to complete an authentic Pre-Raphaelite painting.

Rossetti's current water-colours did not bring in much of an income. For his livelihood Rossetti still looked to relatives, most especially to Aunt Charlotte and William. His finances became even more shaky after Lizzy left her millinery job towards the end of 1851; and William said, 'how he managed to support himself, much less Miss Siddal, is a mystery'. She earned some money from modelling, but not much—Gabriel allowed her to sit only for close friends and associates, such as Millais, who in 1851–2 painted the most celebrated non-Rossettian picture of Elizabeth Siddal.

When he returned from Surrey to London late in autumn, Millais had completed the elaborate background for *The Death of Ophelia,* and he asked Lizzy to pose for the drowning girl. She had to lie, fully clothed, in a large bathtub filled with water, which was heated by lamps beneath the tub. During the last session, the lamps burned out; but Millais, engrossed in his work, was unaware of the mishap, and Lizzy, fearful of disturbing him, said nothing, and lay still for several hours in cold water. She contracted a severe cold, and her father—who did not take kindly to his daughter's association with artists—threatened to bring suit for £50; but the matter was settled amicably when Millais paid for Lizzy's medical expenses.

Although she had sat constantly for Gabriel, Lizzy appeared on a gallery wall in the summer of 1852 only in the role of Ophelia, for again Rossetti submitted nothing to an exhibition. His friends, however, were well represented in Trafalgar Square, with three entries from Millais, three from Collins, two from Brown, and one each from Stephens (his R.A. debut), Cave Thomas, the Pre-Raphaelites' associate from the days of *The Germ,* and Hunt.

Before the opening of The Exhibition, the Pre-Raphaelites had noted several encouraging signs of a new attitude towards them. In December 1851, the first serious and sympathetic magazine article on their movement was published—a twenty-two-page critique in the newly established *Irish Quarterly Review.* The writer, making a commendable effort to understand the objectives and evaluate the achievements of the Pre-Raphaelite Brothers, recognized that these young men were controversial because their work embodied 'peculiarities of style and a departure from the beaten track', and because they 'seem energetically to strive by careful study of nature to substitute some better methods' of painting for those taught by the Royal Academy. Instead of being reviled, the article said, they should be applauded for trying to free themselves from Academic conformity, for it had always been 'the besetting sin of Academies' to insist on 'the study of art' rather than 'the study of nature', and because 'Academies are admirably adapted for the producing of a certain mediocrity in art, but are uncongenial to higher development'.

The author judged the Pre-Raphaelites to be men of 'very keen vision', and, he concluded, whether they 'will realize the high hopes and expectations Mr Ruskin indulges in—and "found a new and noble school in England", remains to be seen, but that they possess the essential qualities likely to lead them to greatness—industry, perseverance, and earnestness, is undeniable'. A few months earlier, it would have been inconceivable for a serious writer—even in Ireland—to prophesy possible greatness for the Pre-Raphaelite Brotherhood. More doors than one had been opened by John Ruskin—and some rather closer to home than Liverpool or Dublin.

Soon after sending-in day, Millais went to a party in London, and the next morning he wrote, 'I heard many very cheering remarks about my pictures from Academicians, one of whom went so far as to say they were the best paintings in the Exhibition.'[1] The pictures alluded to were *The Death of Ophelia*, and *A Huguenot on St Bartholomew's Day Refusing to Shelter Himself from Danger by Wearing the Roman Catholic Badge*, which together with Hunt's *The Hireling Shepherd* were the principal Pre-Raphaelite paintings of 1852. (Millais's third exhibited work was a small portrait of Mrs Coventry Patmore.) Inspired by Queen Gertrude's beautiful speech at the close of Act IV of *Hamlet*, which begins with 'There is a willow', *Ophelia* shows Shakespeare's heroine, an excellent likeness of Lizzy, floating on a stream, surrounded by perhaps the most painstakingly detailed landscape that had ever been seen on the walls of the Academy. Indeed on at least one occasion a professor of botany who had been prevented by bad weather from conducting a field trip, lectured before Millais's painting, from which, he said, his students could learn as much as from nature. But the great popularity of this picture has resulted less from its extraordinary vegetation (painted along the Ewell River near Kingston), than from its human figure. Not only is she an excellent likeness of Elizabeth Siddal, but this young lady with the finely formed face (whose open mouth signifies that she is still singing), the exquisite floating hair, and the expressive hands, seems surely to represent just how the mad Ophelia must have looked just before she died. One of Millais's most lauded works, *The Death of Ophelia* has been called 'a picture of uncanny beauty'[2] and 'the supreme achievement of Pre-Raphaelitism.'[3]

Millais began his other major work of the season, *A Huguenot*, by carefully and faithfully painting an ivy-mantled wall in Surrey, intend-

[1] Some of the R.A.s, however were still far from cordial towards Millais and his fellow innovators. At about this time James Ward, R.A. wrote thus to H. W. Pickersgill, R.A. concerning artistic reform: 'I *abominate* the movement, and shall heartily rejoice in finding in *that*, and *every other spirit of innovation* DESTROYED.' M. H. Spielmann, 'Behind the Scenes of the Royal Academy Exhibition', *Pall Mall Gazette*, 1901, p. 102.

[2] *Saturday Review*, 15 January 1898, p. 74. [3] *Nation*, 27 August 1896, p. 157.

ing it to be the background for a scene with two indeterminate lovers. When he had drawn pencil sketches of the lovers he showed them to Hunt, who, Millais's son related,

strongly objected to his choice, saying that a simple pair of lovers without any powerful story, dramatic or historical, attaching to the meeting was not sufficiently important. It was hackneyed and wanting in general interest. 'Besides', he quietly added, 'it has always struck me as being the lovers' own private affair, and I feel as if we were intruding on so delicate an occasion by even looking at the picture. I protest against that kind of art.'[1]

While discussing this question with Hunt and Collins, Millais suddenly recalled Meyerbeer's opera *The Huguenots*, and, in the words of his son, 'bethought him that a most dramatic scene could be made from the parting of the two lovers'. (Like a good Pre-Raphaelite, Millais attended a performance of the opera in order to study the actions and costumes of the lovers.) The historical basis for the opera and the painting lies in the sixteenth-century conflict between French Catholics and Protestants, specifically the proclamation issued by Parisian Catholic Duke of Guise in August 1572: 'When the clock of the Palais de Justice shall sound upon the great bell at daybreak, then each good Catholic must bind a strip of white linen round his arm, and place a fair white cross in his cap.' The painting itself was described by the artist, while still in Surrey, thus:

It is a scene supposed to take place (as doubtless it did, on the eve of the massacre of St Bartholomew's Day. I shall have two lovers in the act of parting, the woman a Papist and the man a Protestant. The badge worn to distinguish the former from the latter was a white scarf on the left arm. Many were base enough to escape murder by wearing it. The girl will be endeavouring to tie the handkerchief round the man's arm, so to save him; but he, holding his faith above his greatest worldly love, will be softly preventing her. . . . The figures will be talking against a secret-looking garden wall, which I have painted here.

Millais' painting is a splendid realization of his intentions. The Huguenot—immovable, placid, tender but firm, fully cognizant of what awaits him on the following day—might have been the personification of Richard Lovelace's lines

I could not love thee, dear, so much,
Loved I not honour more.

The crowning feature of this picture is the Huguenot's pleading, adoring mistress who embraces him for the last time, and shares with

[1] *The Life and Letters of Sir John Millais*, p. 136.

Ophelia the chronological priority among her creator's excellent portraits of young women. When the two works were first exhibited, *A Huguenot* was even more highly praised than *Ophelia*. 'One such picture', William Rossetti wrote in *The Spectator*, 'tells us more of what Pre-Raphaelitism *is* than all the arguments of four years.' A less subjective writer than William Rossetti observed at the end of the season that 'almost unanimously critics have pronounced this picture the gem of the Exhibition'.[1]

Hunt's painting, *The Hireling Shepherd*, also represents—as mentioned before—a pair of lovers, but they contrast strikingly with the Huguenot and his mistress. The idea for this picture came initially from a portion of Edgar's song in *King Lear*:

> Sleepest or wakest thou, jolly shepherd?
> Thy sheep be in the corn;
> And, for one blast of thy minikin mouth,
> Thy sheep shall take no harm.

In the painting a young shepherd and his country girl are shown idling away their time beneath a tree while the sheep wander unattended. She is shrinking back from the death's-head moth he has just caught, while at the same time feeding unripe apples to a lamb in her lap. The picture, a characteristic exemplification of Hunt's didacticism, is one of the highly realistic allegories for which he became celebrated. Its intended moral lesson was set forth in the exhibition catalogue: 'Mr Holman Hunt painted his picture in rebuke of the sectarian vanities and vital negligence of the nation.' Although it is clear that by allowing the sheep to run free and the lamb to eat green apples, the shepherd and his lass have neglected their duties, it would seem difficult without the help of the catalogue to interpret the picture in accordance with Hunt's stated purpose. (Indeed it might take some doing after reading the quoted sentence to relate it to the picture.) In order fully to grasp Hunt's object lesson one probably would have to be as perceptive, or imaginative, as one of his biographers, who wrote thus:

> Regarded in a wider sense the moral of *The Hireling Shepherd* may be applied to the world at large. Human affairs are characterized by perpetual disorder because of the tendency of individuals to ignore their most important duties —those which consist in service of others—and, instead, to concentrate their thoughts on selfish and useless pleasures. Restraint becomes irksome,

[1] 'Pre-Raphaelitism in Art and Literature', *British Quarterly Review*, August 1852, p. 218.

important matters of life are forgotten since pleasure and amusement have usurped their place, and while the mind is absorbed in trifles, essentials are becoming more and more neglected, until irreparable harm is done to society, and until the disorder produced by this lack of restraint constitutes a problem with which no government can deal.[1]

Perhaps Hunt was thinking of something like this when he painted *The Hireling Shepherd*, but it is by no means necessary to see in the picture an admonition of any kind. One certainly should be permitted to regard the painting only as a fine Wordsworthian pastoral scene whose realistic details—the vegetation, the animals, and, especially, the sunlight—show a fine feeling for and love of nature. As a contemporary writer said, 'Such corn, such sheep, such meadows, such rows of trees, and such cool grass and wild flowers to sit amidst, are not to be found in any painting that we know.'[2] And thirty-four years later, when the picture again was exhibited J. B. Atkinson passed the following judgment on it:

A more solid and brilliant piece of realism was never thrown out of hand: neither Van Eyck nor Memling, Bellini nor Basaiti, in his landscape accessories carried out naturalism with greater force or detail. This nature-study rivals the exactitude of science; yet, though conducted fearlessly and fiercely, permitting no compromise or surrender; the picture comes together with little sacrifice of the unity imperative in art. The sunlight scorching the rank verdure is as terrific as a sunstroke, yet the cool shadows cast by overhanging trees go far to mitigate the intolerable heat.[3]

Although the painting did not escape censure—*The Athenaeum*, for example, complained that Hunt 'revels in the repulsive' and that his rustics 'are of the coarsest breed—ill favoured, ill fed, ill washed', whose faces 'suggest their overattention to the beer or cyder keg on the boor's back'—*The Hireling Shepherd* was Holman Hunt's most favourably received work up to this time. *The British Quarterly Review* voiced the opinion of many by declaring that 'The picture is, in all respects, one of the best in the exhibition.'

In 1852, the Council abolished the much-criticized privilege of three varnishing days for R.A.s and A.R.A.s, and so all of the exhibiting artists gathered on opening morning to touch up their paintings. This time Hunt's and Millais' pictures were ideally hung at eye

[1] A. C. Gissing, *William Holman Hunt*, p. 77.

[2] 'Pre-Raphaelitism in Art and Literature', *British Quarterly Review*, August 1852, p. 216.

[3] J. B. Atkinson, 'Mr Holman Hunt: His Work and Career', *Blackwood's Magazine*, vol. 139, April 1886, p. 544.

level, and the artists received warm congratulations from many fellow exhibitors, including several R.A.s—one of whom prophetically remarked, 'Well, it seems as though the P.R.B. are looking up.'

For the entire Pre-Raphaelite circle, only one incident marred the 1852 opening: an episode involving Ford Madox Brown, whose exhibited pictures were *Christ Washing Peter's Feet* and *The Pretty Baa Lambs.* The former with its eye-catching vitality, its incisive realism, its excellent heads, and its rich colours, was probably his best work up till then, and has been one of the most highly praised of all English religious paintings.[1] *The Pretty Baa Lambs* depicts a mother and her baby (posed by Brown's new wife and daughter) playing on a lawn with two lambs. It was painted entirely out-of-doors, and because of its depiction of nature, including the sunshine, Stephens said it 'might have been a chef-d'oeuvre of Mr Holman Hunt's realistic theories'. The meticulous details show, as the author of the first illustrated book on the Pre-Raphaelites, Percy Bate observed, 'that if the teachings of Madox Brown influenced the young artists of the Pre-Raphaelite Brotherhood, their love of minuteness of realization reacted on the older artist'. Unlike Hunt, however, Brown attached no symbolic significance to his painting; he said he intended only to show a mother and daughter playing together and to portray this open air scene 'as well as my powers in a first attempt of this kind would allow'. On varnishing day when the future President of the Academy, Francis Grant, R.A., came over to speak to him, Brown, without saying a word, astonishingly turned his back and strode from the building, later vowing that never again would he submit anything to this exhibition. The traditional explanation of this extraordinarily rude behaviour is that Brown was infuriated to discover both of his paintings near the ceiling, and was sure their positioning had been malicious. In point of fact, many pictures, including Brown's were not ideally hung because of a shortage of space allotted to the Academy, which still shared a building with the National Gallery. Neither of his works, however, was hung, as his grandson insisted, 'next the ceiling'. *The Pretty Baa Lambs* was placed in the Octagon Room, which, to be sure, was the R.A.'s least desirable gallery, but it stood in a fairly good light about two feet from the floor. As for *Christ Washing*

[1] Among the models for this painting were Stephens, who sat for Christ; William Rossetti and Holman Hunt, who posed for the second and third apostles from the left; and Deverell and Gabriel Rossetti, who represented the first and second apostles from the right.

Peter's Feet, it was exhibited in the coveted West Room, along with Hunt's picture and both of Millais's major paintings. Although it did not hang at eye level, it was in a good light with its lower margin no more than six feet from the ground. It hardly could have been 'skied' since on varnishing day a couple of drops of wet paint fell onto it from a picture directly above that was being touched up. When Grant approached Brown, he came to apologize for the accident and to assure him that since the picture had been cleaned at once, no damage had been done to it. But before Grant could speak, Brown had left the room.[1]

With this exception, 1852 was a year of almost unqualified success for the whole Pre-Raphaelite coterie. There were, to be sure, some half-hearted attempts to ridicule them. It was said that Ophelia could not have floated so comfortably, that the Huguenot's arm could not have extended so far around his mistress's neck, and that nasturtiums (seen in *A Huguenot*) are not in bloom on 24 August. This last rebuke made by the critic for *The Athenaeum* showed how hard pressed he was to find fault; it revealed only that he was ignorant of the fact that in France, where the scene was set, these flowers *do* blossom in August. None of the unfriendly journals, however, not even *The Times*, could forestall the triumph of 1852. As *The British Quarterly Review* observed, 'The Pre-Raphaelite paintings of the present year, and especially those of Millais, have been more widely commented on, and more heartily praised than any others in the Exhibition. Millais and Pre-Raphaelitism have, indeed, been the talk of this metropolitan season.'[2] The most eloquent example of this new opinion of Millais was a column in *Punch*, written by Tom Taylor:

I have this year experienced a new sensation at the Exhibition of the Royal Academy, and I hasten to record my sense of the obligation to Mr Millais. I offer my hand to that Pre-Raphaelite brother. I bow down to him, and kiss the edge of his palette. I have rapped him over the knuckles, in former years, with my pen. He is at liberty to return the compliment, this year, with his maul-stick. Before two pictures of Mr Millais I have spent the happiest hour that I have ever spent in the Royal Academy Exhibition. . . .

In those two pictures I find more loving observation of Nature, more mastery in the reproduction of her forms and colours . . . a deeper feeling of human emotion, a happier choice of a point of interest, and a more truthful

[1] For an authoritative account of the Brown-Grant incident, see *The Athenaeum*, 13 March 1897, p. 353.

[2] 'Pre-Raphaelitism in Art and Literature', August 1852, p. 213.

rendering of its appropriate expression than in all the rest of those eight hundred squares of canvas put together . . . I may be heretical. I cannot help it. R.A.s and A.R.A.s I admire you—I respect you—I appreciate your skill; and I would gladly purchase your works, if I could afford it. But for this year give me Mr Millais. He has painted 'Ophelia' . . . Talk as you like . . . about the needless elaboration of those watermosses, and the over making out of the rose-leaves, and the abominable finish of those river-side weeds matted with gossamer, which the field botanist may identify leaf by leaf. I tell you I am aware of none of these. I see only that face of poor drowning Ophelia. My eye goes to that, and rests on that, and sees nothing else, till . . . the tears blind me, and I am fain to turn away from the face of the mad girl to the natural loveliness that makes her dying beautiful. . . . Of [*A Huguenot*] also, I boldly say, as I said of the other, there is not a whit too much of nicety, or precision, or finish in the details and accessories. Here, again, what I first see, in spite of myself, is the subtle human emotion of those two faces. All the rest I may find out when I have satisfied myself with that. . . . There is all that accuracy of eye and power of hand can do in these pictures, but there is still more of thought and brain. The man who painted these pictures thought them out. He had a meaning to express, and he expressed it. He felt his subject and he makes me feel it. . . . To all R.A.s and A.R.A.s, whether their subjects be rustic or heroic, fanciful or historical, of the past or present, I say, go and do likewise. Unless you can give me a pleasure of the same kind as these pictures give me you do nothing. Before them, I commune with the painter's thoughts; before your works I criticize coloured canvas.

Other critics were less expansive than Taylor, but most acknowledged that Millais had scored a spectacular victory. Even *The Athenaeum*'s reviewer grudgingly owned that he was 'the Raphael of our Pre-Raphaelites, whose powers of thought, execution and industry are undeniable'; and admitted that Millais and his brothers 'are not losing ground; their strict observations and minute imitation of Nature seem even to have awakened some of the "older masters" of the Royal Academy to the necessity of paying more attention than they hitherto have to colour and detail'. One sign indeed of the Pre-Raphaelite success was their influence upon artists who were in no way connected with them. This phenomenon was noted by various commentators, such as, for example, a writer for *Fraser's Magazine*, who said:

The pre-Raphaelites have already outlived the scorn and sarcasm of the public, and extorted from the profession the most remarkable recognition of their influence. The last exhibition teemed with little scraps of pre-Raphaelitism, scattered over works entirely different in spiritual character; and Mr Maclise himself has not hesitated to take a hint from their labours . . . We shall see these pre-Raphaelites working out a revolution to which the Royal Academy itself must at last reluctantly submit.[1]

More important to Millais than critical approval was his overwhelming public popularity. Taylor did not exaggerate when he mentioned 'the thousands' who had stood before his paintings: from the opening of the Exhibition on 3 May until its close on August Bank Holiday, there was scarcely a moment when crowds were not gathered around *Ophelia* and *A Huguenot.* The pictures were being reproduced by the thousands, and the dealer who had bought *A Huguenot* sent Millais an additional fifty pounds because of his profits earned from engravings of the painting. Suddenly Millais was the toast of the art world, and—with the possible exception of the animal-painter Edwin Landseer—was the most highly acclaimed youth in the history of British painting.

His conquest provided him with an uninhibited, boyish delight. On 9 June he wrote, 'The immense success I have met with this year has given me a new sensation of pleasure in painting. I have letters almost every day for one or other of the pictures.' In October, he declared, 'It's quite a "lark" now to see the amiable letters I have from Liverpool and Birmingham merchants, requesting me to paint them pictures, of any size, subject, and amount I like—leaving it all to me. I am not likely to let them have anything, as they would probably hawk it about until they obtained their profit.' *A Huguenot* was exhibited in Liverpool, and won the fifty-pound prize; in Birmingham, *Ophelia* barely missed winning a similar award, which went to a historical painting *Charlotte Corday Going to Execution*, by Edward M. Ward, A.R.A. That Millais's name also would soon be followed by initials was taken for granted, and indeed before the end of the year he came close to becoming an Associate of the Royal Academy. On 1 November the Council met to fill a vacancy in the ranks of the A.R.A.s; on the first ballot the painter Frederick Goodall led with seven votes, followed by Millais and a younger brother of the well-known painter Frederick Pickersgill, A.R.A., each with five votes. While the R.A.s were deliberating on who would oppose Goodall in the run-off election, the secretary announced, rather belatedly, that Millais was below the minimum age (twenty-four) for an A.R.A. Subsequently, Goodall became the victorious candidate. Millais was

[1] 'Art and the Royal Academy', *Frazer's Magazine*, August 1852, pp. 233, 235.

furious because of the way in which he had been defeated, and, William Rossetti reported in a lettter to Stephens, he was even 'roused to reopen the often vexed question of setting up a P.R.B. exhibition'. He became 'somewhat calmed', William added, 'by [Charles Robert] Leslie's assurance that his age alone caused his claims to be overlooked'. When an election was next held, he surely would be the most likely person to be selected.

Millais's colleagues also shared in his success. It was altogether a good year for five of the seven P.R.B.s. Although Hunt was overshadowed by Millais, and his picture was occasionally disparaged, *The Hireling Shepherd* received more praise than any of his earlier works; his reputation spread, and at last he was without serious financial worries. Stephens exhibited his first picture at the Academy (a portrait of his mother), and his and William Rossetti's stature as critics increased because of their membership in the Brotherhood. Even Collinson, the only Pre-Raphaelite to enter the National Institution show, tasted some success with his painting, *The Emigration Scheme*, which *The Athenaeum* called a 'great advance upon [his] previous efforts'. The Brothers' closest colleague, Charles Collins, was applauded for his three exhibited paintings, especially the minutely detailed view of Regent's Park as seen from a house in Sussex Place, *May in the Regent's Park*. Further, the Brotherhood as a whole was lauded by the important *British Quarterly Review*, which devoted twenty-four pages to a friendly article on the Pre-Raphaelites; and their doctrines were in a sense vindicated by the Royal Academy itself, when it announced the establishment of a School of Painting from the Living Model.

Only two of the Brothers were left out of this season's good fortune: Thomas Woolner and Gabriel Rossetti.

Although Woolner had six entries in the 1852 R.A. Exhibition, they were minor works which aroused no notice: three portrait medallions, two designs for medals and a sketch for a monument to Wordsworth.

He had never been able to earn much of a livelihood, but he had persevered in his studio until late in the spring of 1852. Then his entry in the competition to erect a statue over Wordsworth's grave, upon which he had staked all his future hopes, was rejected by the Wordsworth Memorial Commission, which selected a contribution from an especially undistinguished competitor. Woolner reacted by angrily smashing a large clay model, the work of many months, and booking passage on a ship bound for Australia. In 1851 gold had been discovered in Australia, and now Britons regarded the southern continent in much the same light as Americans had looked on California. Woolner hoped that after a few years of prospecting he would return, with his fortune made, to his sculpture in London.

Rossetti, too, was contemplating his future. By summer's end, in addition to the earlier mentioned works, he had completed two more water-colours: *The Annunciation*, whose Virgin (modelled by Lizzy) is bathing her feet in a stream; and perhaps his best picture thus far, *Giotto Painting the Portrait of Dante*. This work was inspired by a passage from Dante's *Purgatorio*, and by the 1839 discovery of Giotto's famous portrait of Dante on a wall of the Bargello in Florence. (One of those who had uncovered the picture had sent old Gabriele Rossetti a copy of his finding, and Gabriel had been lastingly impressed by the portrait.) Gabriel's own painting also embodies the well-known lines in Canto XI of the *Purgatorio* concerning the impermanence of artistic or literary fame:

> Cimabue thought
> To lord it over painting's field; and now
> The cry is Giotto's, and his name eclipsed.
> Thus hath one Guido from the other snatch'd
> The lettr'd prize: and he, perhaps, is born,
> Who shall drive either from their nest.[1]

The lines tell of how the reputation of Florence's great painter, Cimabue, was overshadowed by that of his pupil Giotto, and of how the poet Guido Guinicelli was excelled by 'the other' Guido, Dante's friend Cavalcanti, who in turn might some day be surpassed by another (as indeed he would by Dante himself).

Rossetti's picture shows Giotto, on a scaffold, painting the portrait of Dante who is seated to his left cutting a pomegranate. Behind Giotto Cimabue gazes at his work, while leaning behind Dante, Cavalcanti holds a book of poems by Guinicelli. Dante's eye has been caught by a procession of young women, and especially one of them—a girl with reddish-gold hair, holding a book of devotions. She is Beatrice, posed by Elizabeth Siddal. The painting was planned as part of a triptych, which was not completed, but in itself—its figures, its

[1] Dante Alighieri, *Purgatorio*, canto XI, lines 93–98, translation by the Rev. Henry Francis Cary.

composition, and its realization of the underlying idea—it marked a notable step forward in Rossetti's painting career.[1]

Upon completing this work, in September, Rossetti decided to remain aloof no longer from public exhibitions, particularly since it had become profitable to be a Pre-Raphaelite. He would display something as soon as possible; he would not wait for the next summer, but would submit several pictures to a minor exhibition which would begin in December. Also, in the autumn of 1852 Rossetti made a second decision: he felt that he had lived long enough with his family, and so now at the age of twenty-four decided on a home of his own. In November he moved his belongings into new quarters, three rooms and a balcony overlooking the Thames.

[1] Of the significant works from Rossetti's early years as an artist, only *Giotto Painting the Portriat of Dante* is currently unlocated. Even Virginia Surtees, that indefatigable authority on Rossetti's pictures, has no knowledge of its present whereabouts, nor has she met or corresponded with anyone who has seen the picture.

11

The End of the Brotherhood

About the time that Rossetti left his family home, his poetic career received some stimulus with the publication, on October 23, of a poem for the first time in a journal not partly owned by himself. Interestingly, Gabriel was given his first sizeable reading audience by that unbending foe of the Pre-Raphaelites, *The Athenaeum*. But the editor probably did not know the identity of the author, for Rossetti, ever reluctant to commit himself publicly, signed his contribution 'H. H. H.' having taken the initials from the hardest grade of lead pencil because, he said later, 'people used to say my style was hard'. The poem was 'The Card-Dealer', sub-titled 'Or Vingt-et-un. From a Picture.'

It had been composed several years earlier, but it expresses an attitude which typified Rossetti at all times, though especially pertinent to that period when he began his life in the world at large. According to his introductory note, the poem (whose metre is that of 'The Blessed Damozel') was based on a picture by Theodore von Holst[1] which represents a beautiful, richly-dressed woman sitting at a lamp-lit table, dealing out cards, with a peculiar fixedness of expression. In the game she is playing—Vingt-et-un, often called Twenty-One—it is mathematically certain that all players will eventually be subdued by the dealer. No system has been devised to conquer the dealer of Vingt-et-un; the most one can hope for is a brief spell of excitement before going down to inevitable defeat. For Rossetti, Vingt-et-un stands for the game of life, whose dealer is Fate:

[1] It may be remembered that in his first letter to Brown, Rossetti, wrote, 'The outline from your *Abstract of Representation of Justice* . . . constitutes, together with an engraving after that great painter Von Holst, the sole pictorial adornment of my room.'

Whom plays she with? With thee: thou lov'st
    Those gems upon her hand;
With me: I search her secret will.
    All deem her bosom grand.
We play together, she and we,
    Within a vain strange land:

A land without any order,—
    Whose substance is as breath
Where one lying down ariseth not
    Nor the sleeper awakeneth;
A land of darkness as darkness itself
    And of the shadow of death.

. . .

And do you ask what game she plays?
    With *him*, 'tis lost or won;
With *him* it is playing still; with *him*,
    It is not yet begun;
But 'tis a game she plays with all
    The game of Twenty-One.[1]

Three weeks after the publication of his poem, Gabriel acted as imprudently as might be expected of a man to whom life was a capricious game, by moving to new lodgings when he had little money and less hope of future income. His new residence was the third floor of a house in Chatham Place, a handsome residential quadrangle which lay alongside the Thames immediately north of Blackfriars Bridge. The house, number fourteen, stood beside the bridge and overlooked the river.[2] Rossetti was delighted with his residence. He liked the picturesque area; he enjoyed the splendid view from Blackfriars Bridge of the Houses of Parliament, Westminster Abbey, the Tower, St Paul's Cathedral and more; and he revelled in his situation on the river. A large French window in his studio opened onto a balcony from which he had a clear view of the water highway crowded with barges and paddle-wheeled steamboats; the recently constructed pier just beyond the bridge, where steamers discharged and received

[1] These passages are from the 1852 text, which differs from the later, customarily anthologized version of the poem.

[2] Among the other tenants in the building were six life assurance companies, the 'Lord's Day Observance Society', and, in Number 3, the 'London Society for Promoting Christianity among the Jews.' Chatham Place was demolished shortly before the end of the nineteenth century, and the location of Rossetti's house is now covered by the Victoria Embankment.

Courtesy of the Manchester City Art Galleries.

The Hireling Shepherd by Holman Hunt.

Courtesy the Huntingdon Hartford Collection, Gallery of Modern Art, New York.

A Huguenot by Millais.

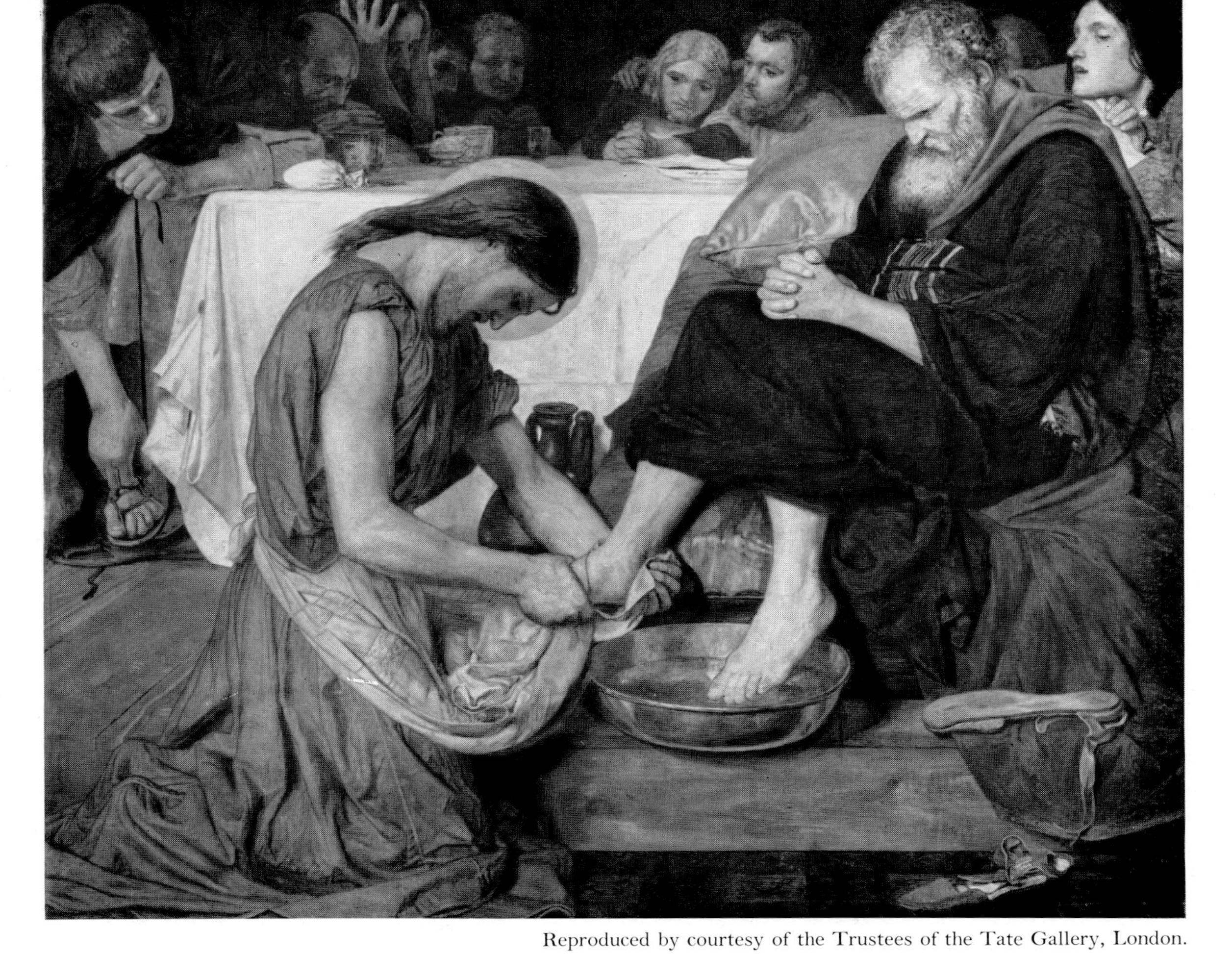

Reproduced by courtesy of the Trustees of the Tate Gallery, London.

Christ Washing Peter's Feet by Ford Madox Brown.

Ashmolean Museum, Oxford.

Beatrice at a Marriage Feast denying her Salutation to Dante by Rossetti.

Ashmolean Museum, Oxford.

Dante Drawing an Angel on the Anniversary of Beatrice's Death by Rossetti.

Reproduced by courtesy of the Trustees of the Tate Gallery, London.

Claudio and Isabella by Holman Hunt.

Reproduced by courtesy of the Trustees of the Tate Gallery, London.

The Strayed Sheep by Holman Hunt.

Reproduced by courtesy of the Trustees of the Tate Gallery, London.

The Order of Release by Millais.

passengers; and the handsome old bridge itself,[1] which teemed with traffic. Rossetti constantly sat on the balcony or stood by one of several windows watching the sights and listening to the sounds. It was a scene of unending fascination.

But living on the river at Blackfriars Bridge was not without drawbacks. A bitterly cold wind blew intermittently throughout the year; the nearby wharves of coal firms, lime and iron establishments, and the Gas Light Company, combined with the river's mud flats at low tide, produced an unsavoury odour; and since the Thames was almost an open sewer, 14 Chatham Place was hardly the healthiest place in London. Rossetti, however, whose weakest sense was that of smell, was no more perturbed by these inconveniences than by his annual rent of forty pounds, payable quarterly, which usually was taken care of by William. To tolerate an unpleasant odour was a small price to pay for complete freedom.

'You can't imagine what delightful rooms these are for a party, regularly built out into the river, and with windows on all sides', Rossetti wrote to Woolner; and on 29 November, six days after his move, he sent a note to Brown, inviting him to his first party, whose guests would also include Hunt, Millais, Stephens, Deverell, Collins and others. During his first few months of residence, Gabriel often celebrated his liberty and relieved his loneliness with festivities in his 'delightful rooms'. He was not always eager, however, to welcome visitors. Thus on only his third day in his new quarters he wrote to William, 'In case I should not see you before then, I write to beg that you will avoid asking [Hunt] (should it enter your head) to come down here on Saturday, as I have Lizzy coming, and do not of course wish for anyone else. I have written to him that I am engaged that evening . . .'[2]

In his 29 November letter to Brown, Rossetti mentioned his first artistic creation on Chatham Place, inspired by an event of 18 November which *The Illustrated London News* called 'one of the most impressive ceremonials ever witnessed in this country; one which, if the moral and personal considerations involved be considered, may be said to have surpassed in significant grandeur any similar tribute to greatness ever offered in the world'. These lofty words referred to the

[1] This was the original structure, which was opened for traffic in 1766 and was demolished and replaced by the present Blackfriars Bridge in 1864.

[2] *Letters of Dante Gabriel Rossetti*, Edited by Doughty and Wahl, vol. 1, p. 115.

state funeral of the greatest nineteenth-century English hero, The Duke of Wellington. In its coverage of the funeral, *The Illustrated London News* remarked that 'the whole of this great British nation had been stirred and moved as by a common impulse'. As if to illustrate this generalization, Rossetti, who was normally oblivious of public affairs, wrote a poem of seventy-eight lines entitled 'Wellington's Funeral'. In a letter to Woolner, he almost apologetically referred to it as 'something *de rigueur* on the Duke of Wellington, which I keep as a monument of the universal influence of public frenzy even on the most apathetic'.

'Wellington's Funeral' was an occasional piece called forth by an exceptional occurrence; its composition did not mean that Rossetti's paramount interest was now literary. On 13 August, indeed, he had written, 'I have abandoned poetry'; and although occasionally he would dash off a poem such as his parody of *Uncle Tom's Cabin* which began 'Dere was an old nigger, and him name was Uncle Tom', for several years thereafter his creative talents would be centred on his painting. When he moved into his new home, and while he was writing the Wellington poem, his most compelling concern was the opening on 6 December of the first exhibition he had entered since the summer of 1850.

In 1849 a Regent Street dealer named Grundy had decided to hold a show in winter when most other galleries were closed, and in November of that year he had sponsored his first exhibition. It had proved to be successful for the artists, and also for the dealers and agents, who received 10 per cent of all sales receipts. In the following winter a competitive Exhibition of Modern British Art was held in the Gallery of the Old Water-Colour Society, at 5 Pall Mall East, where no deductions were taken from sales and no charges imposed for hanging and disposing of works. (All costs, including those of mounting and framing, were covered by revenue received from the sale of admission tickets and catalogues.) Any artist could enter three pictures owned and painted by himself, which might be drawings shown for the first time or sketches for larger pictures that had appeared elsewhere. The exhibition was vastly heterogeneous: works of unknown youngsters hung side by side with those of well-known R.A.s.

In 1852, the Exhibition of Modern British Art was renamed The Winter Exhibition of Sketches and Drawings, and its locale was changed to a gallery at 121 Pall Mall, opposite the Colonnade, where 280 works went on display. Although the show did not measure up to the important summer exhibitions, it was generally well received. *The Literary Gazette* called it 'a select choice from the average productions of some of our best artists'. In its critique, *The Illustrated London News* noted that 'there are pre-Raffaelite efforts in the room, most of which are already ticketed "sold"—an unmistakable evidence of the tendency of the public taste in that direction'. Among the 'pre-Raffaelite efforts' were Brown's sketch for *The Pretty Baa-Lambs* and his 1843 drawing of an infant; Hunt's sketch of *Valentine Reproaching Proteus for His Falsity*; and three works by Rossetti—the water-colour drawings *Rossovestita* and *Beatrice at a Marriage Feast Denies Dante Her Salutation*, and an early pen-and-ink sketch of *Giotto Painting the Portrait of Dante*.

Rossetti's pictures could be called Pre-Raphaelite only by association: in creating them he had paid little heed to Hunt's formulated principles. All three, each of which was priced at twelve pounds or less, found ready buyers and, on 8 January 1853, Rossetti wrote to Woolner, 'I feel I am pretty certain of selling any water-colour drawings I make, and advantageously, the two exhibited having excited a good deal of attention and (unpalatable) praise.'

Rossetti's confidence was swelling, not only because he had sold his currently hanging works but also because, as he told Woolner, 'I have got rid of my white picture to an Irish maniac.' The 'white picture' was *Ecce Ancilla Domini*, and the 'Irish maniac' was Francis MacCracken, the man who had bought Hunt's Liverpool prize painting and who, late in 1852, had bought Brown's *Wickliffe*, which he had seen in Dublin. On Hunt's recommendation, MacCracken became Gabriel's first real patron by agreeing, without seeing it, to pay the original price of fifty guineas for the painting—which Rossetti now called *The Annunciation*, because, William wrote in the *P.R.B. Journal*, he wanted to 'guard against the imputation of "popery".' On 29 January, after he had spent nearly a month retouching the picture, he was sufficiently satisfied with 'the blessed white daub' to ship it to Belfast—and was probably glad to see it go. Of all his creative works it had been the greatest source of annoyance and distress.[1]

[1] Forty-three years later, *The Saturday Review* said the following concerning the picture whose sale Rossetti had thought was a forlorn hope: 'But there must already be quite a number of persons who have seen in Rossetti their first Annunciation. It stands in the National Gallery, it appears in at least one shop window in every street in London; the young person who is now growing up cannot help seeing it, and seeing it before any other Annunciation.'

MacCracken was now corresponding with Ruskin, whose artistic judgment he swore by; before buying *The Annunciation*, he had asked Rossetti for permission to seek Ruskin's opinion of the painting. The permission was promptly denied. Although he paid for the picture without Ruskin's approval, after he received it MacCracken quickly shipped it to Denmark Hill and asked 'the Graduate', as he usually called Ruskin, for his comments. Ruskin praised the oil painting highly, and also spoke well of Rossetti's contributions to the Winter Exhibition. MacCracken immediately sent this news to Rossetti, who on 1 March in a postscript to a letter to Brown made his first written mention of Ruskin in connection with himself:

Please let me know (as soon as possible) whether you ever named to McC. anything regarding the *prices* which I took for those sketches now exhibiting. Ruskin has written him some extravagant praises (those with obtuse accompaniments) upon one of them—I cannot make out which—and McC. seems excited, wanting it, and not knowing (or making believe not to know) that it is sold. I therefore want to be sure whether he is actually acquainted with the price I had; as, in answering him, were I to propose to do him a similar one, I should not think of undertaking it at anything like a similar price, and want to know whether it is necessary to specify that those sketches were sold to *friends*.

The picture that Ruskin extravagantly praised was *Beatrice at a Marriage Feast*.

Rossetti had always maintained a flippant attitude towards critics and patrons,[1] but he was well aware of their importance. On 16 April, he wrote to Woolner:

M'C. sent me a passage from a letter of Ruskin's about my Dantesque sketches exhibited this year . . . Ruskin goes into raptures about the colour and grouping which he says are superior to anything in modern art—which I believe is almost as absurd as certain absurd objections which he makes to them. However, as he is only half informed about Art anything he says in favour of one's work, is of course sure to prove invaluable in a professional way, and I only hope, for the sake of my rubbish, that he may have the honesty to say publicly in his new book what he has said privately, but I doubt this. Oh! Woolner, if one could only find the 'supreme' Carlylian Ignoramus, him who knows positively the least about Art of any living

[1] Perhaps Rossetti's attitude toward patrons, and exhibitions, had been influenced by this passage from Blake's 'Annotations to Sir Joshua Reynolds's Discourses': 'The Rich Men of England form themselves into a Society to Sell and Not to Buy Pictures. The Artist who does not throw his Contempt on such Trading Exhibitions, does not know either his own Interest or his Duty.'

creature—and get *him* to write a pamphlet about one—what a fortune one might make. It now seems that Ruskin had never seen any work of mine before, though he never thought it necessary to say this in writing about the P.R.B.

It was clear that Ruskin could do for Rossetti what already he had accomplished for Hunt and Millais. In his letter to Woolner, Gabriel said that 'Ruskin's opinion (I suppose) has induced [MacCraken] to give me a commission for £150, and I have chosen a subject of the "Virgin in the house of St John" which I am now about.' MacCracken also bought a Rossetti painting for thirty-five guineas; he commissioned the execution of the fallen country girl, *Found*; and throughout the year he sent enthusiastic letters to Chatham Place. On 12 July, Gabriel wrote to his mother,

MacCracken is in a state of wild excitement about some subjects I have been mentioning to him, and wrote me a long letter with full directions as to how I was to get to Belfast at once, and stay with him a little while, when we could arrange everything . . . I shall not go near him for the present, as I think it would be unwise.

But MacCracken was not the only potential patron who had been attracted to Rossetti's work. As Gabriel told Woolner, 'there is another man at Liverpool who has seen the white abomination and wants a picture of mine'. The Liverpudlian was a merchant named John Miller, from whom Rossetti was 'in a fair way', he told Brown, to obtain an even better commission than the best he had received from MacCracken. MacCracken and Miller were typical of their time. All over Great Britain, especially in the manufacturing cities, industrialists were vying with one another to accumulate works of art, an activity of great benefit to the artists. A young painter was fortunate simply to be alive then—but he was thrice blessed if he had gained the approval of Ruskin, whose pronouncements were almost holy writ to the largely uncultivated patrons of art.

One would think that Rossetti would seize on this opportunity to gain fame and fortune. And, for a while, he did work with enthusiasm: 1853 was his most prolific year thus far, for he completed at least a dozen pictures. Only one of these, however, could be called a major work—MacCracken's fine thirty-five-guinea water-colour, *Dante Drawing an Angel in Memory of Beatrice*. This sixteen by twenty-four inch depiction of a passage from the *Vita Nuova* shows a visibly perturbed Dante turning towards three untimely visitors who have called while he was in the midst of drawing a portrait of Beatrice, on the first anniversary of her death.[1] The painting is a vividly coloured, dramatic representation of the incident which two years later Browning would treat in 'One Word More'; and the care Rossetti gave to secondary details—the room furnishings, the River Arno seen through the window, the garden behind the open door—makes this more nearly a 'Pre-Raphaelite' picture than most of his other works.

For several months Rossetti worked on *Dante Drawing an Angel*, and when he completed it, in September, he told William that because the finished product greatly exceeded his original conception, 'the stipulated thirty-five guineas is absurdly under its value now, and I think I must give MacCracken to understand as much'. *Dante Drawing an Angel* was Rossetti's only ambitious, time-consuming endeavour of 1853. His other works were small water-colour drawings or pen-and-ink sketches, none more than ten inches in height or width, all turned out quickly without models. Several of these are interesting, such as the pen-and-ink sketch *Hesterna Rosa* (Yesterday's Rose), which, illustrating one of Rossetti's favourite themes, depicts two dice-throwing gamblers and their mistresses, one of whom embraces her lover while the other, 'yesterday's rose', hides her head in shame. Providing a commentary on the artist's imagination, two other figures complete the picture: a young child playing a lute and an ape idly scratching himself.

Hesterna Rosa was intended to be a sketch for a large oil-painting; but, characteristically, Rossetti never began this work. Nor did he make much effort to fulfil commissions for MacCraken or Miller or any of several other interested patrons. Recognizing that in 1853, as always, he would be impeded most of all by the inability to apply himself, he wrote to Woolner that 'there is a prospect of my getting on all right if I can make myself work'. In January he had told Woolner that he was 'working with a vague reference to the Exhibition', but by the end of the year he had submitted nothing to the Royal Academy or any other exhibition. In autumn, he confessed, 'I have been work-

[1] This is Rossetti's own translation of the *Vita Nuova* passage he illustrated: 'On that day which fulfilled the year since my lady had been made of the citizens of eternal life, remembering me of her as I sat alone, I betook myself to draw the resemblance of an angel upon certain tablets. And while I did thus, chancing to turn my head I perceived that some were standing beside me, to whom I should have given courteous welcome, and that they were observing what I did: also I learned afterwards that they had been there awhile before I perceived them. Perceiving whom, I arose for salutation and said 'Another was with me'.

ing a great deal lately, but somehow it seems impossible to finish anything.' At about the same time, Brown wrote to a friend that 'out of three or four pictures begun he has not finished any, but he has painted and sold three or four lovely Dantesque water-colour drawings'.

The ease with which he now produced small saleable water-colours deterred Rossetti from persevering with more laborious works. And yet, although he received from twelve to twenty-five guineas each for these small pictures, he was not content with what he was doing. He was looking about for more meaningful subjects, and Hunt related that in 1853 Rossetti 'had quite recently read the whole New Testament through from the first word to the last, in the hope of finding some hitherto untreated circumstances suitable for painting'. He was also thinking again about his genuine Pre-Raphaelite painting, *Found*. 'Up to 1853', Hunt remarked, 'Rossetti had not done anything in strict accordance with our exact study of outdoor nature. He had not attempted hitherto to give the truth at first-hand to such accessories.' On 30 September, however, a letter to his mother (who was staying with Mr Rossetti and Christina in the rural town of Frome, in Somerset) showed his desire to follow nature faithfully as he looked forward to painting *Found*:

> I believe I shall be wanting to paint a brick wall, and a white heifer tied to a cart going to market. Such things are I suppose to be had at Frome, and it has occurred to me that I should like if possible to come and paint them there . . . Have you ever seen such an article as the heifer in question, and have you or Christina any recollection of an eligible and accessible brick wall? I should want to get up and paint it early in the mornings, as the light ought to be that of dawn. It should be not too countrified (yet beautiful in colour), as it is to represent a city-wall. A certain modicum of moss would therefore be admissible, but no prodigality of grass, weeds, ivy, etc. Can you give me any information on these heads?

We do not know what information his mother sent him, but, true to form, Gabriel did nothing during the rest of that year to put his ideas onto canvas.

Since in truth he had almost 'abandoned poetry', in 1853 Rossetti wrote only a few short poems, including the spontaneously composed 9 February sonnet 'To Thomas Woolner, inspired by the season's first snowfall', and two or three pieces that were related to his painting. One of these was a parody of Tennyson's youthful study of a legendary Scandinavian sea monster, 'The Kraken'. Rossetti's poem, called 'MacCracken', poked fun at his patron's greedy acquisition of paintings.[1] 'As a picture of facts', William commented, 'the value of "MacCracken" is less than nil; except indeed for its clear implication that Rossetti would have liked to get bigger prices for his performances, from MacCracken or from any one, if only he could have got them.' The poem also shows Rossetti's disdain for those businessmen who recently had become patrons of art—an attitude which he often expressed in conversation and letters, as in a note to Brown on 4 May 1853, where he referred to several merchants, including a Mr T., who were interested in buying paintings:

I understand they have *plenty of tin to begin with*, and I suppose would of course pay well. We agreed that T. had better call on you and come to some understanding . . . The chief thing is, to *lay it on* thick as to payment, as I believe they really have tin. T. is, of course, an ass, and should on principle be treated with ignominy.

[1] Tennyson's poem reads as follows:

Below the thunders of the upper deep,
Far, far beneath in the abysmal sea,
His ancient, dreamless, uninvaded sleep
The Kraken sleepeth: faintest sunlights flee
About his shadowy sides; above him swell
Huge sponges of millenial growth and height;
And far away into the sickly light,
From many a wondrous grot and secret cell
Unnumber'd and enormous polypi
Winnow with giant arms the slumbering green.
There hath he lain for ages, and will lie
Battening upon huge sea-worms in his sleep,
Until the latter fire shall heat the deep;
Then once by man and angels to be seen,
In roaring he shall rise and on the surface die.

And here is Rossetti's parody:

Getting his pictures, like his supper cheap,
Far far away in Belfast by the sea,
His watchful one-eyed uninvaded sleep
MacCracken sleepeth. While the P.R.B.
Must keep the shady side, he walks a swell
Through spungings of perennial growth and height;
And far away in Belfast out of sight,
By many an open do and secret sell
Fresh daubers he makes shift to scarify,
And fleece with pliant shears the slumbering 'green'.
There he has lied, though aged, and will lie,
Fattening on ill-got pictures in his sleep,
Till some Preraphael prove for him too deep.
Then, once by Hunt and Ruskin to be seen,
Insolvent he will turn, and in the Queen's Bench die.

Another 1853 poem prompted by his artistic life was the sonnet now listed as LXV in the *House of Life*, 'Known in Vain':

> As two whose love, first foolish, widening scope,
> Knows suddenly, to music high and soft,
> The Holy of holies; who because they scoff'd
> Are now amazed with shame, nor dare to cope
> With the whole truth aloud, lest heaven should ope;
> Yet, at their meeting, laugh not as they laugh'd
> In speech; nor speak, at length; but sitting oft
> Together, within hopeless sight of hope
> For hours are silent:—So it happeneth
> When Work and Will awake too late, to gaze
> After their life sailed by, and hold their breath.
> Ah! who shall dare to search through what sad maze
> Thenceforth their incommunicable ways
> Follow the desultory feet of Death?

The central idea of this sonnet, as William stated, 'is that of a man who in youth has been feeble in will, indolent and scattered, but who, when too late, wakes up to the duty and privileges of work'. Surely autobiographical, the poem is a fine expression of remorse caused by wasted hours and neglected opportunities.

Rossetti's squandered time resulted in part from his own indolent nature, but was also an effect of the presence of Elizabeth Siddal. They were together even more constantly than in 1851 and 1852, since Gabriel was living alone and Lizzy had moved from her family home into a room of her own on Rossetti's side of the river. She spent most of her time at 14 Chatham Place, for, as William said, Gabriel's rooms 'were now Miss Siddal's chief shelter from an unsympathetic world'. Here she was a model, a companion, a mistress, and a creative artist.

Rossetti had begun earlier to encourage Lizzy to draw and to paint, and was delighted to discover that she had a real aptitude for art. She enjoyed sketching, and within a few months she was showing considerable proficiency. Although she had never done any drawing, and received no instruction other than informal lessons from Rossetti, by the end of 1853 she had created a number of surprisingly good pen-and-ink and water-colour drawings—including her fine self-portrait, which William called 'an absolute likeness', and scenes from various poems. She was an avid reader of verse and before the end of 1853—again urged by her lover—she began to compose poems, generally mournful lyrics which seemed to serve as an outlet for some of her innermost feelings.

Rossetti's enthusiasm for the creative efforts of his protegé, who he was convinced was no less than a genius, caused him to neglect his own work in order to help her. In August he wrote to Brown, 'Liz has made a perfect wonder of her portrait, which is nearly done, and which I think we shall send to the Winter Exhibition.' (Neither the portrait nor any of her other drawings was submitted to the exhibition.) Later he told Brown that 'her power of designing ever increases greatly, and her fecundity of invention and facility are quite wonderful, much greater than mine'. This outburst, William said, may 'be a lover's exaggeration, but not mere nonsense'. Hunt, too, saw Lizzy's gift when, on Rossetti's request, he looked at some of her drawings. 'I complimented them fully', Hunt related, 'and said that had I come on them without explanation I would have assumed they were happy designs by Deverell. "Deverell!" he exclaimed, "they are a thousand times better than anything he ever did".'

Because of Rossetti's sensitivity towards Lizzy, and because it was evident he wished to be alone with her, his friends seldom visited 14 Chatham Place after his first few months there, and the once frequent parties became rare occurrences. The couple whiled away their time sketching, reading, talking, and sitting on the balcony watching the rest of the world pass beneath them. Rossetti's way of life was as unmethodical and unsystematic as ever: he drew, wrote, retired, and ate (usually in restaurants because his apartment had no cooking facilities) whenever he felt so inclined; his rooms remained in a notorious state of disorder; and, perhaps to symbolize his new freedom, he grew a full beard. Lizzy apparently never complained about these living conditions. She rarely had visitors of her own, and apparently her only friend was Brown's wife, the former Emma Hill. (Since their mothers had known each other, Lizzy's friendship with Emma probably antedated her introduction to Gabriel, and perhaps it was because of this earlier acquaintance that Rossetti was often furiously jealous of Emma, and objected to any familiarity between the two young women.)

The most frequent guest at 14 Chatham Place was William, who sometimes slept in this conveniently located apartment, a few minutes' walk from his office in Somerset House, where in late summer he was promoted to a position with a salary of £250. As for his parents and

Christina, Gabriel occasionally saw them early in the year, but hardly at all after mid-spring, when they had moved to Somerset. The Arlington Street day-school had not been profitable, and Mr Rossetti's health had steadily declined, so Mrs Rossetti seized the chance offered by a clergyman friend to open a school in Somerset. Maria remained in town, but she and Gabriel, hardly birds of a feather, saw little of each other. At the end of 1853 the senior Rossettis and their daughters had still not been introduced to Miss Siddal, although for well over a year they had known about her, since Gabriel's letter to Christina on 4 August 1852, refers familiarly to her (as 'the Sid'). And Gabriel had not yet visited the Southwark home of the Siddals.

During most of 1853 Rossetti remained in London, occasionally visiting Brown and other friends in Hampstead. But once he left the city for four weeks. On 15 June, he wrote to his financial mainstay, Aunt Charlotte,

> I am going to or near Newcastle with our friend Mr Scott for a week or so . . . I am obliged to leave town without more delay, by continually returning illness, which I ought to have tried to shake off before by change of air. I am doing some work which will not take long to finish on my return, and for which I shall get paid immediately. Meanwhile, if you could increase my obligations to you by a loan of ten or twelve pounds, I would engage faithfully to return it as soon as I get the money in question, of where there is no doubt . . . I think I am going to start tomorrow for Tynemouth, which is a watering-place near Newcastle. I hope the sea-air will do me some good, as I have long been in want of it. I shall bathe, and try to set myself up.

This letter seems to be the only documentary evidence of Gabriel's 'continually recurring illness' of 1853. The £12 arrived forthwith, and on the morning of 17 June Rossetti and William Bell Scott left by train for Newcastle-upon-Tyne, 272 miles north-west of London.

After a daylong journey in a wooden-benched third-class coach, which Rossetti called 'disgusting work', they arrived in Newcastle, one of Victorian England's typically dingy, smoky industrial cities. Rossetti instantly detested Newcastle, which in letters he termed 'dreary', 'horrid', and 'beastly'. In a few days he wrote to his mother, 'I do not know exactly what my next move will be, but I do not think of staying here . . . this atmosphere is so stagnant (intellectually speaking) that I really scarcely know, nor can exert myself to think whether I have anything to say.' He reported to William that he found 'the general stagnation too like the spirit of Banquo, except for a strenuous dog, from whom also I suffer much'. He wrote Aunt

Charlotte as well—thanking her for the money and adding: 'I fancy the sea-air at Tynemouth will be the thing for me.'

Gabriel soon left Newcastle, without having breathed any of the invigorating sea-air of Tynemouth. With Scott he paid leisurely visits to the towns of Carlisle, Hexham, and Wetherel, and then travelled alone by train to Coventry, where he began a walking tour of Warwickshire. The tour took him to such places as Warwick and Kenilworth—and, surprisingly, he enjoyed the exercise. After walking twelve miles from Kenilworth to Stratford, he wrote to his mother, 'I never feel in the least tired, as it is in London, or about beastly Newcastle.' After several days in Stratford, on 14 July he returned to London.

Rossetti intended his trip to be a holiday, but not without some artistic efforts. He did some sketching and drew two small watercolours—*Carlisle Wall*, originally known as *The Lovers*, and a study in yellow entitled *Girl Singing to a Lute*; he finished the earliest version of one of his best known poems, the imaginative ballad 'Sister Helen', which at the suggestion of his friend Mary Howitt he sent to a small German publication, the *Dusseldorf Artists' Annual*, where it was published later in the year. Also, he composed two sonnets—'On the Site of a Mulberry-Tree', which expressed his anger over the cutting down (by an eighteenth-century clergyman) of a tree planted by Shakespeare, and 'The Hill Summit', now LXX of *The House of Life*, described by the poet in 1854 as 'one which I remember writing in great glory on the top of a hill I reached one after-sunset in Warwickshire':

This feast-day of the sun, his altar there
In the broad west has blazed for vester-song;
And I have loitered in the vale too long
And gaze now a belated worshipper.
Yet may I not forget that I was 'ware,
So journeying, of his face at intervals
Transfigured where the fringed horizon falls,—
A fiery bush with coruscating hair.

And now that I have climbed and won this height,
I must tread downward through the sloping shade
And travel the bewildered tracks till night.
Yet for this hour I still may here be stayed
And see the gold air and the silver fade
And the last bird fly into the last light.

William Rossetti commented:

> In its immediate primary meaning, this sonnet describes a resplendent day nearing its close, and the poet, on a day-long journey, contemplating the sunset from a height: and I have no doubt the sonnet was the direct outcome of an incident. On the other hand, I am equally satisfied that the implied or analogous meaning is likewise intentional—that of a career which, having reached its shining culmination, has thereafter to decline into the shade, and close in the night of the tomb.

The sonnet clearly grew out of Rossetti's inner turmoil as he made ready to return home from his vacation.

Shortly after he had arrived in Newcastle, Gabriel wrote to William, 'I want to tell you that Lizzy is painting at Blackfriars while I am away. Do not therefore encourage anyone to go near the place. I have told her to keep the doors locked, and she will probably sleep there sometimes.' Lizzy apparently slept most of the time at 14 Chatham Place while her lover was away from London, and when he entered his apartment on 14 July, he was pleasurably surprised to see her admirable, though still incomplete, self-portrait.

He also discovered that Elizabeth was suffering from the effects of consumption.

Rossetti mentioned in a letter to Brown in August, 1853, that Lizzy was very ill. In fact, it had become clear that Lizzy's malady was neither temporary nor trivial. A physician who examined her feared that she might never again enjoy good health; a change of climate was recommended, and later in the year she visited the channel resort town of Hastings. The illness itself may have resulted from a variety of factors: inherited consumptive tendencies, unwholesome living conditions in Southwark and at Chatham Place, notoriously long hours in the millinery shop, extended periods of modelling, the bitingly cold balcony overlooking Blackfriars Bridge, where sometimes she sat for hours posing for Gabriel, and her irregular way of life genrally.

Lizzy's illness imposed great strain and nervous tension onto Rossetti. He was genuinely anxious about her—of this there can be no doubt—but he was shocked and depressed to realize that now in fact his supposedly flawless blessed damozel was a melancholy semi-invalid—and perhaps doubly depressed when he considered the fact that Lizzy was well past her twentieth birthday, and for more than three and a half years had been his friend and for more than two years had been his fiancée. Undoubtedly she was expecting soon to become a married woman—otherwise her behaviour would have been unthinkable—and Gabriel just as surely was cringing at the thought of giving up his free and easy bachelorhood. In all likelihood the couple already had had some exchange of words on the question of just when they would legalize their relationship.

So all this mental turbulence during the last few months of 1853 made it more than ever difficult for Rossetti to persevere with his work. He soon abandoned all thought of his (or Lizzy's) participation in the Winter Exhibition. Although, as we have noted, from at least one point of view he had had a successful year, he was far from satisfied with his achievements—especially in contrast with those of his friends.

For the Pre-Raphaelite circle, 1853 more than reaffirmed the triumph of 1852. Walter Deverell after an absence of five years returned to the Royal Academy Exhibition with two of his pictures. Charles Collins contributed one of the most popular works in the Exhibition, a small picture of a child saying a prayer, of which one reviewer said, 'grace and innocence have rarely found a more lovable or lovely interpretation'. Ford Madox Brown, whose anger of the preceding summer had subsided (perhaps because 1852, thanks to MacCracken, had been his most remunerative year) returned to the R.A. with a superbly executed little picture called *Waiting*, showing a young wife with a baby sleeping on her lap, crocheting as she awaits the arrival of her husband. More important still, to Brown, were two pictures he had begun, which, when completed, would be two of his finest works. One was *The Last of England*, inspired by Woolner's departure for Australia, showing a young English couple and their baby at the railing of an emigrant ship, gazing on their native land for the last time. In order, Brown said, 'to ensure the peculiar look of light all round which objects have on a dull day at sea [*The Last of England*] was painted for the most part in open air on dull days, and, when the flesh was being painted, on cold days'. The other was that enormous painting which is generally regarded as Brown's masterpiece and even as the *chef d'oeuvre* of Pre-Raphaelitism—that tribute to all labourers, *Work*, which, as the Victorian art critic Sidney Colvin said, 'was designed to be a complete and pregnant drama of nineteenth-century life, having for its central figures a group of navvies at their noonday labour, and full of all sorts of contrasts between rich and poor, weak and strong, rough and fastidious, idle and busy, thoughtful and contemplative'.[1]

Holman Hunt enjoyed his most productive year to date, with three works exhibited in the Academy—a portrait of an Oxford don entitled *New College Cloisters, 1852*, and his principal paintings of the season, *Claudio and Isabella* and *Our English Coasts, 1852* (the latter being popularly known as *The Strayed Sheep*). For the first time Hunt scored a resounding critical and popular success. *Claudio and Isabella*—based, as noted in an earlier chapter, on the prison scene in *Measure for Measure*—drew huge crowds and attracted more attention than the picture hanging beside it, which was the best current production of the ever-popular Edwin Landseer. In this highly dramatic picture the imprisoned Claudio (posed by Deverell) has frighteningly exclaimed that 'Death is a fearful thing!' and Isabella, stunned by the realization that her brother would sacrifice her virtue to save his own life, replies 'And shamed life is hateful.' As always Hunt expertly handles his colours and light and shade, and he skilfully represents the secondary details, such as the flower in the window and the church-spire in the background. His finest achievement in this picture, however, in the words of a later reviewer, was his first 'expression of inward thought and feeling through the outward form'.[2] The vividly contrasting faces were hypnotic in 1853 and have been the main basis for the high praise that has been given to *Claudio and Isabella.*

Hunt's other principal painting of 1853 covered only a square foot of canvas, *The Strayed Sheep*. Unlike most of his works, this picture is without symbolic meaning; it simply depicts a flock of sheep atop a cliff on England's southern coast, is a perfect embodiment of Pre-Raphaelitism, and was one of the most warmly lauded works in Trafalgar Square. *The Illustrated London News*, in a typical comment, said:

> Let no visitor pass without examining this little picture, upon which labour appears to have been bestowed for pure love of labour; and every colour of the rainbow comes in for a share. . . . Nothing can be imagined greener, softer, more tempting than the herbage of those downs, where golden-fleeced sheep are herding, various hues of sunlight playing fitfully across their woolly coats:—nothing calmer than the clear blue sky beyond.

In *The Spectator*, William Rossetti was ecstatic in his praise of *The*

[1] 'Ford Madox Brown', *Portfolio*, June 1870, p. 85.

[2] 'Mr Holman Hunt: His Work and Career', *Blackwood's Magazine*, April 1886, p. 544.

Strayed Sheep, which he deemed 'the most perfect' work in The Exhibition. His panegyric said, in part:

We look in vain for a blemish or a shortcoming. We rate it the most triumphant vindication yet seen of the Pre-raphaelite principle; showing how much of the new, the beautiful, the significant, may be educed from the simplest materials by the determination to represent everything faithfully and thoroughly.

Both of Hunt's major works earned prizes for him—*Claudio and Isabella* won the £50 award in Liverpool, and *The Strayed Sheep* carried off a similar £60 laurel in Birmingham—and both quickly found eager purchasers. Financially comfortable at last, Hunt at the end of the year was giving the finishing touches to two paintings as he prepared to leave, in a month or two, on a long-projected trip to the Holy Land.

In 1853, as in 1852, the most triumphant Pre-Raphaelite was Millais, who exhibited two paintings, *The Proscribed Royalist*, and *The Order of Release*, both of which like *A Huguenot*, are historical love scenes. The former picture depicting an imagined episode from the mid-seventeenth-century Parliamentary wars, shows a Cavalier hidden in a tree trunk kissing the hand of an attractive young Puritan woman who has secretly brought him food and, fearful for his safety, is anxiously vigilant. As in all of Millais's pictures, the figures are well done, but here, uniquely among his early works, they are overshadowed by the superbly painted natural background, which a contributor to *Fraser's Magazine* called 'absolute nature', and which William in *The Spectator* characterized as 'perhaps the most lovely and the most perfectly printed which Mr Millais has produced'. But while that painting was well received and fetched a good price, its reception could not be compared with that of the painting which gave Millais his greatest success till then, and was perhaps the most spectacularly popular painting of his entire career—*The Order of Release*. The picture represents a Highlander, taken captive in the Civil Wars, being released from prison because of an order obtained by his wife, who stands barefoot with her baby, thrusting the order at the jailer. The painting was an almost unprecedented popular hit. *The Illustrated London News* reported that Millais had

certainly a larger crowd of admirers in his little corner of the Middle Room than all the Academicians put together command; any, and a crowd intent on what they are about—a good sticking crowd, who, having once taken up their position opposite the subject of their homage, are not inclined very soon to move on, but stand there gaping, and staring, and commenting upon the wondrous effects, without any regard to the pressure from behind of crowds preparing to occupy their place.

The size and immobility of these throngs forced officials of the Academy, for the first time in its history, to station a uniformed guard beside a painting to move the spectators on.

This arrestingly dramatic picture surely has deserved its continuing popularity because of its excellently arranged and superbly painted figures. The jailer, who is minutely examining the paper; the exhausted and weakened prisoner, who is emotionally overcome by this long-awaited moment of liberation; the sleeping child, who one would never suppose had been the most troublesome individual Millais had yet painted;[1] the exultantly leaping collie dog, who might have come from the brush of the great animal-painter, Edwin Landseer—all of them, one feels, have been presented precisely as they would have appeared if the incident as such had actually taken place. Rising above all of the others, however, is the highlander's magnificent wife, whose face splendidly reveals both her feelings of joy and elation at the sight of the husband whose freedom she has secured, and her effort to control her emotions until they are away from the jail. This portrait surpassed even those of Ophelia and the Huguenot's mistress and convinced most of his detractors that Millais was England's foremost painter of young women. (The portrait is an excellent likeness of the painter's model, Mrs John Ruskin, though Millais changed the colour of her hair from golden auburn to black.)

The Order of Release sold for the remarkable price of £400, which capped the year's almost unqualified success for Millais and for the Brotherhood. To be sure, a few daily newspapers still indulged in some half-hearted carping, but ineffectually. It would seem, as Hunt said, that 'the converted oracles were guarding themselves against signs of too sudden a conversion' to Pre-Raphaelitism.

In January 1854, Woolner wrote from Australia, 'I saw by the

[1] In a letter of 12 December 1852, Millais wrote, 'I have a headache and feel as tired as if I had walked twenty miles . . . All the morning I have been drawing a dog, which in unquietness is only to be surpassed by a child. Both of these animals I am trying to paint daily, and certainly nothing can exceed the trial of patience they occasion. The child screams on entering the room, and when forcibly held in his mother's arms struggles with such successful obstinacy I cannot begin my work till exhaustion comes on, which generally appears when daylight disappears. A minute's quiet is out of the question . . . This infant I could almost murder, but the dog I feel for, because he is not expected to understand.'

papers the P.R.B.s did great things at the R.A.Ex. Millais seems to be looked on as one of the great London Lions. I should wonder but little if the Queen knighted him soon.' Indeed, it did seem probable that soon he would gain an honour which had been denied him in 1852 and which most twenty-four-year-old artists would then have regarded as only slightly less exalted than a knighthood. William Frith, A.R.A., had been chosen by the Royal Academicians in February to fill a long-standing vacancy in their ranks; and his promotion necessitated an election, in November, of a new Associate. Now that he had reached the prescribed minimum age, Millais was the leading candidate for the position.

The coming election may have influenced Millais in painting *The Order of Release*. In *The Spectator*, William Rossetti noted disapprovingly that the picture has 'no background, properly so called, but merely a laying of dark colour', and that 'the wife's feet are preternaturally delicate and unsoiled for one who has been walking barefoot'. With the associateship almost within his grasp, Millais must have deliberately made a few compromises to avoid alienating those who would cast the votes. He may have decided it would be risky to exhibit two pictures with elaborately detailed backgrounds; and although a Pre-Raphaelite desire for realism prompted him to find a genuine order of release and copy it faithfully, he may have given the woman improbably clean and dainty feet because he remembered the uproar caused by his picture of Christ in the carpenter's shop.

Late in July, while he was impatiently waiting for November, Millais and his brother were invited by the Ruskins to spend a Scottish holiday with them at Glenfinlas, in the Trossachs. During his five weeks in Scotland, Millais began his famous portrait of John Ruskin standing on rocks beside a stream;[1] somewhat more importantly, he fell in love with Mrs Ruskin. While Ruskin was busily preparing a series of lectures to be delivered in Edinburgh, the Millais brothers and Euphemia Ruskin defied the almost constant rain by hiking, sketching, fishing, and picnicking during the day, while at night they laughed and joked and played battledore and shuttlecock, games which were too frivolous for Euphemia's husband. Married to a solemn, humourless, impotent, considerably older man, who usually seemed unaware of her existence, the gregarious and beautiful

[1] In July 1965, at an auction sale held at Christie's, this portrait of Ruskin fetched a price of 24,000 guineas.

Euphemia was thoroughly happy for the first time since her marriage, and before long she too was very much in love. When Millais returned to London in early September, they were both wondering how Mrs Ruskin could become Mrs Millais.

Millais's thoughts during the next two months were divided between Euphemia, of whom he drew a number of sketches, and the 7 November election. When the momentous day arrived, he was much too nervous to remain at home, and so he and his brother joined Charles and Wilkie Collins for a day in the country. When they returned to town that evening, they called at the Academy and were greeted by Charles Landseer, who said, 'Well, Millais, you are in this time *in earnest,*' alluding to the preceding year's election and also making a pun on the form in which his name had been mistakenly registered, 'John Ernest Millais'. In the final ballot Millais defeated J. C. Horsley, thirteen votes to nine, and thus at the age of twenty-four years and five months he became an Associate of the Royal Academy.

When Rossetti learned the next day of his colleague's good fortune, he realized that in honouring Millais the Royal Academicians had sounded the death knell of the Brotherhood. For many months, as we saw earlier, the society had been moribund: only once in 1853 had it held a meeting, late in April; then the members had drawn portraits of each other to send to Woolner, who had abandoned gold mining and opened a studio in Australia, and then 'informed us', Hunt recounted, 'that as our names appeared so often in the home newspapers it would be an advantage to him with the colonists to have visible evidence of our friendship'. Now with Hunt preparing to leave for Palestine, and Millais joining the enemy camp, one could only write 'finis' to the story of the Pre-Raphaelite Brotherhood.

'Millais, I just hear, was last night elected Associate,' Gabriel wrote to Christina, adding, ' "So now the whole Round Table is dissolved." '

Two days later, Christina answered her brother's letter and enclosed a sonnet which still is the most fitting epitaph to the P.R.B.:

> The P.R.B. is in its decadence:
>   For Woolner in Australia cooks his chops,
>   And Hunt is yearning for the land of Cheops;
> D. G. Rossetti shuns the vulgar optic;

While William M. Rossetti merely lops
His B's in English disesteemed as Coptic;
Calm Stephens in the twilight smokes his pipe
But long the dawning of his public day;
And he at last the champion great Millais,
Attaining Academic opulence
Winds up his signature with A.R.A.
So rivers merge in the perpetual sea;
So luscious fruit must fall when over-ripe;
And so the consummated P.R.B.[1]

[1] Many years after the sonnet had been composed, William wrote, 'The only point in it which in our time seems rather obscure is the reference to myself—which must mean that I, in my press-criticisms, made light of my P.R.B. colleagues (which is joke, not fact), and that my utterances met with no public regard (which is partial but not entire fact; for these criticisms, appearing in a paper of such high repute as *The Spectator*, and being, in 1850 to 1852, nearly the only press reviews which upheld the Preraphaelite cause, did excite some attention, and I suppose some anger).'

12

Postscript

Two events occurring less than three months after Millais's election might serve as footnotes to Christina's sonnet on the dissolution of the Round Table.

First, there was Hunt's departure, in January, for the Near East. A devout Christian, Hunt had long desired most of all to interpret visually the life of Christ, which he was convinced he could do faithfully only in the land where the episodes actually took place. In the summer of 1853, he decided that as soon as he had finished his current pictures, he would leave for the Holy Land, and would stay for at least two years. Nearly all of his friends tried to change his mind, not only because of the hardships and dangers he would face, but because of the recent recognition and future prospects which he might forfeit by leaving England. But no one, not even John Ruskin, could dissuade him. As he told his painter-friend Augustus Egg,

> . . . my desire is very strong to use my powers to make more tangible Jesus Christ's history and teaching. Art has often illustrated the theme, but it has surrounded it with many enervating fables, and perverted the heroic drama with feeble interpretation. We have every reason to believe that the Father of all demands that every generation should contribute its quota of knowledge and wisdom to attain the final purpose, and however small my mite may be, I wish to do my poor part, and in pursuing this aim I ought not surely to serve art less perfectly.

After this moving declaration of faith, Egg said only, 'Well, perhaps you're right.'

The two paintings Hunt was completing at the end of 1853 were *The Light of the World* and *The Awakened Conscience*. Based on a line from the Book of Revelations—'Behold, I stand at the door and knock: if any man hear my voice, and open the door, I will come in unto him, and will sup with him, and he with me'—and showing Christ in a moonlit orchard holding a lantern and knocking on a door, *The Light of the World* is probably the most famous and the most widely produced English painting of the nineteenth century. Nothing can better illustrate Hunt's dedication to his art than the nearly three years of labour he spent on this picture. He began its background in 1851 when he and Millais and Collins were in Surrey, where in order to gain the best possible mixture of light and shade, he spent every full-moonlit night painting in an orchard, though the weather was cold enough to permit ice-skating. He later wrote:

For my protection from the cold, as far as it could be found, I had a little sentry-box built of hurdles, and I sat with my feet in a sack of straw. A lamp, which I first tried, proved to be too strong and blinding to allow me to distinguish the subtleties of hue of the moonlit scene, and I had to be satisfied with the illumination from a common candle. I went out to my work about 9 p.m., and remained till 5 a.m. the next morning, when I retired into the house to bed till about ten, and then rose to go back to my hut and devote myself for an hour or two to the rectifying of any errors of colour, and to drawing out the work for the ensuing night.

When he returned to London, Hunt resumed his labours: 'On moonlight nights at Chelsea I was able by some dried clinging tendrils of ivy, which I had brought from the door in Surrey and fastened to an old board, to advance what I had done on the spot itself.' For another two years when the moon shone, Hunt, working with a lay figure, was a nocturnal artist: on 3 March 1853, Rossetti wrote to Brown, 'I have just come from Hunt's, who is dreadfully fagged, sitting up all night to paint his moonlight.' Writing to Stephens on 23 October 1853, Hunt referred to his many months of work on *The Light of the World* and ended his letter thus: 'I am tired—oh so tired! I wish I could rest, sleep, or die, from my wearing labour.' Incidentally, both the women whose names are associated with the P.R.B. were used by Hunt in this picture. 'Miss Siddal', he said, 'came to let me study the effect of light and shade on her beautiful copper-coloured locks.' When he painted Christ's head, he asked Christina to sit for it, because of 'the gravity and sweetness of [her] expression'.

The work is remarkable in many respects, but especially in its extraordinary illumination, which comes from Christ's head, from his lantern, from the jewels on his robe, from the stars, from the indiscernible moon, and even from the frost on the ground. Ruskin called it nothing less than 'the most perfect instance of expressional purpose with technical power which the world has yet seen'.[1]

The Awakened Conscience was to hang in Trafalgar Square in 1854 and received high praise from Ruskin. It represents a wealthy young man seated before a piano in his luxurious parlour, with his mistress rising from his lap as the words of the song on the sheet of music before her, 'Oft in the Stilly Night', summon up memories of childhood and awaken her conscience to the sinfulness of her present life. Hunt intended this painting to complement *The Light of the World*: he said that 'my spiritual subject called for a material counterpart in a picture representing in actual life the manner in which the appeal of the spirit of heavenly love calls a soul to abandon a lower life'. Much discussion has centred on the question of whether Hunt began *The Awakened Conscience* before or after Rossetti drew his first design for *Found*; Hunt, however, pointed out that he had not known of the existence of *Found* until he returned from the Near East. The inspiration for his painting, he said, came from his reading of *David Copperfield*, and the story of Mr Peggotty's search for Little Em'ly; he explained: 'My object was not to illustrate any special incident in the book, but to take the suggestion of the loving seeker of a fallen girl coming on the object of his search.' But the question of 'who was first?' is really unimportant—for, as we have noted, the theme was a familiar one in Victorian art and literature.

Hunt finished *The Awakened Conscience* in January 1854, and before the end of the same day, he was aboard the night mail train on the first leg of his trip to the Holy Land. Because of his hasty departure he had not eaten; and he recounted how Millais, who had accompanied him to the station, 'rushed to the buffet and seized any likely food he could, tossing it after me into the moving carriage'. Thus, with his fellow Pre-Raphaelite running beside the train and throwing food at him, Holman Hunt set off on the most important journey of his life.

Rossetti's parting present to Hunt was a daguerrotype of *The Girlhood of Mary Virgin*, his only artistic product of their shared studio,

[1] We will return to this work in the next volume, when we come to its exhibition at the Royal Academy in 1854.

along with four lines copied by hand from Sir Henry Taylor's verse drama *Philip van Artevelde*:

> There's that betwixt us been, which men remember
> Till they forget themselves, till all's forgot,
> Till the deep sleep falls on them in that bed
> From which no morrow's mischief knocks them up.

Saddened by Hunt's departure, within the next month Rossetti was shattered by a more devastating blow, the death of Deverell.

As early as 1852 Deverell's health had started to decline, and in 1853—after his father's death had left him the sole support of his younger brothers and sisters—he began to weaken swiftly from the illness, Bright's disease. The affliction did not affect his good spirits, nor his willingness—against doctor's orders—to support the family by drawing and painting for many hours every day. He commuted in all kinds of weather between London and his suburban home in Kew, usually riding in a third-class carriage with open sides, occasionally, when he missed the last train, walking for more than ten miles. Finally, in December, his heath completely gave way, and he was confined to bed. His last, unfinished picture, *The Doctor's Last Visit*, ironically represents a physician informing his patient's family that there is no hope of survival for the invalid. As he wasted away, Deverell faced death with equanimity; his only concern was the financial state in which he would leave his brothers and sisters. At this critical time, Millais came to his aid: busy though he was, he spent many hours reading to Deverell; he paid for a private nurse; and he conspired with Hunt to buy their friend's major unsold painting, *The Pet*, sending an acquaintance to act as buyer, thus giving Deverell the pleasure of knowing he would provide at least something for his survivors.[1] On the morning of 2 February, the twenty-six-year-old Deverell was told he would die before the end of the day; seemingly unaffected by the news, he remained conscious until four o'clock, when he closed his eyes for the last time.

Rossetti found it painful to attend Deverell's funeral on 7 February, because, as he told Scott, he had 'no older or more intimate friend', and because he felt guilty for not having visited the dying man during the last fortnight of his life. 'I should have gone much oftener lately,'

[1] The picture shows a woman standing with her caged bird in front of an open doorway which leads onto a bright, cheerful, luxuriant garden; it intrinsically was well worth purchasing and now hangs prominently in the Tate Gallery.

he wrote apologetically to Scott, and then, as if to ease his conscience, he added, 'but the doctor had given express orders he should see no one; and the last time I saw him was contrary to that injunction'. What most distressed Rossetti was his knowledge that the lowering of the coffin symbolized the end of an era. Woolner was in Australia, Hunt was on his way to Syria, Brown was living in seclusion in Hampstead, Millais was sitting with fellow A.R.A.s, and now Deverell was dead. After the funeral of the man who had introduced him to Elizabeth Siddal, Rossetti wrote to Woolner, 'if I live even to middle age, his death will seem to me a grief of my youth'. He might have written, 'his death will seem to me the end of my youth', for when he left the cemetery, he knew that the curtain had fallen on the final scene of the P.R.B. drama.

It was inevitable that the Pre-Raphaelite Brotherhood would not outlive the salad days of its founders: the society was the personification of the spirit of youthfulness. But the Pre-Raphaelite movement was more than just another juvenile rebellion. In the five years of its life, this organization of seven fledglings—only four of whom had more than a modicum of talent—had successfully challenged the conventions and formulae of the omnipotent Royal Academy; by insisting upon originality and sincerity, it had helped to stave off the fulfilment of Constable's prophecy of 1821 that 'in thirty years English art will have ceased to exist'; it had proved the truth of Ruskin's injunction to 'go to Nature in all singleness of heart, and walk with her labouriously and trustingly'. Achieving for England's painters what Wordsworth and Coleridge had done half a century earlier for her poets, it had helped to clear the way to individual freedom in an age increasingly dominated by what Matthew Arnold called philistinism. It had changed public taste in contemporary art and had begun to exert an influence on other artists. In 1853, Hunt wrote, British art exhibitions all 'contained examples of attempts to work from Nature, in avowed, and still more often in unavowed, accordance with our principles'.[1] Finally, the P.R.B. had given the world more than a dozen outstanding works of art.

[1] In his discussion of the 1853 R.A. Exhibition, the reviewer for *Fraser's Magazine* made this observation: 'There are fewer pictures *de genre* than ordinary, for which we have as much right to be thankful as for anything we have gained. The absence of the worn-out Vicars of Wakefield, and the eternal scenes out of the Spectator, reproducing the same affectations with scarcely a solitary modification of design or manipulation, is all clear profit . . . To be relieved from the meretricious monotony of these simpering faces and theatrical misrepresent of humanity, affords us considerable satisfaction . . .'

Although we are concerned only with the active period of the Brotherhood, it should be said, in passing, that London's Tate Gallery and principal galleries in Manchester, Birmingham, Liverpool, and Oxford contain many proofs of the scope and durability of Pre-Raphaelitism.[1] Even art instruction came within the Pre-Raphaelite orbit in 1914: George Dunlop Leslie, R.A., wrote:

Throughout Sir Francis Grant's Presidency [1866–78] and for several years after Lord Leighton's accession to the Chair [in 1878], the predominating influence that the Pre-Raphaelite movement had over the work done in our Schools was plainly manifest. That it was an influence for good I firmly believe, for it promoted accurate and painstaking work and absolute fidelity to nature, 'the Old Mistress', as Millais used to call her in contradistinction to 'the "Old Masters" . . . and under its influence the Academy Schools certainly produced a large percentage of students who in after life greatly distinguished themselves.'[2]

The suddenly erupting force of Pre-Raphaelitism was truly a remarkable phenomenon. As a twentieth-century commentator said of the principal Brothers, 'How these three lads had the knowledge, the intuition, and the technical ability to challenge the whole established art of the mid-nineteenth century, and to put in its place something so original and so accomplished, is one of the marvels of the age.'[3] (Pre-Raphaelitism, it should be noted, was strictly a British movement; it did not noticeably affect Continental art, nor were the Brothers associated with or influenced by non-British contemporaries —such as the French realist Gustave Courbet, who after shocking his native Academicians with his paintings scored his initial success in the Paris salon of 1850, when the Pre-Raphaelites were losing their first battle in London.)

But the crowning achievement of the Pre-Raphaelite Brotherhood lay not in its influences, important though they were, but rather in the artistic development of its three principal members. Millais, already an accomplished artist when the P.R.B. was formed, probably owed less to the society than his colleagues; but without his Pre-Raphaelite adventure, he might well have become just another conventional academic artist. Had Hunt been working alone, he might not have painted as successfully as he did—and, what is more, he might have

[1] The Tate Gallery owns forty-seven pictures by Rossetti, but it was not until 1966 that a wholly Pre-Raphaelite room was opened there. Many works are still in storage.

[2] George Dunlop Leslie, *The Inner Life of the Royal Academy*, p. 53.

[3] Percy Dearmer, 'Holman Hunt and the Pre-Raphaelite Movement', *The Contemporary Review*, vol. CXXXIV (July 1928), p. 75.

been at least temporarily compelled to abandon art as a profession.

But it was Rossetti who was most indebted to the Pre-Raphaelite Brotherhood. Not that he was, as some writers have made him out to be, the principal Pre-Raphaelite: indeed, properly speaking, he was not even a lesser Pre-Raphaelite. Only twice was he artistically motivated to leave his studio for nature—when he painted the vine in *The Girlhood of Mary Virgin*, and when he accompanied Hunt to Sevenoaks—and in his studio it was only in his first oil-paintings, under Hunt's eye, that he made more than a half-hearted attempt to follow the principles of Pre-Raphaelitism. Yet, though he was no Pre-Raphaelite painter, if it had not been for the Brotherhood and its artistic and social relationships he would almost certainly never have been a painter at all. The five years of the P.R.B. were his art school, his training ground.

So for him and for those others that remained, the P.R.B. had served its purpose, opening the doors to an apparently rosy future. Early in 1854, Thomas Woolner was preparing to return to England and a fresh start as a sculptor; Holman Hunt was approaching Syria and the beginning of the most serious phase of his life; John Everett Millais was looking forward to the first exhibition in which his name would be followed by the initials 'A.R.A.'; and Dante Gabriel Rossetti, having finished his apprenticeship, and encouraged by wealthy patrons and the nation's foremost critic, could (if he so willed) begin in earnest his artistic career, with all the best prospects for independence, productivity, and success.

Four voices might have joined their laureate in singing, 'Ring out wild bells, to the wild sky. . . . Ring out the old, ring in the new.'

SELECT BIBLIOGRAPHY

Angeli, Helen. *Dante Gabriel Rossetti*. London: Hamish Hamilton, 1949.
'Art and the Royal Academy', *Fraser's Magazine*, vol. 46, August 1852.
Athenaeum 1848–1853 *passim*.
Atkinson, J. B. 'Mr Holman Hunt: His Work and Career', *Blackwood's Magazine*, vol. 39, April 1886.
Baldry, Alfred. *Sir John Everett Millais*. London: Bell, 1899.
Banner, Delmar Harmood. 'Holman Hunt and Pre-Raphaelitism', *Ninteeenth Century*, vol. 102, October 1927.
Bate, Percy. *The English Pre-Raphaelite Painters*. London: Bell, 1901.
Benson, Arthur C. *Rossetti*. London: Macmillan, 1904.
Bertram, Anthony. *A Century of British Painting*. New York: Studio Publications, 1951.
Bickley, Francis. *The Pre-Raphaelite Comedy*. London: Constable, 1932.
Boase, T. S. R. *English Art, 1800–1870*. Oxford: Clarendon Press, 1959.
Burd, Van Akin. 'Background to Modern Painters: The Tradition and the Turner Controversy', *Publication of the Modern Language Association*, vol. 74, June 1959.
Carr, J. Comyns. 'Some Recollections of Millais', *The Living Age*, vol. 224, January 1900.
Cary, Elizabeth L. *The Rossettis*. New York: Putnam, 1900.
Collingwood, W. G. *The Life and Works of John Ruskin*. London: Methuen, 1893.
Colvin, Sidney. 'Ford Madox Brown', *Portfolio*, vol. 1, June 1870.
Cook, E. T. *The Life of John Ruskin*. London: Allen, 1911.
'Dante Gabriel Rossetti', *Quarterly Review*, vol. 184, July 1896.
Dearmer, Percy. 'Holman Hunt and the Pre-Raphaelite Movement', *Contemporary Review*, vol. 134, July 1928.
De La Sizerrane, Robert. *English Contemporary Art*. London: Constable, 1898.
Doughty, Oswald. *A Victorian Romantic: Dante Gabriel Rossetti*. London: Muller, 1949.
Fish, Arthur. *John Everett Millais*. New York: Funk and Wagnalls, 1923.
Frith, William P. *A Victorian Canvas*. London: Bles, 1957.
Ford, Ford Madox. *Ford Madox Brown*. London: Longmans, 1896.
The Pre-Raphaelite Brotherhood. London: Duckworth, 1907.
Rossetti: A Critical Essay on Art. London: Longmans, 1896.

Gissing, A. C. *William Holman Hunt*. London: Duckworth, 1936.

Hodgson, John E. and Frederick A. Eaton. *The Royal Academy and Its Members*. London: Murray, 1905.

Horsley, John Calcott. *Recollections of a Royal Academician*. London: Murray, 1903.

Hough, Graham. *The Last Romantics*. London: Duckworth, 1949.

Housman, Laurence. 'Pre-Raphaelitism in Art and Poetry', *Essays in Divers Hands*. London: Oxford University Press, 1933.

Hubbard, Hesketh. *A Hundred Years of British Painting, 1851–1951*. London: Longmans, 1951.

Hunt, William Holman. 'The Pre-Raphaelite Brotherhood: A Fight For Art', *Contemporary Review*, vol. 49, April, May, June 1886.

Pre-Raphaelitism and the Pre-Raphaelite B rotherhood. London: Chapman and Hall, 1913.

Illustrated London News 1843–1853 *passim*.

Ironside, Robin. *Pre-Raphaelite Painters*. London: Phaidon, 1948.

Knight, Joseph. *Life of Dante Gabriel Rossetti*. London: Scott, 1887.

Lamb, Walter R. M. *The Royal Academy*. London: Maclehose, 1835.

Laver, James. *Victorian Vista*. London: Hulton Press, 1954.

Leslie, Charles Robert. *Autobiographical Reflections*. London: Murray, 1860.

Leslie, Charles Dunlop. *The Inner Life of the Royal Academy*. London: Murray, 1914.

Literary Gazette 1848–1853 *passim*.

Leon, Derek. *Ruskin: The Great Victorian*. London: Routledge, 1949.

Marillier, Henry C. *Dante Gabriel Rossetti*. London: Bell, 1899.

Masson, David. *Memories of London in the 'Forties*. London: Blackwood, 1908.

Megroz, Rodolphe L. *Dante Gabriel Rossetti*. London: Faber, 1928.

Millais, John G. *The Life and Letters of Sir John Millais*. London: Methuen, 1899.

'Modern Painters, Etc.', *Fraser's Magazine*, vol. 33, March 1846.

Parkes, Kineton. *The Pre-Raphaelite Movement*. London: Reeves and Turner, 1889.

Perugini, Mark. *Victorian Ways and Days*. London: Jarrolds, 1932.

Phythian, John E. *The Pre-Raphaelite Brotherhood*. London: Newnes, 1905.

'The Pre-Raphaelite Brotherhood', *Nation*, vol. 56, February 1893.

'Pre-Raphaelitism', *Irish Quarterly Review*, vol. 1, December 1851.

'Pre-Raphaelitism', *The Spectator*, Vol. 24, October 1851.

'Pre-Raphaelitism from Different Points of View', *Fraser's Magazine*, vol. 53, June 1856.

'Pre-Raphaelitism in Art and Literature', *British Quarterly Review*, vol. 16, August 1852.

Quilter, Harry. *Preferences in Art, Life and Literature*. London: Swan Sonnenschein, 1892.

'Radical Romantics: Pre-Raphaelites at New York', *Art News*, vol. 63, May 1964.

Reid, J. Eadie. *Sir J. E. Millais*. London: Scott, 1909.

'The Relation of Art to Nature', *Cornhill Magazine*, vol. 14, July 1866.

Reynolds, Joshua. *Discourses* (ed. Roger Fry), London: Seeley, 1905.

'Rise and Progress of the Royal Academy', *Dublin University Magazine*, vol. 60, December 1862.

Rossetti, Dante Gabriel. *Collected Works* ed. by William M. Rossetti. London: Ellis, 1886.

Family Letters, ed. by W. M. Rossetti. London: Ellis, 1895.

Rossetti, William M. *Dante Gabriel Rossetti as Designer and Writer*. London: Cassell, 1889.

Pre-Raphaelite Diaries and Letters. London: Hurst and Blackett, 1900.

Some Reminiscences. New York: Scribner's, 1902.

'The Royal Academy Exhibition', *Fraser's Magazine*, vol. 47, June 1853.

Ruskin, John. *Pre-Raphaelitism*. London: Smith, Elder, 1851.

The Three Colours of Pre-Raphaelitism', *Nineteenth Century*, vol. 4, November–December 1878.

Scott, William Bell. *Autobiographical Notes*. London: Osgood, 1892.

Sharp, William. *Dante Gabriel Rossetti*. London: Macmillan, 1882.

Short, Ernest. *A History of British Painting*. London: Eyre and Spottiswoode, 1853.

The Spectator 1849–1853 *passim*.

Spielmann, Marion H. *Millais and His Works*. London: Blackwood, 1898.

Stephens, Frederick George. *Dante Gabriel Rossetti*. London: Seeley, 1894.

Thornbury, Walter. *Old and New London*. London: Cassell, 1893.

Troxell, Janet Camp. *Three Rossettis*. Cambridge: Harvard University Press, 1937.

Vincent, Eric R. *Gabriele Rossetti in England*. Oxford: Clarendon Press, 1936.

Waller, Ross D. *The Rossetti Family, 1824–1854*. Manchester University Press, 1932.

Waugh, Evelyn. *PRB*; *An Essay on the Pre-Raphaelite Brotherhood*. Graham, 1926.

Rossetti :His Life and Works. London: Duckworth, 1928.

Welby, Thomas Earle. *The Victorian Romantics, 1850–1870*. London: Howe, 1929.

'What Are the Functions of the Artist', *Fraser's Magazine*, vol. 55, June 1857.

Woolner, Amy. *Thos. Woolner, R.A., Sculptor and Poet*. London: Chapman and Hall, 1917.

Wilson, H. S. 'Millais', *Magazine of Art*, vol. 3, January 1879.

INDEX

Academy, 177
Albert, Prince, 155–6
Alfred, King, 79
Angeli, Helen, xii, 93
Angelico, Fra, 34, 48, 49, 50, 79, 111, 115, 116, 132
Antwerp, 33, 112
Arlington Street, 149, 203
Armitage, Edward, 137
Arnold, Matthew, 217
Art and Poetry, 124
Art Journal, The, 103, 107n., 172, 173n.
Athenaeum, The, 12, 33, 70, 71, 96, 104, 106, 125, 133–4, 135, 137n., 139, 154, 155, 156, 166, 167–8, 171, 172, 183, 185, 185n., 186, 188, 191
Atkinson, J. B., 183
Aylott and Jones, 120

Bacon, Francis, 79
Bartoli, Taddeo, 115
Bartolomeo, Fra, 115
Basati, Marco, 183
Bate, Percy, 184
Bath, Marchioness of, 31, 107, 108, 174
Beatrice (Dante's), 154, 175–6, 189, 198
Behnes, William, 69, 70, 89
Belfast, 174, 195, 197, 200n.
Bellini, Giovanni, 64n., 79, 183
Benson, Arthur C., xii, 26, 74, 91, 92, 147
Bernini, Giovanni, 116
Birmingham, 13, 174, 187
Birmingham City Art Gallery, xi, 218
Birmingham Prize, 187, 208
Blackfriars Bridge, 192, 193, 205
Blackheath, 54
Blackwood's Magazine, 141–2, 183n., 207m.
Blake, William, 5n., 11, 22–23, 178
Annotations to Sir Joshua Reynolds's Discourses, 23–24, 87n., 196n.
Boccaccio, Giovanni, 3, 79, 97
Bonnard, Camille, *Costumes*, 99
Boulogne, 109
Brighton, 148
British Institution, 12, 43, 47, 58, 69
British Museum, 47, 48, 60, 87, 118, 150
British Quarterly Review, The, 151, 182n., 183, 185, 188
Brookes, Peter Cannon, xi
Brown, Emma Hill, 175, 202
Brown, Ford Madox, 31, 44, 52, 53, 54, 56, 67, 88, 106, 117, 118, 130, 132, 148, 150, 152, 153, 154, 158, 163n., 165, 174, 179, 191n., 193, 196, 197, 199, 200, 202, 205, 214, 217; art education in Europe, 33–34, 41; earliest ideas on realistic painting, 34–35; exhibition career prior to 1848, 36; first meeting with D. G. Rossetti, 36–38; tutors Rossetti in his studio, 38–39, 41–42; first meeting with Hunt, 54; opinion of Campo Santo frescoes, 65; reasons for not becoming a P.R.B., 67–69; and the German Pre-Raphaelites, 74–75, 88; influence over Rossetti, 102; contributions to *The Germ*, 121, 123, 124; second marriage, 175; angry departure from 1852 Exhibition, 184–5
Paintings:
Abstract of Representation of Justice, 31
Christ Washing Peter's Feet, 35, 184–5
Cordelia Watching at the Bedside of Lear, 95–96, 159
Death-bed of the Giaour, 31, 35, 36
Execution of Mary Queen of Scots, 31, 54
Geoffrey Chaucer Reading the 'Legend of Custance . . .', 39, 158–9, 159n., 166
Justice, 36
Last of England, The, 35, 206
Manfred on the Jungfrau, 35
Our Lady of Saturday Night, 31
Parisina's Sleep, 31, 33n., 54, 54n.
Pretty Baa-Lambs, The, 184, 195
Waiting, 206
Wickliffe Reading His Translation of the New Testament, 40, 54, 195
Work, 35, 206–7

Brown, Ford Madox—*cont.*
Poem:
'The Love of Beauty', 121
Browning, Elizabeth Barrett, 79
Browning, Robert, 22, 24, 28, 79, 146
Blot in the 'Scutcheon, A, 90
'Fra Lippo Lippi', 77n.
'Laboratory, The', 145
'One Word More', 198
Paracelsus, 90, 115
Sordello, 90
Bruges, 112–13, 124
Brussels, 111–12
Brussels Museum, 112
Builder, The, 103, 123, 132
Bulwer-Lytton, Edward, 106
Rienzi, 84
Burger, Gottfried, 24
Burlington House, 10
Byron, Lord George Gordon, 28, 36, 79

Camberwell, 169
Camden Town, 149
Campbell, Calder, 123
Campbell, Thomas, 2
Campo Santo frescoes, 63–66
Departure of Hagar from the House of Abraham, The, 64
Sacrifice of Isaac, The, 64, 65
Canaletto, Antonio, 64n.
Caracci, Annibale, 169
Carlyle, Thomas, 165, 196
Cary, F. S., 6
Cary, Henry Francis, 2, 189n.
Cavalcanti, Guido, 189
Cervantes Saavedra, Miguel de, 79
Charlotte Street, 3, 6, 26, 37, 81, 93, 113, 114n., 148, 149
Chartism, 81
Chatham Place, 192, 193, 197, 201, 202, 205
Chaucer, Geoffrey, 79, 159, 160
Chelsea, 113, 214
Cheyne Walk, 113, 114
Chinese Gallery, The, 13, 101, 103, 104
Chronicle, Morning, 103
Cima da Conegliano, 49
Cimabue, Giovanni, 189
Clarendon Square, 70
Claude Lorrain, 64n.
Cleveland Street, 56, 57, 94, 101, 113, 114
Clipstone Street, 36, 37, 38, 42, 52, 53, 56, 81
Clough, Arthur Hugh, 122
Coleridge, Samuel Taylor, 2, 145, 217
Collins, Charles, 78, 154, 165, 167, 179, 206, 211; close relationship to the P.R.B., 151, 152, 158, 159, 163n., 193; paints in Surrey with Hunt and Millais, 169, 214
Convent Thoughts, 158, 160, 162, 166, 168
May in Regent's Park, 188
Collins, Wilkie, 151, 211
Collins, William, 151
Collinson, James, 72, 73, 80, 83, 91, 93, 94, 107, 112, 117, 143, 154, 168; proposed for P.R.B. membership, 70–72; religious beliefs, 71, 75, 144; and Christina Rossetti, 71, 149; his lethargy, 71–72, 89, 90; contributions to *The Germ*, 118, 123, 125; resignation from the P.R.B., 144
Paintings:
Answering the Emigrant's Letter, 137
Charity Boy's Debut, The, 71
Emigration Scheme, The, 188
Image-Boys at a Roadside Alehouse, 107n.
Incident in the Life of St. Elizabeth of Hungary, An, 155–6
Rivals, The, 71
Columbus, Christopher, 79
Colvin, Sidney, 96, 206
Combe, Thomas, 117n.
Connoisseur, xi
Constable, John, 11, 11n., 46, 217
Contemporary Review, 218n.
Cook, E. T., 50, 171
Cornelius, Peter, 74–75
Corregio, 23, 64n., 169
Courbet, Gustave, 218
Cranbourne Street, 128, 176
Critic, 123, 125, 148, 149
Cromwell, Oliver, 79
Cuyp, Albert, 64n.
Cyclographic Society, 44, 53

Dante, 3–4, 5n., 25, 79, 145, 154, 175
Divine Comedy, The, 3–4, 189
Vita Nuova, La, 25, 146, 147, 175, 197, 198n.
Dearmer, Percy, 218n.
De La Sizeranne, Robert, 132
Delacroix, Eugène, 111
Delaroche, Hippolyte, 111
Della Robbia, Andrea, 48
Denmark Hill, 169, 170, 196
Deverell, Walter, 118, 119, 123, 131, 134, 150, 154, 168, 174, 193, 202, 206, 207; nearly becomes eighth P.R.B., 128, 136, 151, 174; first sees Elizabeth Siddal,

128–9; introduces Rossetti to Miss Siddal, 129; shares studio with Rossetti, 151; models for Brown, 159, 184n.; final illness and death, 216–17
Paintings:
Banishment of Hamlet, The, 155–6
Doctor's Last Visit, The, 216
Pet, The, 216
Twelfth Night Scene, 136
Dickens, Charles, 139, 142; attacks P.R.B. in *Household Words*, 139–41, 146
David Copperfield, 141, 215
Nicholas Nickleby, 141
Oliver Twist, 141
Donatello, 48
Doughty, Oswald, xii, xiii, xiv, 101, 121
Dublin, 159, 180, 190
Dulwich Gallery, 47
Dürer, Albrecht, 98, 116, 163, 171
Dusseldorf Artists' Annual, 204
Dyce, William, 138

Eastlake, Charles, 22, 7 n., 160
Edinburgh Review, 49n.
Egg, Augustus, 106, 213
Emerson, Ralph Waldo, 79
Etty, William, 58, 59
Ewell River, 180
Exhibition of Modern British Art, 194, 202, 206
1852 Exhibition, 194–5
Exhibition, The Great Industrial, 157
Eyck, Jan van, 46, 64n., 99, 111, 112, 113, 183
Ferdinand IV, King of Naples, 1
Fielding Copley, 114n.
Fitzroy Square, 56
Flandrin, Hippolyte, 111
Flaxman, John, 79
Fleet Street, 26
Folkestone, 109
Ford, Ford Madox, 36n., 40n., 175, 184
Francia, 46
Fraser's Magazine, 35, 186, 208, 217n.
Fredeman, William E., xiii, 137n.
Free Exhibition (see also National Institution of Fine Arts), 12–13, 36, 40n., 118, 126
1849 Exhibition, 100–4, 108
1850 Exhibition, 131–4
1851 Exhibition, 155–6
Frere, John Hookham, 2
Frith, William P., 10n., 11n., 15, 210
Frost, William, 60
Fuseli, Henry, 160, 163
Gainsborough, Thomas, 11, 23
Gaunt, William, xii
Géricault, Jean-Louis-André-Théodore, 111
Germ, The, 118–26, 128, 131, 136, 179
German Pre-Raphaelites, 74–75
Ghent, 112
Ghiberti, Lorenzo, 44, 79
Ghirlandajo, Domenico, 49, 50
Giorgione, 79, 80, 111, 124
Giotto, 34, 50, 160, 189
Gissing, A. C., 183n.
Glenfinlas, 210
Goethe, Johann Wolfgang von, 79, 145
Goodall, Frederick, 187
Gower Street, 60, 62, 73, 74, 81, 101, 169
Gozzoli, Benozzo, 50
Granet, Francois, 111
Grant, Francis, 184–5, 218
Grasmere, 152
Greenwich, 54
Gregorius, Professor, 33
Grylls, Rosalie, xiii–xiv, 40n.
Guinicelli, Guido, 189

Hampden, John, 79
Hampstead, 90, 175, 203, 217
Hancock, John, 42, 44, 53, 118, 119
Hardman, Frederick, 141–2
Hastings, 205
Haydon, Benjamin Robert, 12, 79
Highgate, 160
Hilton, William, 79
Hogarth, William, 11, 46, 79, 154
Holbein, Hans, 34, 47
Holborn, 52, 151
Holland, Lord Henry Richard, 2
Homer, 79
Hood, Thomas, 79
Horsley, John Calcott, 15, 211
Houghton, Lord Richard Monckton, 74
Houghton, Walter E., 141
Household Words, 139
Housman, Laurence, 76n.
Howard, Frank, 60
Howitt, Mary, 204
Hunt, Leigh, 28–30, 39, 79, 126
Hunt, Violet, xii
Hunt, William Holman, 58, 59, 69, 73, 78, 79, 80, 84, 89, 90, 91, 97, 98, 99, 102, 105, 106, 113, 128, 129, 134, 135, 137, 141, 143, 145, 146, 149, 151, 152, 154, 156, 159, 160, 161, 165, 167, 169, 170, 172, 177, 179, 181, 184, 184n., 193, 197, 202, 211, 216; youthful opinion of contemporary English art, 10–11, 48; describes

Hunt, William Holman—*cont.*
Rossetti as an Academic student, 18; opinion of Brown's teaching methods, 38–39, 53; acquaintance with Rossetti at school, 44; childhood interest in painting, 44–46, 47; first visit to National Gallery, 46–47; prepares for R.A. entrance examination, 47–48; enrolls as an R.A. student, 48; reads Ruskin's *Modern Painters*, 48–51; Rossetti's first visit to his home, 52–53; guides Rossetti in his early painting, 53–54, 87–89, 105, 117, 178; first meeting with Brown, 54; opinion of Brown's opinions, 54; simple way of life, 54; interest in non-artistic topics, 55; desire to propagate Pre-Raphaelite principles, 55, 66, 118, 152; shares studio with Rossetti, 55–57; early friendship with Millais, 59–61; takes Rossetti to meet Millais, 61–62; examines Campo Santo engravings, 63–66; opposition to Brown's becoming a P.R.B., 68; response to Woolner's candidacy for P.R.B., 70; attitude towards sculptors, 70, 83; opinion of Collinson and his art, 71–72; proposes Stephens for P.R.B. membership, 72–73; called 'Pre-Raphaelite' by fellow Academic students, 75; explains P.R.B. principles to recruits, 76–78; attitude towards Raphael, 76; concern for morality in art, 76–78, 85; response to revolutionary events of 1848, 80, 86; develops new technique of painting, 85–86; troubled by Rossetti while sharing studio, 94–95; reaction to Rossetti's entering 1849 Free Exhibition, 100–1; visits France and Belgium with Rossetti, 109–13; settles in Chelsea, 114; opinion of Rossetti's 'Pre-Raphaelitism', 132, 199; visits Sevenoaks with Rossetti, 146–7; contemplates abandonment of painting, 166; painting in Surrey with Millais and Collins, 169, 214; wins 1851 Liverpool prize, 173; sells first picture to MacCracken, 174; recommends Rossetti to MacCracken, 195; works on *The Light of the World*, 213–15; departs for Palestine, 213, 215–16, 217, 219

Paintings:
Awakened Conscience, The, 213, 215
Claudio and Isabella, 145, 158, 207, 208
Converted British Family Sheltering a Christian Missionary from the Persecution of the Druids, 108, 115, 117, 126, 136, 137, 139, 146
Etchings for *The Germ*, 120, 121, 125
Eve of St. Agnes, The, 43–44, 51, 55, 61, 84
Hireling Shepherd, The, 169, 176, 180, 182–3, 185, 188
Light of the World, The, 213–15
New College Cloisters, 207
Our English Coasts, 1852 (see *The Strayed Sheep*)
Rienzi, 55, 61, 80, 84, 85, 86–87, 95, 106–7, 108
Strayed Sheep, The, 207–8
Valentine Rescuing Sylvia from Proteus, 145, 153, 158, 160, 163, 166, 168, 169, 173, 195

Hyde Park, 157
Hyde Park Corner, 13, 101, 103, 104

Illustrated London News, The, 5n., 36, 134–135, 137n., 138, 156, 166, 193, 194, 195, 207, 208
Ingres, Jean, 111, 124
Irish Quarterly Review, 179–80
Italian Pre-Raphaelites, 34, 63–65, 74, 79, 97; relationship to English Pre-Raphaelites, 65–66, 76, 77

Joan of Arc, 79
Jones, George, 17, 18–19

Keats, John, 22, 29, 74, 79, 106
'Eve of St. Agnes, The', 43–44, 61
'Isabella, or the Pot of Basil', 84, 97
Kent Place, 130n.
King's College (Strand), 5
King's College School, 5–6
Kingsley, Charles, *The Saint's Tragedy*, 155
Knight, Joseph, 71
Kosciusko, Tadeusz, 79

Lambeth, 72
Landor, Walter Savage, 79
Landseer, Charles, 211
Landseer, Edwin, 137, 187, 207, 209
Larg, David, xii
Lasinio, Carlo, 64, 76
Lea marshes, 108, 115
Leicester Square, 26
Leighton, Frederick, 218
Leon, Derrick, 161n., 169
Leonardo da Vinci, 34, 79, 80, 111
Leslie, Charles Robert, 13, 20–21, 188
Leslie, George Dunlop, 13, 20, 218
List of Immortals, 78–80

Literary Gazette, The, 58, 103, 123, 131, 135–6, 137n., 138, 167, 168–9, 195
Liverpool, 13, 174, 180, 187, 197, 218
Liverpool Academy, 173
Liverpool Prize, 173, 187, 208
London Bridge Station, 109
Longfellow, Henry Wadsworth, 79, 166
Louvre Museum, 110–11, 112, 124
Lucas, John, 118
Luini, Bernardino, 34, 48
Luxembourg Palace, 111, 124
Lyell, Charles, 4, 56, 85n., 175

MacCracken, Frances, 174, 195–7, 198, 200
Maclise, Daniel, 58, 59, 186
Maddox Street, 38, 39, 72, 94
Manchester, 13, 174, 218
Mantegna, Andrea, 111, 124
Marillier, Henry C., xii
Masaccio, 34
Mazzolini, Ludovico, 46
Mégroz, Rodolphe, 71, 101
Memling, Hans, 112, 113, 124, 183
Memmi, Lippo, 115, 116
Meyerbeer, Giacomo, 181
Michelangelo, 34, 48, 79, 80
Millais, John Everett, 68, 70, 72, 76, 80, 83, 84, 94, 100, 101, 103, 105, 109, 118, 125, 134, 145, 146, 149, 151, 152, 154, 156, 159, 165, 167, 170, 173, 183, 197, 217, 218, 219; childhood, 5, 57; student at Sass's Academy, 57; student in Royal Academy Schools, 57–58; earliest exhibited paintings, 58–59; 1848 picture rejected by R.A., 58, 102; conventional behaviour and attitudes, 59, 80; interest in physical exercise, 59; early friendship with Hunt, 59–61; earliest attitude towards the idea of a P.R.B., 66, 73, 78; personal relations with Rossetti, 67, 91, 99, 193; his importance to the P.R.B., 67, 142–3; called 'Pre-Raphaelite' by fellow Academic students, 75; interest in music, 79; develops new technique of painting, 85–86; and Pre-Raphaelite social activities, 89, 90, 91, 113; denies influence of Rossetti, 98–99; outburst of anger at 1850 Exhibition, 137; asks Patmore to appeal to Ruskin, 160–61; meets Ruskin, 169; paints in Surrey with Hunt and Collins, 169, 180, 214; defeated in election for A.R.A., 187–8; talks of a P.R.B. exhibition, 188; falls in love with Mrs Ruskin, 210–11; elected an A.R.A., 210–11; sees Hunt depart for Palestine, 215; with Deverell during his final illness, 216

Paintings:
Carpenter Shop, The, 126–7, 136, 137, 138, 139, 141, 142, 143, 210
Christ in the Home of His Parents (see *The Carpenter Shop*)
Cymon and Iphigenia, 58, 60, 61
Death of Ophelia, The, 169, 178–9, 180, 182, 185–7
Elgiva Seized by the Soldiers of Odo, 58
Ferdinand Lured by Ariel, 114–15, 126, 137, 138, 139
Huguenot, A, 169, 180–2, 185–7, 208
Lorenzo and Isabella, 97–99, 106–7, 162
Mariana, 144, 157–8, 162, 163, 168
Order of Release, The, 208–9, 210
Pizarro Seizing the Inca of Peru, 58
Portrait of James Wyatt and Granddaughter, 114, 138
Portrait of John Ruskin, 210
Portrait of Mrs. Coventry Patmore, 180
Proscribed Royalist, The, 208
Return of the Dove to the Ark, The, 157, 160, 163, 166, 168
Tribe of Benjamin Seizing the Daughters of Shiloh, The, 58
Woodman's Daughter, The, 144, 157, 158, 168

Millais, John Guille, 161, 181
Millais, John William (father of John Everett Millais), 57, 146
Millais, Mrs. John William, 57, 146
Miller, John, 197, 198
Milton, John, 2, 5n., 79
Moore, Lady Dora, 1–2
Moore, Sir Graham, 1
Mulready, William, 143n., 163
Munro, Alexander, 135, 136
Murillo, Bartolomé Esteban, 64n., 85n.

Nation, 180n.
National Gallery, 10, 46, 47, 48, 184
National Institution of Fine Arts, The, 131, 134, 155, 188
National Portrait Gallery, 21
Newcastle, 203–4, 205
Newman Street, 114, 148, 151, 174, 175
Newton, Isaac, 79
Nine Elms, 150
Nineteenth Century, 116n.
Notre Dame Cathedral (Paris), 110

Observer, The, 103, 132
Orcagna, Andrea, 50

Overbeck, Johann Friedrich, 74–75, 88
Oxford, 109, 114, 117n., 143, 146, 218
Oxford Street, 126

P.R.B. Journal, 84, 117, 124, 136, 147, 151, 152, 162n., 165, 195
Pall Mall Gazette, 180n.
Paris, 109–12
Parmigiano, Francesco, 46
Parris, Leslie, xi
Patmore, Coventry, 79, 90, 106, 121, 165; and *The Germ*, 118, 122, 123, 125; praises Rossetti's translations, 147; persuades Ruskin to help the P.R.B., 160–1
'Essay on Macbeth', 124
'Seasons, The', 122
'Woodman's Daughter, The', 144
Peckham, Morse, xi
Petrarch, 3
Phidias, 9, 79
Phythian, J. Ernest, 158
Piccadilly, 13, 26
Pickersgill, Frederick, 187
Pickersgill, Henry W., 180n.
Piombo, Sebastian del, 46
Pissarro, Lucien, xii, 105, 132
Poe, Edgar Allan, 79, 90, 145
Polidori, Charlotte, 21, 25, 30, 39, 52, 102, 107, 108, 147, 174; gives financial assistance to D. G. Rossetti, 31, 38, 148, 150, 203, 204
Polidori, Gaetano, 2
Polidori, Margaret, 146
Pollaiuolo, Antonio del, 34
Pope, Alexander, 8
Portfolio, 207n.
Portland Gallery, 147, 155
Poussin, Nicolas, 64n., 79
Pre-Raphaelite Brotherhood, organizational meeting, 73–74, 76–80; selection of name, 74–76; formation unrelated to revolutionary political events of 1848, 80–82; social activities, 89–93, 97; and a P.R.B. house, 113; disclosure of meaning of initials, 133–37
Prospect Place, 114, 169
Pugliesi, Cavalier, 79
Punch, 143, 160, 185

Quarterly Review, 176
Quilter, Harry, 16, 98

Raphael, 9, 34, 44, 49, 61, 64n., 74, 76, 76n., 79, 80, 111, 116, 135, 139, 140, 141, 142, 163, 171, 186
Transfiguration, 75
Reach, Angus B., 134, 135, 137n.
Red Lion Square, 151, 164, 174
Regent's Park, 95, 149
Rembrandt van Rijn, 5n., 23, 33, 64n., 116
Reni, Guido, 46, 135, 169
Reynolds, Joshua, 6–9, 11, 23–24, 87n., 178, 196n.
Discourses, 7–9
Rienzi, Cola di, 79, 84
Risorgimento, 1–2
Robert-Fleury, Joseph, 111
Robsjohn-Gibbings, Terence, xii
Rogers, Samuel, 2
Ross, William, 163
Rossetti, Christina, 3, 4, 5, 21, 27, 53, 93, 118, 148, 199, 203, 213; and Collinson, 71, 72, 149; models for D. G. Rossetti, 94, 116, 132n.; contributions to *The Germ*, 122, 123, 125; teaches in mother's school, 149; models for Hunt, 214
'Dream Land', 122
'End, An', 122
'P.R.B., The', 211–12
'Pause of Thought, A', 123
'Song: Oh roses for the flush of youth', 123
'Sweet Death', 124
'Testimony, A', 123
'Three Stages', 123
Rossetti, Dante Gabriel, xi, xii, 1, 58, 61, 73, 75, 79, 80, 83, 84, 106, 113, 114n., 139, 141, 143, 146, 165, 172, 179, 188, 214, 219; early childhood, 3–5; attendance at school, 5–6; enrolled in Sass's Academy, 14–16; impressions of Westminster Hall competition, 14–15; attends R.A. Antique School, 16–22, 26, 30; dual artistic interests, poetry and painting, 22, 118, 147, 194; early reading tastes, 22–24, 90; influenced by Dante, 22, 175–6, 177, 189, 196, 197–8, 199; influenced by Blake, 22–24, 87n., 178; receives financial assistance from William, 23, 150; influenced by Browning, 24, 28, 90; interest in the theatre, 26, 91; first letter to William Bell Scott, 27–28; first letter to Brown, 31–32; letter to Leigh Hunt, 28–30; receives financial assistance from Aunt Charlotte, 31, 38, 148, 150, 203, 204; first meeting with Brown, 36–38; tutored by Brown in his studio, 38–42, 44; enrolled in Maddox Street drawing academy, 38, 39, 72, 94; praises Hunt's *Eve of St. Agnes*, 43–44; first visit to Hunt's home, 52–53; begins to study under Hunt's tutelage, 53–54;

early friendship with Hunt, 54–55; shares studio with Hunt, 55–57; has dominant role in formation of the P.R.B., 66–67; suggests Brown for P.R.B., 68; proposes Woolner for P.R.B., 69–70; proposes Collinson for P.R.B., 70–72; proposes William for P.R.B., 72; opinion of Keats, 74, 79; disinterest in politics and international affairs, 80–82; guided by Hunt in painting *The Girlhood of Mary Virgin*, 87–89; attitude towards perspective in painting, 88, 117; enjoyment of P.R.B. social activities, 89–93, 97; talent for reciting poetry, 90; youthful temperance, 91–92; conflict with father, 93, 150; proves to be troublesome studio mate for Hunt, 94–95; models for pictures of friends, 95, 158, 159, 184n.; alleged influence on Millais, 98–99; completes *The Girlhood of Mary Virgin*, 99–100; exhibits *The Girlhood of Mary Virgin* in the Free Exhibition, 100–2; suddenly departs from Hunt's studio, 105–6; visits France and Belgium with Hunt, 109–13; rents studio at 72 Newman Street, 114; persuades fellow P.R.B.'s to establish magazine, 118–19; contributions to *The Germ*, 120, 122, 124, 125–6; meets Elizabeth Siddal, 128–9; in love with Elizabeth Siddal, 129–30, 144, 152–153, 201–2; response to *The Athenaeum's* 1850 attack, 134; disinclined to exhibit his pictures, 134, 144, 174, 198; alleged responsibility for revealing meaning of 'P.R.B.', 135–7; visits Sevenoaks with Hunt, 146–7; rents studio at 74 Newman Street, 148; inquires about position as telegrapher, 150–1; shares studio with Deverell, 151; relationship of his work to Pre-Raphaelitism, 152, 177–8, 195, 198, 199, 219; physical relations with Elizabeth Siddal, 153–4; moves into Brown's Newman Street studio, 174–5; exhibits at the 1852 winter exhibition, 190, 194–5; moves into flat in Chatham Place, 192–3; acquires first art patrons, 195–7; pictures receive first public notice from Ruskin, 196–7; attitude towards patrons, 196, 200; enthuasism for Elizabeth Siddal's creative work, 201, 202; visits Newcastle and Warwickshire, 203–5; effect upon him of Elizabeth Siddal's illness, 205–6; response to Millais' becoming an A.R.A., 211; and Hunt's departure for Palestine, 215–16; and the death of Deverell, 216–17

Paintings and Drawings:
Annunciation, The, 189
Beatrice at a Marriage Feast Denies Dante her Salutation, 148, 153–4, 175, 176, 195, 196
Borgia, 148, 175, 176
Carlisle Wall, 204
Dante Drawing an Angel in Memory of Beatrice, 197–8
Ecce Ancilla Domini, 115–17, 131–4, 136, 145, 147, 148, 174, 195–6
Found, 176–7, 197, 199, 215
Francesca da Rimini, 126
Giotto Painting the Portrait of Dante, 126, 176, 189–90, 189n., 195
Girl Singing to a Lute, 204
Girlhood of Mary Virgin, The, 56, 85, 87–89, 92, 94–95, 99–105, 107, 108, 215, 219
Hesterna Rosa, 198
'*Hist, said Kate the Queen*', 115, 126, 146
How They Met Themselves, 176, 177
Laboratory, The, 145
Lovers, The, 204
Portrait of Charlotte Polidori, 21
Portrait of Christina Rossetti, 21, 53
Portrait of Gabriele Rossetti, 56
Portrait of William Rossetti, 21
'*Retro me Sathana*', 21–22
Rossovestita, 152–3, 154, 195
Self-Portrait, 21
Virgin in the House of St. John, The, 197

Writings:
'Autumn Idleness', 147
'Blessed Damozel, The', 24, 25, 105, 123, 126, 191
'Bride's Prelude, The', 25
'Card Dealer, The', 191–2
'Carillon, Antwerp and Bruges, The', 124
'Choice, The', 24
'Dante at Verona', 25, 175
'English Revolution of 1848, The', 81n.
'From the Cliffs, Noon', 124
'Hand and Soul', 120, 122, 130
'Hill Summit, The', 204–5
House of Life, The, 21, 24, 96, 147, 153, 201, 204
'Husbandmen, The', 96, 97
'Jenny', 25, 92, 177
'Known in Vain', 201
'Last Confession, A', 25, 177
'Last Sonnets at Paris', 111–12
'London to Folkestone', 109
'MacCracken', 199–200

Rossetti, Dante Gabriel—*cont.*
'Mary's Girlhood' (written for *The Girlhood of Mary Virgin*), 99–100
'My Sister's Sleep', 24, 25, 102, 105, 122
'Not as These', 96, 97
'Old and New Art', 96
'On the Site of a Mulberry-Tree', 204
'On the "Vita Nuova" of Dante', 175
'Pax Vobis', 124
'Portrait, The', 24, 25n.
'Retro Me, Sathana', 24
'Sacred to the Memory of Algernon Stanhope', 25
'St. Luke the Painter', 96–97
'Sea-Limits, The', 124
'Sister Helen', 176, 177, 204
'Sonnets for Pictures', 124
Sorrentino, 24
'Stealthy School of Criticism, The', 153n.
'To Thomas Woolner', 199
Translations of Italian Poetry, 25, 147, 175, 198n.
Uncle Tom's Cabin, parody of, 194
'Wellington's Funeral', 193–4
'World's Worth', 124
'Young Fir-Wood, A', 147
Rossetti, Frances (Mrs Gabriele), 2–3, 14, 27, 149, 199, 203
Rossetti, Gabriele, 1–5, 14, 27, 93, 150, 189, 199, 203; writings on Dante, 3–4
Rossetti, Maria, 3, 4, 27, 93, 149, 203
Rossetti, William, 3, 4, 5, 11, 21, 24, 40, 67, 71, 73, 78, 80, 82, 83, 88, 89, 90, 92, 95, 102, 110, 112, 117, 118, 124, 125, 132n., 142, 147, 148, 151, 153, 162n., 165, 178, 188, 193, 195, 198, 200, 201, 202, 203, 212n.; gives financial assistance to brother, 23, 150; position in the Internal Revenue Office, 27, 149, 202; proposed for P.R.B. membership, 72; chosen secretary of the P.R.B., 84; provides financial support for his family, 93, 108; models for Millais, 99; models for his brother, 116; named editor of *The Germ*, 119; contributions to *The Germ*, 120–1, 122, 123; becomes art critic for *Critic*, 125; on Elizabeth Siddal, 129–30; becomes art critic for *The Spectator*, 148–149; writings in *The Spectator*, 156, 167, 173, 182, 207, 208, 210; models for Brown, 159, 184n.
Royal Academy of Art, 6–13, 57, 58, 70, 71, 102, 128, 179, 183, 217
Exhibition of 1848, 43–44
Exhibition of 1849, 82, 95, 96, 97, 99, 103, 106–7
Exhibition of 1850, 124, 127, 136–53
Exhibition of 1851, 157–60, 165–7
Exhibition of 1852, 179–87
Exhibition of 1853, 206–10
Royal Academy Schools, 6, 16, 19, 75, 81, 102, 218
Antique School, 15–16, 18–21, 58, 60, 69, 72
Life School, 16, 86
Painting School, 16
Painting School from Living Model, 188
Rubens, Peter Paul, 23, 46, 47, 58, 64n., 112, 113
Ruisdael, Jacob van, 64n.
Ruskin, Euphemia, 169, 209, 210–11
Ruskin, John, 12, 61, 165, 178, 179, 180, 200n., 213, 217; opinion of Campo Santo frescoes, 63–64; on Rossetti's *Ecce Ancilla Domini*, 116; persuaded by Patmore to help the P.R.B., 161; meets Millais, 169; refers to Pre-Raphaelites in revised edition of *Modern Painters*, 170; first public notice of Rossetti's paintings, 196–7; in Scotland with Millais, 210
Letters, to *The Times*, 161–4, 166–7, 170n.
Modern Painters, 48–51, 61, 77, 161, 170, 172
Pre-Raphaelitism, 170–3
Seven Lamps of Architecture, The, 161
Stones of Venice, The, 161

St. Germain des Prés, Church of, 111
Santi, Giovanni, 116
Sarto, Andrea del, 64n., 116
Sass's Academy, 6, 14, 15, 47, 58
Saturday Review (London), 114n., 180n., 195n.
Savonarola, Girolamo, 104
Schafer, Ary, 76n., 111
Scott, William Bell, 26, 35, 37, 90, 145, 203, 204, 217; receives first letter from D. G. Rossetti, 27–28; expresses opinion of Rossetti's poetry, 28; and *The Germ*, 118, 123
'Rosabell,' 177
Sevenoaks, 146–8, 158, 219
Shakespeare, William, 5n., 79, 204
Hamlet, 155–6, 180
King Lear, 95–6, 182
Measure for Measure, 145, 207
Much Ado About Nothing, 146
Twelfth Night, 128, 136
Two Gentlemen of Verona, 145
Sharp, William, xii, 122

Shee, Martin, 57
Shelley, Percy Bysshe, 5n, 22, 29, 79, 94
Siddal, Elizabeth, 144, 193, 217; discovered by Deverall, 128–9; meets D. G. Rossetti, 129; physical characteristics, 129, 130; family background, 130; in love with Rossetti, 130–1, 152–4, 174, 175, 201; models for P.R.B. group, 131, 153, 158, 159, 178–9, 180, 214; models for Rossetti, 152–3, 189, 201; creative work, 201–2, 205; paints self-portrait, 201, 202, 205; relations with Rossetti family, 203; illness, 205–6
Society of Art, 69
Society of British Artists, 12
Somerset, 199, 203
Somerset House, 175, 202
Southwark, 130, 203, 205
Spectator, The, 122, 134, 135, 136, 137n., 148–9, 156, 167, 173, 182, 207, 208, 210, 212n.
Spenser, Edmund, 79
Spielmann, Marion, H., 180n.
Stanhope, R. S., 177
Stanhope Street, 70
Stephens, Frederic George, 40, 53, 56, 59n., 65, 67, 68, 78, 80, 83, 84, 88, 89, 90, 95, 96, 98, 99, 116, 117, 118, 132, 132n., 145, 147, 151, 174, 184, 193, 214; proposed for P.R.B. membership, 72–73; models for Millais, 115; and *The Germ*, 123, 125; hired by *The Critic*, 149; models for Brown, 184n.; makes debut in R.A. Exhibition, 188
Stone, Frank, 104, 133, 138–9
Strachey, Lytton, xiv
Strand, The, 6, 26
Surrey, 169, 173, 180, 181, 214
Surtees, Virginia, 189n.

Tate Gallery, xi, 104, 216n., 218, 218n.
Taylor, Sir Henry, *Philip van Artevelde*, 216
Taylor, Tom, 185–6, 187
Tennyson, Alfred, 29, 79, 117, 144, 147, 219
'Kraken, The', 199–200
'Mariana', 144, 157–8
Thackeray, William Makepeace, 79
Thames River, 50, 190, 192
Thomas, Cave, 118, 179
Thorburn, Robert, 163
Times, The, 132–3, 138, 159–60, 161, 166–167, 170n., 171, 185
Tintoretto, Jacopo Robusti, 64n., 79, 80, 116
Titian, 5n., 23, 34, 46, 47, 64n., 79, 80, 111, 135
Tottenham Court Road, 152
Tower of London, 87
Trafalgar Square, 10, 15, 17, 99
Tupper, Alexander, 124
Tupper, G. F. & Sons, 120
Tupper, George, 119
Tupper, John, 118, 124, 125, 147, 148, 174, 177n.
'The Subject in Art', 121–2
Turner, J. M. W., 5n., 9–10, 49, 137, 167, 171, 172

Uccello, Paolo, 34

Van Dyck, Anthony, 46, 64n.
Van Hanselaer, Professor, 33
Vasto, Marquis of, 1
Velasquez, Diego, 64n.
Veronese, Paolo, 64n.
Victoria, Queen, 81, 141, 142, 157
Von Holst, Theodore, 31, 37, 191

Wahl, John Robert, xiii
Wappers, Baron, 33
Ward, Edward M., 137, 187
Ward, James, 180n.
Washington, George, 79
Waterloo, 112
Watts, George Frederick, 15, 20, 137, 177
Waugh, Evelyn, xii
Wellesley Index to Victorian Periodicals, 141, 142
West, Benjamin, 76n., 114
Westminster Hall Competition, 13, 14–15, 36
Wigmore Street, 99
Wilkie, David, 72, 79
Windus, William L., 173n.
Winwar, Frances, xii
Wiseman, Cardinal, 71
Wood, Esther, xii
Woolgar, Miss, 26
Woolner, Thomas, 72, 73, 80, 89, 91, 113, 116, 118, 147, 165, 193, 195, 196, 197, 198, 199, 210, 211, 217, 219; career prior to formation of P.R.B., 69; proposed for P.R.B. membership, 69–70; his sculpture unrelated to Pre-Raphaelitism, 83, 90, 117, 125, 152; writes 'Pre-Raphaelite' poetry, 90, 118, 121, 123, 125; and the Wordsworth competition, 152, 188–9; departs for Australia, 189, 206
'My Beautiful Lady', 121
'Of My Lady in Death', 121
Wordsworth, William, 5n., 79, 134, 152, 183, 217